GLOBAL FINANCIAL PERSPECTIVES

Jagdish N. Sheth
Brooker Professor of Research
Graduate School of Business
University of Southern California

Abdolreza Eshghi
Associate Professor of Marketing
Bentley College

Published by

GN62AA **SOUTH-WESTERN PUBLISHING CO.**

CINCINNATI   WEST CHICAGO, IL   CARROLLTON, TX   LIVERMORE, CA

PREFACE

International finance and global financial practices have become critical to corporate survival and profitability for a number of reasons.

First, private foreign investment by corporations has been steadily increasing on a worldwide basis. The equity positions in different countries require a significant amount of long-term commitment and often create exit barriers. Consequently, a significant percentage of total capital is tied up in international operations. Furthermore, private foreign investment is not limited to less developed countries. It is now extended to advanced countries such as the U.S., Japan and those in Europe. As more offshore competitors invest in domestic capacities in other countries, the total capital portfolio with international investment rises dramatically. For example, recently virtually all European countries and Japan have started investing heavily in the U.S. Similarly, many U.S. firms are continuing to invest in Europe and Japan.

Second, since the floating of the dollar and the liberalization of monetary flows across national boundaries, managing equity and debt capital portfolios on a global basis has become a specialized function that is critical to corporate performance: profits or losses of a corporation can be determined by currency fluctuations as well as stock market prices in various stock exchanges of the world. This was clearly demonstrated in the stock market crash of 1987, during which New York, London, and Tokyo stock exchanges were virtually reacting to each other on an hour-by-hour basis.

Third, the costs of capital and foreign investment incentives are becoming more and more diverse. For example, the traditional risk-return model of investment is breaking down as countries begin to provide unorthodox incentives, such as tax havens, countertrade, and capital repatriation in exported products or services. In short, international finance is becoming more and more context-driven and less and less investment-theory-driven.

Finally, the diversity of political risks associated with both investment and working capitals across national boundaries is increasing at an alarming rate. The traditional notion that there are high investment risks in less developed countries and virtually no risks in Western bloc nations are no longer so clear cut. For example, when a country like the United States becomes the largest debtor nation in the world and is unable to reduce the biggest trade deficit in the world as well as federal budget deficit, it becomes less clear how the U.S. is structurally different from any less developed country such as Brazil, Argentina or India.

What we need, therefore, is a specialized understanding of corporate finance in the international context. International finance even affects companies not engaged in international business because global financial markets have an impact on their cost of capital, both short term and long term, as well as their offshore procurements of parts, materials and products.

This volume is designed to be a supplement to a textbook in the required finance courses at the M.B.A. level, as well as at the advanced undergraduate level. It is intended to fulfill the accreditation requirements of internationalizing the finance curriculum in the schools of business and management.

The volume is prepared to serve several educational needs in finance.

- It details the complexity of the international environment for financial decisions and practices. Special emphasis is placed on political risks, economic incentives, and governmental control of flow of funds in the international arena.
- It provides a strategic and managerial perspective on international finance through readings that are practical and contain good case histories as well as conceptual frameworks.
- It includes an annotated bibliography, which will facilitate self-study by students or encourage them to undertake special projects related to international finance.

A number of criteria were used in the selection of articles included in this volume.

- They must have a managerial orientation, which makes them relevant to the practice of corporate finance.
- The authors must be well recognized for their contributions to the field.
- The perspective on international finance should be worldwide rather than limited to the U.S.

Although the volume is designed to supplement the required finance classes at the M.B.A. and the advanced undergraduate level, it can also satisfy the needs of Executive M.B.A. programs, as well as corporate executive education seminars on international finance.

We are grateful to Ramona Newman, now a Ph.D. student at the University of Illinois, Urbana, for her invaluable assistance in searching for articles and references included in this volume.

The editors and the Publisher are also grateful to the authors and publishers who granted permission to reprint articles included in this volume.

Jagdish N. Sheth
Abdolreza Eshghi

CONTENTS

INTRODUCTION

Diversity and Volatility of International Finance _____

The diversity and volatility of the investment environment for corporations involved in international markets is truly bewildering. In fact, it is no exaggeration to state that a multinational corporation's strategic competitive advantage rests much more in its ability to manage its financial portfolio than in the experience curves and quality circles associated with manufacturing excellence or in competitive positioning and the product differentiation concepts associated with marketing excellence. The diversity and volatility of corporate finance in the international arena make the position of the Chief Financial Officer (CFO) both more critical and vulnerable.

The factors responsible for this diversity and volatility are the subject matter of this section. We have identified at least four major forces: global mergers and acquisitions, global financial markets, government regulations, and currency exchange rates (Figure I.1).

In recent years, perhaps the single most dramatic factor in international finance has been mergers, acquisitions, and strategic alliances among foreign corporations. As a given industry becomes global in competition, customers, and capacity, consolidation and rationalization of the industry through global mergers and acquisitions becomes more prevalent. This is evidenced in such diverse industries as steel, semiconductors, oil, petrochemicals, machine tools, consumer electronics, pharmaceuticals, and automobiles.

Global mergers, acquisitions and strategic alliances add diversity with respect to calculating asset values, tax write-offs, depreciation schedules, and multiple tax

Figure I.1
_____

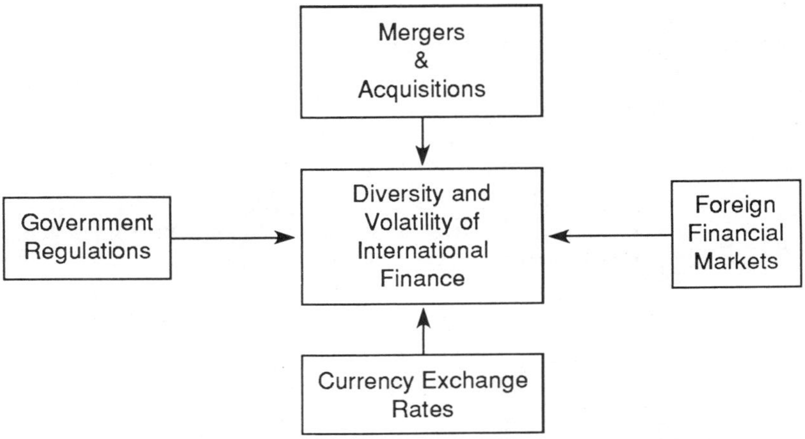

vii

structures of different countries. The traditional concepts of risk and return used in making capital decisions are likely to be relegated to more strategic issues of global competitiveness and market domination.

Another major factor in international finance is access to foreign capital markets for both debt and equity capitals. As more and more nations allow their stock exchanges to list and trade foreign stocks and bonds, and as world stock markets operate on a real time basis, what happens in one capital market will have an immediate impact on all capital markets. This increases the volatility of foreign investment decisions. Access to world capital markets is a double-edged sword. On the one hand, it increases capital options available to a corporation; on the other hand, it makes the corporation much more dependent on foreign investors, who may have different financial expectations from domestic investors.

To compound the volatility and complexity of the situation, the floating currency exchange rates in operation since the late seventies have blurred working capital, fixed capital, and cashflow management issues. It is less and less clear whether short-term working capital decisions are less critical to the financial performance of the organization than long-term debt and equity issues. Indeed, it is becoming increasingly necessary for a multinational enterprise to develop in-house expertise in managing daily currency fluctuations, just to deliver quarterly financial objectives.

Finally, both the diversity and complexity of foreign investment decisions and capital markets is enhanced by the significant role played by the host governments. On the one hand, host governments want multinationals to invest in their countries, so they offer numerous incentives to attract investment capital. On the other hand, host countries seem to be afraid of the enormous employment and capital powers of the multinationals. This is especially true of several emerging nations, such as India, China, and Brazil. At the same time, it is increasingly difficult to predict and manage the political risks associated with foreign private investments, since many countries are unwilling or unable to repatriate dividends, capitals, or both, in hard currency. In fact, it has become fashionable for many governments, in both developing and advanced countries, to insist on countertrade or offset agreements as means for repatriation.

International Strategies for Financing and Investment

The context of international finance and investment is complex and volatile, to say the least. Therefore, it is even more desirable for the practitioners to develop and utilize some conceptual frameworks—a theory of international finance—for their foreign capital decisions.

Although the traditional measures (net present value, internal rate of return, payback period, etc.) based on risk and return analysis are still useful, they must be modified to take into account the complexity and volatility of foreign capital and investment decisions. Perhaps the best method may be to include factors peculiar to foreign capital and investment in the definitions of risk and return. For example, political risk is a very key and unique aspect of risk. Similarly, monopoly rents and profits in many less developed countries are a significant element of return on investment unique to international investment. A comparable analysis is appropriate for offshore capital sources. If a company borrows from foreign countries, its cost of capital is likely to be subject to influences generally not present in domestic borrowings.

We have developed a simple but powerful framework to incorporate all the risk and return issues specific to international finance. It is based on two factors: source of capital and source of investment (Figure I.2).

Businesses that rely primarily on domestic sources of capital to finance domestic investments are likely to rely on industry-specific risks and returns criteria. For example, utility companies will have different financial criteria than biogenetics or high tech industries, even though they may all be domestic borrowers and domestic investors.

Recently however, more and more domestic investment companies are obtaining their debt and/or equity financing from foreign countries. In this case, cost of capital risk and return issues must be added, in addition to industry-specific risk and return issues. Obtaining financing from foreign sources is becoming more common among telecommunications companies such as AT&T, as well as the divested seven regional holding companies. The financial performance of these companies cannot be judged purely on the merits of their domestic investments. In fact, they are highly dependent on foreign stock markets, currency rates, inflation, and economic policies.

More commonly, however, a company takes its domestic sources of financing and invests in foreign countries. This is typical of most multinationals, who begin to do business all over the world by private foreign investment strategy. In this situation, the political risks associated with foreign countries and the market returns associated with foreign markets must be examined, above and beyond the traditional industry-specific risks and returns criteria.

Finally, the most complex reality for truly global enterprises (and one that is more and more common) is the situation in which both capital borrowing and capital investment take place on a worldwide basis. This is more prevalent for several European enterprises, and it is becoming more and more prevalent for some Japanese and the U.S. multinationals. Indeed, it is not unusual to see a company's stocks and

Figure I.2

	Source of Capital	
	Domestic	Worldwide
Source of Investment — Domestic	Industry Risk-Return	Cost of Capital Risk-Return
Source of Investment — Worldwide	Country Risk-Return	Global Risk-Return

bonds listed in the three major stock exchanges of the world: London, New York, and Tokyo. In a global risk-return environment, we must understand, identify, and qualify the main effects of industry, cost of capital, and country specific risks and returns, as well as their interactive effects.

We hope this simple but potentially powerful framework will enable students and instructors to evaluate specific decisions that businesses make about foreign investment and foreign capital.

Book Summary

This book consists of three parts. Part I focuses on the environment of international finance. The emphasis on private foreign investment, internationalization of American businesses, and the rapid expansion of European and Japanese multinationals, as well as emergence of multinationals from less developed countries, suggests that we are evolving toward a multibusiness, multisector era, in which national economic policies, external debt of developing nations, and global competition are likely to encourage strategic alliances. Therefore, in addition to industry-specific factors influencing the financial ratios for debt and equity, it is important to understand country-specific factors. For example, debt to equity ratios vary significantly among U.S., German, and Japanese corporations.

We must also understand the economic risks associated with businesses in less developed nations, especially those with very high inflation rates. Successful economic exposure must incorporate at least two principal protective mechanisms: operational mechanisms such as lead and lagging payments; balance sheet management and pricing policy that pegs domestic prices to the exchange rate; and financial mechanisms such as forward contracts and other hedging tactics.

Part II discusses foreign investment decisions and practices. Despite the complexity and volatility of international investments, companies still use internal rate of return and payback period as the predominant measure of risks and return. They do, however, vary discount rates by subjectively estimating the weighted average cost of capital based on local rates. Furthermore, the primary methods of adjusting for different levels of risk in foreign projects are to borrow funds from local sources or to adjust the required accounting rate of return on investment. A key aspect of foreign private investment is the government incentives that foreign countries offer. While economic stability, infrastructure, production costs, and proximity to market are key rational criteria for private foreign investment, many companies are shrewd enough to encourage intense bidding wars among governments eager to attract companies and offer whatever incentives are necessary. For example, Mexico, Malaysia, Singapore, and Taiwan have offered some very attractive incentives in recent years. This is also true of some of the East European countries.

No matter what the methods and the processes of making private foreign investments, it is essential to estimate the political risks inherent in such investments. The political economy models suggest that the type of risk (destination of plant and equipment, exchange controls, taxes and tariffs, export controls, or labor relations) are due to different nations' political philosophies. For example, a country dominated by state-controlled international politics is likely to generate different types of risks than a country governed by bureaucratic organizational politics.

Part III focuses on financing decisions in the international context. Although market-based forecasts implicit in the term structure of interest rates and of forward exchange rates are quite reasonable in a competitive and efficient market, a company must examine any specific competitive advantages it may have due to its legal structure, geographical location, or an unusual forecasting ability, and use those advantages to adjust market-based forecasts for financing its operations.

A significant influence on corporate financing decisions is the structure of capital markets. Is there an optimal capital structure for the multinational firm? How does multinationality affect the company's cost of equity? Is the multinational firm's cost of capital affected by its debt financing decisions? Does currency of denomination exert an influence of its own? If so, what is the nature of this influence? Can the multinational firm benefit from international differentials in nominal interest rates? Underlying these specific issues is the basic theoretical and empirical question of the degree of segmentation or integration of international money and capital markets and the efficiency of the foreign exchange market.

In addition to the complexity and volatility of investing and financing in the international arena, there is a more fundamental question: Where is additional financing likely to come from? The traditional sources of financing, such as banks and securities markets, seem to have reached their limits. What is likely to emerge are some innovative methods of financing. These include underwriting price-indexed securities, realigning regulatory arrangements to facilitate more efficient deployment of bank capital, leverage buyouts, and creation of junk bonds. Furthermore, it is very likely that investment houses will emerge as powerful intermediaries to bridge the gap in financing.

I. ___ THE MULTINATIONAL CORPORATION AND ITS ENVIRONMENT ___

Trends in Multinational Business and Global Environments: A Perspective
William A. Dymsza

The Relationship of Headquarters Country and Industry Classification to Financial Structure
J. Markham Collins and William S. Sekely

Risk Assessment for U.S. Affiliates Based in Less Developed Countries
John Whitcomb Kennedy

1. TRENDS IN MULTINATIONAL BUSINESS AND GLOBAL ENVIRONMENTS: A PERSPECTIVE

WILLIAM A. DYMSZA*

William A. Dymsza is Professor of International Business at the Graduate School of Management, Rutgers, The State University. He has served as Editor-in-Chief of JIBS since 1975 and is a Fellow of the Academy of International Business. Dr. Dymsza has been an advisor to the OECD and the United Nations and has written widely on international management. Professor Dymsza wants to express his appreciation to 2 reviewers who contributed many valuable suggestions to improve this article.

Abstract. This article reviews and synthesizes the emergence and growth of U.S., Western European, and Japanese MNCs in the postwar environment, the growing role of state enterprises, and the recent emergence of Third World MNCs. While U.S. foreign direct investments have expanded and continue to be highly significant, some important recent developments are the more rapid growth of Western European and Japanese MNCs, the increased role of the U.S. as a host country for investments, the emergence of multibusiness by MNCs, the more numerous actors involved in global business, and the dramatic, more rapid changes in the world environment. This article explores developments in host- and home-country policies, some of the other major actors in international business, "newer" forms of international participation along with some hypotheses, and concludes by analyzing a few major changes in global environments and multinational management.

Introduction

The growth of multinational corporations (MNCs) has been one of the landmark developments of the post-World War II period. The postwar setting provided a highly favorable atmosphere for MNCs, and, although not completely new, their rapid expansion globally, their capability to integrate business across national frontiers, and their economic power have had significant repercussions on the world economy. The research and writing about multinationals have long been growth undertakings, producing volumes of books and articles on the subject. Further, MNCs have generated considerable controversy and conflict, provoking a variety of regulations by host and home countries and interaction with many other actors.

Relying on many studies available, this article will highlight postwar trends in the development of MNCs, the involvement of various actors, recent changes in global and national environments and some recent developments in strategic planning and

Reprinted from *Journal of International Business Studies,* Winter 1984, 25–46, by permission of the University of South Carolina, College of Business Administration.

organizational change. This article is a combination review, synthesis, and essay based upon my personal interpretation. In addition, it states certain hypotheses and speculations on recent trends and developments in multinational business. The literature available is vast, and thus the focus must be limited to a relatively small number of trends and developments in multinational business and global environments.

Early Postwar Developments

International business in the postwar period was characterized by rapid expansion of international trade, fostered by the more open world trading system after reconstruction. The United States was in a predominant economic position during this period and led the way. At the same time, many U.S. companies were multiplying direct investments in mining, petroleum, and other primary activities in the late 1940s and in the early 1950s. Some U.S. companies—such as Singer, International Telephone and Telegraph, and General Electric—had undertaken direct investments in manufacturing during the latter part of the 19th century and continued to make such investments before and after World War II. After economic reconstruction, in the early and mid 1950s, these and other American industrial enterprises began a strong expansion of direct investments in manufacturing in Canada and then in Western Europe.

Internationalization of American Business

The strongest rise of multinational enterprise, however, took place between the mid 1950s and 1970, with U.S. companies predominant. U.S. industrial enterprises expanded direct investments in manufacturing affiliates in Canada, and with the establishment of the European Common Market, they escalated such investments in Western Europe to establish production within the free trade area and to take advantage of rapid economic growth and increased market potential in the region. Further, to protect themselves against the loss of export markets and from the threat of higher trade barriers, American companies undertook direct investments in import-substituting manufacturing in certain developing countries with larger markets, such as Mexico, Brazil, Argentina, and the Philippines. U.S. electronic and other companies facing increased import competition undertook offshore investments in Asian countries in labor-intensive, quite standardized products to take advantage of the supply of low cost, relatively unskilled labor available. These MNCs started generally with simple assembly and then shifted to testing and more complex manufacturing over time [Moxon 1975].

Because the Japanese government placed restrictions for many years on incoming direct investments, the major involvement of American companies in Japan was in trade and thousands of licensing agreements. By the 1960s, U.S. MNCs were undertaking direct investments in manufacturing in Japan, primarily through the minority-owned joint ventures required by the government.

Meanwhile, American and other Western natural resource companies continued to undertake direct investments in Venezuela, other Latin American countries, and elsewhere. They particularly expanded direct investments in crude oil operations in Saudi Arabia (through the ARAMCO consortia of major oil producers), Iran, Kuwait, other Middle East countries, Libya, Nigeria, Algeria, Indonesia, and other nations. In what Vernon terms the "obsolescing bargain," the Third World oil producing nations squeezed a growing share of the profits from the crude oil and mining operations of the MNCs and exacted other concessions, such as placing nationals into key managerial and technical positions and some increase in refining activities in their countries [Vernon 1971 and 1977]. After the emergence and rapid growth of the European Economic Community, U.S. petroleum companies expanded their investments in petroleum refining and marketing operations in Western Europe.

Finally, American commercial banks, insurance companies, investment houses, accounting firms, advertising agencies, consulting firms, market research agencies, and other service establishments undertook direct investments and expanded their business in Europe in the 1960s and 1970s as part of the internationalization process. In almost every field, the multinationalization of American business was one of the spectacular phenomena of the time.

Emphasis Upon Foreign Direct Investments

This multinationalization of business from the 1950s to the 1970s was characterized by an expansion of foreign direct investments. These investments transfer capital (including foreign exchange), but more significantly they transfer scarce technology, management, business knowhow, and training capabilities, along with specific control of the foreign affiliates. Some of these direct investments were based upon the international product cycle [Vernon 1966 and 1971]. U.S. companies developing new products began by exporting to Western European and other developed nations; however, after they encountered trade barriers to their exports, stronger competition from local firms entering production, and products that became somewhat more standardized, U.S. companies entered into direct investments in manufacturing affiliates in Western Europe and at a later stage in developing countries.

Most industrial MNCs engaging in foreign direct investment were oligopoly firms that exploited such firm-specific advantages as technology, organizational capabilities, product differentiation, promotion, brand names and other marketing expertise, and economies of scale. These industrial companies internalized or kept control of advantages based upon their knowledge within the enterprise by transferring these scarce resources to foreign subsidiaries, which they controlled, through direct investments. Locational factors, such as market size and potential growth, labor, material, and other costs, availability of natural resources, government policy, and the existence of trade barriers, also played a significant role in foreign investment decisions [Dunning 1980; Calvet 1981].

Rapid Expansion of Western European MNCs ————————————————————————

Western European firms—for example, Unilever, Nestle, Siemens, Phillips, Ciba, and Imperial Chemicals (or predecessor companies)—had a long history of involvement with manufacturing in foreign nations in the 19th century. They continued to expand direct investments in manufacturing along with exports until World War II. Although their initial emphasis in the postwar period was on exports, Western European industrial companies increased foreign direct investments through new ventures or acquisitions, particularly after the late 1950s [Franko 1976]. These companies initially expanded foreign manufacturing in other Western European nations, spurred by trade barriers that impeded exports and by the emergence of the European Economic Community. Later, Western European MNCs expanded direct investments in developing countries, often involving joint ventures. British and French companies invested primarily in former colonies while other Western European nations expanded manufacturing production in Latin America and elsewhere.

By the late 1960s and the 1970s, Western European MNCs were undertaking major industrial direct investments in the United States through new establishments or acquisitions. In a number of cases the sequence of involvement of these firms, particularly in specialty chemicals, pharmaceuticals, electrical equipment, and tires followed a pattern: distinctive innovation, export, and then manufacturing production [Franko 1976]. American trade barriers or the threat of such barriers, along with a weakening of the U.S. dollar, played an important part in such direct investments. Further, the large Western European oligopoly firms had developed considerable technological, marketing, management, and production advantages, along with broad international experience; they decided to exploit these firm-specific advantages by penetrating the substantial American market. Part of this was an oligopolistic reaction by Western European companies to the increased competition from U.S. MNCs in their home countries. Thus, Western European industrial companies became global enterprises that competed effectively with U.S. MNCs in the American market, in developing countries, and in Europe. By the 1970s Western European MNCs were expanding globally more rapidly than American enterprises.

Expansion of Japanese MNCs ————————————————————————————————————

After reconstruction and the rapid economic growth in the 1950s and 1960s, Japanese firms concentrated on exports of textiles, consumer electronics, steel, automobiles, and other products to Asian developing countries and to the United States and other industrial nations. Huge Japanese trading companies, reemerging in the 1950s, played a major role in imports of required raw materials and exports of standardized products, along with financing trade. These huge trading companies established many branches and offices in key trade centers in foreign countries. During the mid and late 1950s, Japanese industrial firms undertook direct investments in manufacturing in nearby Asian countries in order to protect markets that were being lost because of increased trade restrictions. Japanese investments in Asian developing countries were primarily in manufacturing standard products—textiles, apparel, consumer electronics, fabricated metals, and so on—and involved minority-owned joint ventures [Tsurumi 1976; Yoshino 1976]. These investments were generally export oriented since they placed high reliance on the parent company's exporting intermediate materials and components to the affiliates. Many small Japanese firms spearheaded manufacturing investments in Asian countries in conjunction with the major trading companies in the 1960s (which helped to finance their investments), but the large enterprises assumed a major role later. Further, with increased labor costs in Japan and more substantial competition in the late 1960s, Japanese companies undertook offshore investments in manufacturing in low-wage, Asian countries to produce consumer electronics at competitive prices for the American market.

From the 1970s to the 1980s, Japanese industrial companies such as Sony, Matsushita, Honda, and Mitsubishi undertook manufacturing investments in the United States in order to gain greater access for their high quality, differentiated products in the substantial American market. By that time the large oligopoly Japanese enterprises had become more multinational in their organization, strategy, and integrated approach to international business [Yoshino 1976; Tsurumi 1976].

Internationalization of State Enterprises _____

In the postwar period, state enterprises became a more important factor in international trade and in other types of international business. Wholly- or partially-owned state enterprises—long active in oil production—such as ENI, Compagnie Francaise des Petrole, and ELF-Equitane expanded their direct investments and international trade in petroleum in the 1950s and 1960s. These state-controlled oil enterprises in industrial nations have to deal increasingly with state-owned enterprises in the oil-producing countries and with the OPEC cartel. Other partially- or wholly-owned state enterprises have participated to an increasing extent in international business, but it is a mixed and complex picture.

Based upon 304 open-end interviews of officials of state enterprises, governments, and other relevant groups in Europe, Mazzolini found that state-controlled enterprises were constrained in their foreign involvement, particularly in direct investments abroad, by government policies that favor domestic growth over foreign expansion, by the bureaucratic, decision-making structure, and by political conflicts, rivalries, and compromise [Mazzolini 1979 and 1980]. Yet, governments of industrial nations have encouraged their controlled natural resource enterprises to undertake investments in exploration and extraction of oil and minerals while they have also pressed for refining in the home country. In the manufacturing field, the pressure of labor unions about losses of jobs and political preferences for location of enterprises within the country rather than in foreign countries, has constrained some direct investments by state-controlled firms abroad.

On the other hand, the managers of European state-controlled enterprises have pushed aggressively for expansion of manufacturing in foreign countries in order to take advantage of opportunities for growth; many government officials have supported such expansion which would promote increased exports. In their initial foreign direct investments, a number of industrial state enterprises have experienced difficulties in scanning the foreign investment climate, in evaluating overseas projects in a systematic fashion, in obtaining approval through the bureaucratic structure, and in implementing projects; but after they gained experience, they overcame many of these problems and adopted more efficient processes such as those used by private MNCs [Mazzolini 1979 and 1980].

Partially- or wholly-owned industrial state enterprises, such as Renault, Volkswagen, and DSM, undertook major direct investments in manufacturing in foreign countries and became highly multinational in their business. By the 1980s many state enterprises had become multinational enterprises with substantial direct investments, a network of foreign affiliates, and major involvement in international trade and contractual arrangements. According to the last survey of the U.N. Centre of Transnational Corporations, about one tenth of the world's 295 largest industrial MNCs were state enterprises (wholly or partially state owned) [U.N. Centre on Transnational Corporations 1983].

State enterprises have many other complex effects on international business that can only be touched upon here. In many cases state enterprises prefer to conduct business with other state-owned firms rather than with private companies [Vernon 1979]. Governments find it convenient to have their state enterprises act for them in major business deals, such as exchanges of oil for technology. Further, state enterprises may find dealing with each other in longer-term commercial arrangements rather than with private firms convenient because such agreements reduce planning uncertainties, promote semi-official goals, and provide more stability in their business operations. Nevertheless, state-owned enterprises find entering into various relationships with private MNCs to be advantageous. State-owned oil and mining enterprises have worked out arrangements for MNCs to market and distribute their products. A number of industrial state enterprises have entered into joint ventures, licensing, management contracts, and other arrangements with MNCs to obtain modern technology, to improve the performance of their business, and to compete more effectively in world markets. Thus, state enterprises and MNCs have been working out links with each other.

Recent Rise of Third World MNCs _____

In recent years, many hundreds of companies from Third World nations—including Argentina, Brazil, Hong Kong, India, South Korea, and Taiwan—have undertaken direct investments, primarily in manufacturing, in other developing countries. According to Wells, most of these manufacturing direct investments have been motivated by the effort to maintain markets that were being lost to exports as a result of increased trade restrictions; further, these developing-country firms have sought to reduce costs of production and to diversify their business [Wells 1983]. The generally smaller Third World companies undertaking these investments have scaled down their manufacturing operations for the smaller-sized markets of host developing countries. As a result of their scaled down, more labor-intensive technology and lower management and overhead costs, these companies have manufactured products at relatively low cost and have competed largely on the basis of price [Wells 1983]. The Third World manufacturing investments overseas are predominantly joint ventures—more than 90 percent of the companies for which data are available [Wells 1983]. The affiliates are managed largely by expatriates from the home developing countries, but these multinationals grant considerable autonomy to their managers.

Based upon their research of Third World multinationals from India, Hong Kong, Argentina and Brazil, Lall and his collaborators do not accept that developing country MNCs are primarily small scale producers of standardized products, which scale down their technology and compete largely on the basis of price [Lall 1983]. They found a number of diverse patterns of investments by developing country MNCs. Hong Kong firms, which have a substantial number of investments abroad, specialize in textiles, garments, consumer electronics, and other light consumer products which they export to a considerable extent. A number of the companies included, however, are foreign expatriate firms that locate in Hong Kong. Indian firms invest in diverse manufacturing abroad, including capital goods that involve fairly high technology, textiles, and food products. To some extent the pattern of Indian foreign investors is determined by the inward-looking, protectionist policies of the government which led to the development of such industries. Argentine firms, which initiated some manufacturing investments earlier in this century, have in recent years invested primarily in the engineering and metal-making industry, food processing, publishing, and pharmaceuticals abroad. Brazilian companies, which developed considerable industrial capabilities, have not been particularly active in manufacturing investments; rather, the major thrust of Brazilian enterprises has been in heavy civil construction, engineering consulting, and design of projects. Petrobas, the government-owned oil company of Brazil, has invested in oil exploration and drilling in other Latin American countries, Africa, and the Middle East. Other state-owned oil enterprises, for example those from India, Argentina, and Taiwan, have undertaken ventures in oil exploration, seeking secure, less expensive sources of supply [Wells 1983].

Inherently, foreign investments by Third World firms, like those of MNCs from industrial nations, are highly complex phenomena with many variations. Scholars can differ in conceptualizations and interpretations about patterns, motivations, and characteristics; but in my judgment, the Wells study, based upon a data bank on 963 parent firms in Third World nations, containing information on 1964 overseas affiliates located in 125 host countries, with 938 of the affiliates engaged in manufacturing supplemented by interviews of 150 managers of enterprises and much additional research, has a strong empirical and conceptual framework for its major findings: that MNCs from developing countries have engaged in manufacturing operations abroad with scaled-down, more labor-intensive technology and have competed primarily on the basis of price.

Based upon these characteristics, a major issue is whether the advantages of developing-country investors in scaled-down production of fairly standardized products and lower prices will be eroded over time as a result of competition from local firms. Another issue is whether Third World MNCs can complete effectively with the much larger Western and Japanese MNCs that utilize modern technology, economies of scale, and much more sophisticated marketing and other expertise. Although the evidence is far from clear, I would speculate that Third World MNCs have found a niche in more appropriate, labor-intensive technology and will improve their product adaptation, marketing, and management capabilities. This will enable them to continue to expand their manufacturing investments despite the competition of Western MNCs and local enterprises.

Multibusiness, Multi-actor Era

In essence, the growth of multinational enterprises and other types of international business produced a multibusiness, multi-actor setting with rapid changes in global, regional, and national environments [Robinson 1981]. MNCs have interacted with numerous actors—host nations, home countries, international organizations, the EEC and other regional groups, the Group of 77, OPEC, state enterprises, financial institutions, labor unions, consumers, environmentalists, intellectuals, and others. Further, MNCs have been entering into a wider range of contractual arrangements and different types of trade, along with direct investments. Distinctions in investments between home and host countries have blurred to some extent as many nations have become both. A number of the key international business actors have been mentioned previously. The balance of this article turns to a fuller discussion of developing country and developed country governments and several other key factors. Then, discussion will focus on MNC involvement in multibusiness, a few key changes in global environments, and recent trends in multinational management.

Host Developing Nations

Although U.S. and Western European MNCs have undertaken their most substantial direct investments in developed countries, the major problems have emerged in developing nations. While there is some lessening of confrontation, certain rhetoric and important conflicts continue to exist between developing nations and multinational companies. Given that developing countries vary in major ways with respect to levels of development, economic structure, size, national economic planning, and mixes of capitalism and socialism, it is not surprising that they respond in different ways to MNCs. Further, besides government officials, there are many other internal and external actors who influence the foreign investment stance of these countries: businessmen, labor unions, consumers, intellectuals, environmentalists, UNCTAD, the Group of 77, other international and regional organizations, and so on. Thus, various concerns arise, including "dependencia," protection of national sovereignty, aspirations for economic growth and modernization, issues of transfer pricing, knowledge about past abuses and political interference of foreign corporations, fears of the oligopoly power of MNCs, and inherent conflicts between the global strategies of multinationals and the national interests of developing nations. Amid such multiplicity, generalizations are difficult to state; nevertheless, certain trends appear.

Developing nations started to deal with foreign natural resource companies years ago. In Vernon's "obsolescing bargain," Third World countries squeezed a growing share of the profits from these foreign investments through a series of renegotiations;

they also exacted other concessions from these MNCs, including requirements for increased refining operations, joint ventures, service and other contracts, and placement of more nationals in key managerial positions [Vernon 1971 and 1977]. Although a few governments have expropriated mining and petroleum ventures, they have often entered into joint ventures and taken over ownership of the foreign operations in stages while continuing to rely on the MNCs for international marketing, distribution, and technical services.

In recent years the "obsolescing bargain" has been spreading to foreign manufacturing investments as some developing nations have been renegotiating many of the conditions of entry and imposing local ownership requirements and performance restrictions on industrial MNCs.

Benefits/Cost of Foreign Investment Projects

Developing country governments have been striving to obtain more substantial benefits in relation to costs from manufacturing affiliates of MNCs in economic development, national income, technology, balance of payments improvement, and in other ways. The various benefits/costs are closely interrelated and are difficult to ascertain over the short, medium, and longer terms. A number of host developing governments have resorted to social cost/benefit analysis, which strives to determine net social contributions (positive or negative) of investment projects by utilizing opportunity costs, shadow pricing, externalities, and other adjustments. Social cost/benefit evaluations represent a definite advance, but the calculations determine the social value of the project from the standpoint primarily of one criterion: how efficiently does it utilize domestic resources [Wells 1975]. Further, the evaluations make assumptions and judgments, fail to consider the interrelationships of a project to others in the economy, experience difficulties in analyzing projects over their lives, and neglect many dynamic and qualitative impacts of the investments.

The determination of overall benefits of a project in relation to costs of a foreign investment project over the medium and longer term and its various ramifications, qualitative as well as quantitative, presents major difficulties to government policy makers who have perceptions different from those of executives of MNCs. Government officials, intellectuals, labor union officials, local businessmen, and other groups in developing countries perceive MNCs as political actors who exercise decision-making power over important segments of the national economy from a headquarters located outside the country and beyond the jurisdictional authority of their governments [Root 1983]. Developing nations are concerned about the power of MNCs to circumvent national policies through their allocation of resources globally, their possible manipulative transfer pricing, and their integrative global strategies and operations. Thus, government policy makers experience difficulties in determining the trade-offs between economic benefits and possible political and social costs of manufacturing affiliates of MNCs in their countries.

Foreign Investment Policies

Through foreign investment policies and regulations, developing host nations have striven to obtain more substantial perceived benefits in relation to costs from manufacturing investments over time, difficult as these are to measure. From another standpoint, as Robinson states, most foreign investment policies strive to channel investments to priority or desired areas, rather than maximize or minimize inward inflows [Robinson 1976].

Although these many factors produce wide variations in policies and regulations, common choices can be seen: 1) reserving certain sectors and activities, such as public utilities, air transportation, banking, insurance, to the state or national industry, and also excluding foreign investment from certain industries adequately served by national firms; 2) relatively open-door and liberal policies toward foreign investments, supplemented in a number of cases by incentives; 3) entry-screening to permit direct investments that foster vital national objectives; 4) requirements for sharing ownership, particularly through joint ventures with majority national equity at the time of investment or within specified periods; and 5) performance requirements, such as local content, export obligations, employment of nationals, development of local managers, and local R&D.

A number of developing countries in the Pacific, African, and Caribbean regions have followed relatively open-door policies with respect to foreign investments. Countries such as Taiwan, with sizable markets, considerable industrialization, a relatively large supply of low-cost labor, manufacturing free zones, and political stability, have attracted substantial foreign direct investments. Other smaller nations with limited markets, resources, and endowments have obtained small foreign investments in their industries.

In evaluating alternative foreign direct investment projects, we should emphasize that MNCs give particular importance to foreign investment climate, increasingly to political risk, and to market attractiveness, which involves market size, potential growth, and competition. Thus, relatively open-door policies of some host countries do not attract foreign investments nor do incentives. The role of incentives, such as duty-free entry of materials and equipment, protection from import competition, transfer guarantees, and tax holidays, seems to be marginal in foreign investment decisions. Among various considerations, incentives are generally matched by other countries seeking inward investments. Incentives can take on some importance in investment decisions by MNCs between alternative country locations which have equivalent foreign investment climates, political risk, and market attractiveness.

The other foreign investment policies used widely by many of the major developing countries have had mixed results in achieving national objectives. Entry screening requires governments to establish relevant and consistent criteria; it also requires governments to resolve various contradictions and trade-offs in national objectives. Developing nations have been successful in getting MNCs to enter into joint ventures, even those with minority ownership. Yet, some of the benefits that Third World nations have obtained from joint ventures are political and psychological, given the trade-offs involved. For example, MNCs may not provide their most modern technology and business knowhow to joint venture affiliates nor promote exports aggressively. Further, MNCs can retain considerable control over affiliates through their management, technology, marketing and product expertise, and in other ways [Dymsza 1984]. Developing nation governments have multiplied performance requirements on foreign investments in recent years, but many of these regulations have adverse cost effects on local economies, are highly protectionist, and distort trade and investment flows. Certain performance requirements such as export commitments and R&D obligations commonly cannot be attained, or host governments experience difficulties in monitoring them.

Over the last decade or so, a number of developing countries have imposed a combination of severe entry-screening, ownership requirements, and performance restrictions, and limitations on repatriation of earnings with respect to foreign investments. When these countries have administered such policies in a rigid and arbitrary manner, such as in India and Peru, MNCs have shifted their direct investments to other countries that have less onerous and more flexible policies. As a consequence, many developing nations in recent years have established more flexible and to some extent more accommodating foreign investment policies. Further, negotiations between host governments and MNCs have assumed major importance in foreign investment entry. Thus, negotiations between more experienced government officials and executives of oligopoly MNCs often play crucial roles in foreign investment entry decisions, terms, and conditions. Many such host governments have not only developed more consistent policies and administrative procedures, but have also stengthened their negotiating capabilities with MNCs. Nevertheless, developing nation officials and other actors in these countries are still concerned about the impact of MNCs on their economies, cultures, and sovereignty, and about the problems of reconciling integrative global strategies of multinationals with their national interests.

Despite the efforts of a number of such nations to develop more consistent and realistic foreign investment policies, MNCs still find that some regulations are inconsistent, changeable, and highly bureaucratic. They encounter difficulties in dealing with complex bureaucratic organizations—in some cases involving numerous ministries and departments—that reach decisions on foreign investment and technology projects. Further, as Lombard showed in his study of Columbia's foreign direct investment screening process, a major gap can exist between the foreign investment policies and regulations and the administrative practices because of the subjectivity of the decision makers, the considerable concentration of power in a limited number of officials, and the uneven efficiency, speed, and sophistication of the evaluation process [Lombard 1978]. Even though the atmosphere has become somewhat less confrontational, MNCs perceive generally that developing governments impose a greater degree of regulation on their manufacturing investments than they did a decade ago.

Developed Country Governments and Interest Groups _____

The policies of a number of developed nations, such as the United States, West Germany, the United Kingdom, and the Netherlands, are influenced by their dual position as significant investors as well as recipients of foreign direct investments. These countries generally follow policies of neutrality with respect to outward investments and of a relatively open door to inward investment flows.

Regulations by Developed Host Countries

Nevertheless, a number of OECD countries exercise sectoral controls or restrictions in banking, insurance, communications, air transport, tobacco, shipping, natural resources, energy sectors, and nuclear energy. These countries reserve such sectors for exclusive or predominant national ownership, including that of state enterprises, or they impose regulations on their activities. For example, Canada's National Energy Programme in 1980 aimed at Canadianization of the oil and gas sectors by increasing ownership by the Canadian government and private Canadian concerns to 50 percent or more.

Other developed nations have certain screening procedures and performance requirements with respect to inward direct investments. For example, the Foreign Investment Review Board in Australia evaluates the merits of incoming new investments and acquisitions from the standpoint of elaborate net economic and other benefits/costs standards. Several developed nations impose performance requirements on foreign enterprises pertaining to local labor and material content, expansion of exports, and limitations on imports. A number of OECD countries require formal authorizations of inward direct investments. While their industrial and trade policies and their sectoral and other controls have had important impacts on multinational investment and technological arrangements, the overall regulatory framework imposed by developed nations on manufacturing direct investments has been far less restrictive than the controls employed by developing country governments.

Industrial Policies

Many developed countries have played an active role through their industrial policies in encouraging inward foreign investments of technology agreements that contribute especially to their national technological capabilities and development of high technology industries. They have sought also to increase exports, create employment, and improve their balance of payments.

The role of the Ministry of International Trade and Industry (MITI) of Japan and the close cooperation between the government, industry, financial institutions, and trading companies in indicative planning of the future directions of Japanese industrial growth have been major factors in the country's competitive strength in world markets. As is well known, Japanese policies have emphasized acquisition of foreign technology through licensing and cross-licensing agreements with foreign enterprises, rather than through inward direct investments, which until recently were restricted in ownership and other aspects. For example, between 1950 and 1972, Japanese companies entered into 17,600 licensing agreements to obtain technology covering nearly every field of modern industry; for this technology they paid $3.3 billion in royalties [Yoshino 1976]. The Japanese then proceeded to improve and modernize this technology and were able to emphasize improved quality of product through effective quality control.

Through its indicative planning, financing, and other concerted measures, Japan in recent years has been phasing down its declining industries, such as shipbuilding, textiles, steel, and aluminum while concentrating support on more promising, higher technology sectors, such as computers and software, microelectronics, microbiology, genetic engineering, and optical fibers. A central element of this government-industry cooperation to develop industries of the future is emphasis on the widening and deepening of scientific research and technological development in key sectors. To foster this research and development Japan has encouraged information exchange, joint research and development, and cross-licensing between its MNCs and foreign MNCs. For example, Japan's MITI invited foreign computer companies to enter into information exchanges in a joint program to develop a fifth generation computer and joint R&D or cross-licensing between MNCs in such high technology fields as telecommunications, semiconductors, genetic engineering, and robotics [U.N. Centre on Transnational Corporations 1983]. Through such forward looking and coherent industrial policies and through relationships with foreign MNCs, Japan expects to engage in industries with high growth and competitive potential in the future. Japanese MNCs are playing an important part in the technological developments and cooperative arrangements with foreign firms; they expect to play key roles in competing in home and in world markets in the future.

Other countries have focused their industrial policies on development of high technology industries in which MNCs will play significant roles. For example, through its indicative planning, France plans to boost R&D to at least 2.5 percent of its GNP by 1985 and steer industrial development toward high technology sectors such as micro-electronics, bio-technology, and aerospace. To achieve these goals, France grants preferential treatment to MNCs that provide these types of advanced technological knowhow and engage in relevant R&D in contrast to those operating in traditional sectors [U.N. Centre on Transnational Corporations 1983].

Policies of Capital-Exporting Nations

Developed home-country policies have generally supported outward direct investments by MNCs and have strengthened the competitiveness of their enterprises by official trade and investment financing, assistance for technological development, and various industrial policies. Developed nations have also encouraged foreign investments to Third World countries by financing, risk insurance, and occasional tax incentives while striving to obtain national treatment for their enterprises overseas and to protect their investments. A few countries such as Sweden require prior authorization of direct investment outflows. However, industrial nations have imposed some restrictions on outgoing investments for balance-of-payments reasons. For example, the United States imposed mandatory controls on direct investments from 1965 to 1974 to deal with balance-of-payments deficits. Other developed countries have given particular attention to foreign direct investments that promote their exports.

Financing Related Foreign Direct Investments and Other International Business

More significantly, developed nations have used packages of financing and export credits, often at concessional interest rates along with other indirect subsidies, to promote exports that are related to their foreign direct investments. Close links exist between exports and direct investments because the major contribution by MNCs of equity capital is often the machinery and equipment supplied. Commonly, developed nations tie their export credits, financing, and foreign aid to capital goods exports. Further, the financing arrangements and the terms, involving mixes of export financing, longer-term credits, and official aid, may play decisive roles in the decisions of developing and state socialist nations in the selection of foreign companies for joint ventures, turnkey projects, and various industrial cooperation agreements. The U.S. government has protested about various OECD governments' mixing of long-term financing and official aid at interest rates below the market rates on various major industrial cooperation and other projects in Eastern European socialist nations. Under the auspices of the OECD, a broad agreement that aims at narrowing interest rate differentials between the United States and other OECD countries was reached in 1982, but the conflicts with respect to financing of East-West trade have not been resolved.

As another example, the Japanese government has strongly supported the increased involvement of Japanese MNCs and smaller firms in direct investments, trade, and other business in Asian countries. The Japanese Export-Import Bank's lending increased two-and-a-half times in the 1981 fiscal year to more than $2 billion a year [U.N. Centre on Transnational Corporations 1983]. These loans finance primarily Japanese exports of industrial machinery and plants, often related to manufacturing investments by Japanese firms. The Bank extends loans also to Japanese companies to finance their equity participation in manufacturing investments or to foreign borrowers who enter into joint ventures with Japanese enterprises.

U.S. Antitrust Policy

The U.S. government extends its antitrust policy to the entire multinational system of companies throughout the world, including its affiliates and licensees in foreign nations; it applies this policy also to mergers with or acquisitions of foreign firms and to foreign companies operating abroad where their behavior has actual or potential anticompetitive effects in the United States. Made highly complex, perplexing, and uncertain as a result of numerous court decisions and administrative interpretations, U.S. antitrust policy is more restrictive than that of the EEC and other Western nations. The extraterritorial application of U.S. antitrust laws engenders conflicts with other nations. Furthermore, American MNCs and many authorities in the field believe that U.S. antitrust policy is unrealistic, weakens the competitive strength of U.S. companies operating abroad, and hinders the international economic position of the nation.

U.S. Labor Unions and MNCs

Since the late 1960s, labor unions in the United States along with some intellectuals and other groups have become increasingly disturbed about the displacement of jobs by direct foreign investments abroad. U.S. labor unions contend that U.S. MNCs have exported jobs by direct investment and by transferring technology abroad. Various studies have concluded that the employment effects of American foreign direct investments are somewhat positive, based upon exports related to the direct investments and the defensive reaction of many companies to increased trade restrictions abroad. The assumptions of various studies have been challenged, but the net employment effects of foreign direct investments and technology transfers are minor compared with the employment effects of economic recessions, technological change, and shifts in consumer demand. Although little empirical support exists for

U.S. and Western labor union contention that direct investments lead to major unemployment, the labor union leaders continue to maintain their positions about the detrimental impact of foreign investment on the domestic economy.

Labor unions maintain also that MNCs obtain major advantages because U.S. tax policy allows them to defer their taxes until profits are repatriated home. Although modifications in U.S. policy have been proposed and considered, the existing tax policy has been continued in order not to place American companies in a disadvantageous position in relation to foreign competitors in international business.

More recently, U.S. labor unions have concentrated more on increased protection against competitive imports and pressures on foreign MNCs to invest in manufacturing in the United States. Partly as a result, a number of Japanese and other MNCs have undertaken manufacturing investments in the United States. Pressures from labor unions, workers, and some firms have led the American government to negotiate "voluntary" export restraints on a number of competitive import products such as those that the Japanese government accepted on automobile exports during the last 3 years. More seriously, the United Automobile Workers Union has pressed strongly for performance requirements legislation that would require progressively more local content in automobile production from 60 to 90 percent by 1986, depending upon the number of automobiles produced. The U.S. House of Representatives passed this bill in 1982. While this bill has not become law, considerable support exists for increased performance requirements in the United States and other Western nations.

Western labor unions' efforts to create a common front of national unions and to bargain internationally with MNCs have not succeeded because of major differences among the unions. U.S. and other Western unions continue to perceive MNCs as major threats to them. Union argue that MNCs have much greater flexibility than the unions: MNCs can establish production abroad, but the unions cannot shift the workers to follow production in other countries [Root 1983].

Changing Patterns of Foreign Direct Investments _____

By the 1980s, the United States had become both the principal recipient and the major source of foreign direct investments. From 1978 to 1980 the U.S. share of direct investment outflows was a little less than half of the total while its share of the inflow was about 30 percent of the total [U.N. Centre on Transnational Corporations 1983]. A decline in the relative importance of the United States in foreign direct investment outflows took place while the significance of West Germany, the United Kingdom, other Western European countries, Canada, and Japan increased as investor nations. While foreign direct investments in extractive industries declined throughout the 1970s, direct investments in manufacturing, and especially in services, increased rapidly. Particularly notable were the increased investments in banking and insurance. As mentioned previously, state enterprises participated in increased direct investments and other multinational business. Further, Third World nations strongly increased their direct investments in manufacturing in other developing countries although the total magnitude of these investments was relatively small—

only about 2 percent of reported foreign direct investment outflows during the period 1978–1980; but the data on these investments seem to be incomplete [U.N. Centre on Transnational Corporations 1983].

Multiforms of International Business by MNCs

Even though the large industrial MNCs continue to have major involvement in foreign direct investments which they control, they have substantially increased their participation in joint ventures (including minority-owned ones), international licensing, subcontracting, turnkey projects, management contracts and other contractual arrangements in recent years. In an OECD study, Oman terms these arrangements "new forms of investment" [Oman 1984]. Joint ventures, which do involve equity ownership are investments, but the other contractual arrangements comprise nonequity participation, closer to medium-term service contracts. International licensing, management contracts, subcontracting, and other arrangements are not new, for MNCs have long been engaging in them on an intrafirm or arms-length basis. Further industrial cooperation agreements with state socialist nations have involved various combinations of such contracts. What is new, is that MNCs have been participating in joint ventures and contractual agreements to a greater extent over the last decade or so.

Factors Favoring "Newer" Forms of International Participation

MNCs have entered into joint ventures and other types of international arrangements to a greater extent in response to developing host government regulations and also as a result of their own strategies and initiatives. Faced with rapidly changing global environments, increased international competition, greater risk and uncertainty, and a perception of more stringent regulations, many MNCs have been shifting to joint ventures, licensing, and other contractual agreements. The motives of MNCs have been not only defensive reactions but also strategic initiatives to respond more effectively to changing global competitive environments, to new opportunities in OPEC and other countries, and to the goal of greater flexibility in their global operations. For example, a number of Western European, U.S., and other firms have worked out multibillion dollar engineering and turnkey plus projects, involving exports of machinery and equipment and provision of technical assistance and management, with a number of oil-producing countries in the Middle East and North Africa and smaller scale projects in newly industrialized nations. Large industrial cooperation projects by Western nations and Japan undertaken with socialist East European countries in the 1960s and 1970s have involved licensing, co-production, subcontracting, turnkey projects, and occasional joint ventures since traditional direct investments have been excluded. As control of the natural resource industries has shifted to developing nations, MNCs in these activities have concentrated more on processing, manufacturing (for example, petro-chemicals), and marketing. These MNCs have entered into more joint ventures, service contracts, technical assistance and management agreements, and other arrangements.

Increase in Joint Ventures

Available data show that Western European and Japanese MNCs have long found establishing joint ventures to be advantageous, particularly with minority ownership, in developing countries, partly as newer entrants. During the period 1966 to 1970 (the last period for which the author has data), more than four fifths of Japanese manufacturing affiliates established in developing countries and about half of Western European affiliates were either minority owned or 50–50 percent (co-owned) joint ventures [U.N. Centre on Transnational Corporations 1978]. During the same period, 1966–1970, about one third of the U.S. manufacturing affiliates established in developing nations were minority owned or co-owned joint ventures, while in 1971–1975 about two fifths of the U.S. manufacturing affiliates were either minority or 50–50 percent joint ventures [U.N. Centre on Transnational Corporations 1978]. The U.S. Department of Commerce reported that in 1977 American companies abroad had more joint venture affiliates by number, although not by book value, than wholly-owned subsidiaries [U.S. Department of Commerce 1981].

Thus, U.S. MNCs have been participating to a greater extent in joint ventures, particularly minority owned and co-owned ones, in developing countries. Besides reacting to the pressures of host developing governments, U.S. MNCs entered into joint ventures to become more competitive in foreign investment entry with European and Japanese companies. Further, U.S. MNCs found that they were able to exercise considerable control over minority-owned joint ventures through management, product and process technology, product differentiation, promotion, trademarks, brands, and other aspects of marketing and business expertise [Dymsza 1984]. By the late 1960s and 1970s, U.S. companies were finding many more suitable partners available for joint ventures in a number of developing countries. These partners contributed managerial, marketing, financial, and other capabilities as well as contacts with governments and financial institutions. Thus, joint ventures brought definite advantages to U.S. as well as to Western European and Japanese firms even though some of the circumstances varied.

In a recent survey of 51 large multinational companies in the United States, Robinson found that 80 percent of the firms stated that their preferred type of entry relationship was joint ventures (in many cases with minority or co-ownership), licensing and other contracts, or flexible arrangements (various combinations of direct investment, joint ventures, and contractual agreements) [Robinson 1983].

Global Investment Environment

Besides a number of the factors previously mentioned, Oman and others attribute this growing participation of MNCs in joint ventures and various contractual agreements to many other aspects of the changing global investment environment. A whole series of related factors—among them, the stagflaton of the 1970s and early 1980s, the global recessions in the mid 1970s and early 1980s, a slowdown in domestic investments and productivity growth in OECD countries, the shift to floating exchange rates, the relatively high inflation until recently, and the high interest rates—all of these and other factors—have led Western companies "to focus on relatively short-term financial returns" and generally " to shorten overall investment planning horizons considerably" [Oman 1984]. The shorter-term foreign investment planning horizon has been reinforced by the recycling of OPEC and other oil-producing country funds by the multinational banks, the phenomenal expansion of the Euro-currency markets, the short-term character of the bulk of these deposits and loans, and the far greater involvement of multinational banks in international finance in the 1970s and early 1980s. Further, as whole sectors of industry have matured and as technology, marketing, and other business expertise and access to world markets have become widely diffused over time, many leading MNCs, including those which in the past have had policies of entering into wholly-owned production of subsidiaries, have established more flexible strategies to enter into joint ventures, licensing, and various combinations of contractual agreements.

In the past, major impediments to joint ventures and some contractual arrangements included significant transactions costs in finding suitable local partners or associates, and in negotiating, monitoring, and enforcing the agreements. The Westernization and modernization of business in many developing countries and the improvement of communications networks have substantially reduced monitoring costs and facilitated parent-company control of global operations with many affiliates, without having 100 percent or majority ownership [Oman 1984]. On the other hand, the transactions and control costs of traditional foreign direct investments have probably increased because of increased performance and other restrictions by host governments, pressures for renegotiation of conditions of entry, and political risk. As another hypothesis, a number of the large oligopoly MNCs may find that they can partly internalize certain firm-specific advantages—in technology, management, product differentiation, trademarks, and other expertise—with joint venture affiliates or perhaps through international contractual arrangements such as licensing and franchising. In some cases, as in the hotel industry, international franchising can be the most cost-effective way for a hotel enterprise to capitalize on its firm-specific, oligopoly advantages.

Further, as the period of intensive innovation in an industry decelerates and runs its course, many MNCs find that licensing and contractual arrangements become more efficient and profitable ways of undertaking international business. Contractor points out many strategic factors that encourage MNCs and other firms to engage in arms-length licensing [Contractor 1982]. Thus, the policies of host countries, changes in global environments, the strategic responses and initiatives of MNCs, and the more flexible strategies of many MNCs have played a part in the shift to multi-types of international business. Still, MNCs continue to engage in traditional foreign direct investments and to develop global strategies to integrate their business around the world; they also engage in major international trade, which is discussed briefly next.

Changing Character of International Trade

Even though international trade is based upon comparative advantage, reciprocal demand, technological advantage, the international product cycle, internal and external economies of scale, relative income levels, nonprice competition, and other factors, multinational firms have been playing a major part in determining the composition and direction of trade flows. An increasing part of world trade has been intrafirm trade by MNCs between parent companies and affiliates and among affiliates in the MNC system.

The intrafirm trade of U.S. MNCs in 1977 comprised 22 percent of total American foreign trade; if minority-owned affiliates and foreign MNCs are included, 39 percent of total U.S. imports and 36 percent of total U.S. exports were intrafirm transactions in 1977 [U.S. Department of Commerce 1981]. Further, as industrial cooperation projects with socialist nations slowed down after the middle of the 1970s (because of global recessions, increased protectionism, politicalization of East–West business, and substantial foreign debt of certain socialist countries) counter trade and buy-back arrangements have been accounting for a much more significant part of East–West trade. Counter trade has been spreading between MNCs, state enterprises, and various firms in other transactions in developed and developing countries.

As another hypothesis, when industries mature in many developed nations and in newly industrialized nations, certain MNCs may cut back on foreign direct investments and capitalize on their economies of scale in production, marketing, and finance to engage in more international trade. Thus, these MNCs may concentrate on exploiting their oligopoly advantages in international trade and finance. Japan's leading trading companies offer an example of firms that exploit such advantages through a combination of imports, exports, distribution, financing, and direct investments with small manufacturers involving joint ventures.

Japanese trading companies engage in imports of essential materials, export of manufactures, organization and promotion of direct investments involving smaller Japanese manufacturers and foreign partners in joint ventures, arrangement of trade and investment financing, and participation in technology and service contractual arrangements.

Finally, many industrial MNCs continue to engage in traditional foreign direct investments to exploit their unique firm-specific advantages and locational opportunities by creating integrated global production networks to serve multiple regional and national markets [Behrman 1984]. These firms develop global strategies to integrate not only production but also sourcing, finance, R&D, product design, various aspects of marketing, personnel policies, and external relations—although many variations exist from one company to another.

Recent Changes in Global Environment

Multinational business has been affected by rapid and dramatic changes in the global, regional, and national environments in the 1970s and the 1980s, some of them previously mentioned. A discussion of the major changes in environments—economic, political, socio-cultural, competitive, technological, and others—is beyond the scope of this article. Nevertheless, let us consider a few in the 1980s. During the early 1980s a sharp and deep global recession took place with major increases in unemployment in most countries.

External Debt of Developing Nations

In 1984, developing countries had an external debt of more than $800 billion, well over half owed to international commercial banks and other private creditors. The largest part of the debt was concentrated in Latin American countries, particularly Argentina, Brazil, Mexico, and Venezuela; a considerable part of the private debt was short- or medium-term with maturities under 2 years; much of it was at high, floating interest rates tied to the U.S. prime rate or the London interbank rate.

Through multilateral negotiations involving the International Monetary Fund (IMF), in some cases the Bank of International Settlements and the major international creditor banks (some of which had to commit additional funds), the debt of the major Latin American countries has been restructured or rolled over. Under the terms of the restructuring arrangements, the IMF has imposed rather severe conditions on the major debtor nations. These conditions vary, but essentially they require major debtor nations to hold down their governmental expenditures, pursue more effective monetary restraints, reduce inflation significantly, cut down on their imports, and expand exports. These IMF imposed conditions have had serious repercussions and trade-offs on the debtor nations by reducing their economic growth sharply, increasing unemployment, distorting income distribution, and leading to considerable resentment and opposition by the affected groups. Some countries, such as Brazil and Argentina, have experienced difficulty in meeting targets. As a consequence, the IMF and commercial banks have cut off their financing during certain periods while further negotiations were taking place. Several smaller debtor nations, including Chile, Peru, and Bolivia, have not worked out restructuring agreements and ceased payments of interest and principal on their external debt in 1984.

The major internal debt problem of developing countries has had numerous ramifications on multinational business, many more than can be discussed here. It has led to declines in exports to these countries as they have imposed new trade restrictions; it has held back licensing and other contractual agreements with business firms in these nations. Further, with the deterioration in the foreign investment climate and political uncertainties, MNCs have exercised considerable caution in undertaking additional direct investments or expanding existing operations. Further MNCs have faced exchange controls on some of their remittances of dividends, royalties, management fees, and interest on loans advanced. Large debtor nations, such as Mexico, have made excellent progress in reducing imports and expanding exports sharply with rigorous monetary, fiscal, and other measures; but the trade-off in slowing down domestic growth and reducing real income of many people has led to considerable opposition in the country. Brazil and Argentina, while improving their balance of payments, have been unable to control surging inflation; widespread opposition exists within these countries to the economic conditions and trade-offs of the restructuring agreements.

As one scenario, the longer-term resolution of the external debt of developing countries requires sustained economic growth in the industrial nations in the order of 3 ½ percent or more for many years [International Monetary Fund 1984]. As Keynes stated with respect to German reparations after World War I, debtor nations can repay and service debt essentially through exports to the creditor nations. Thus, a second important condition would require the industrial nations to ease their trade restrictions in order to encourage increased exports by the debtor to creditor nations. Other financial experts believe that the major commercial creditor banks will have to increase the maturities of the debt and reduce interest rates substantially. They will also have to lend considerable funds to enable the countries to continue their economic growth and viability—essential for future servicing of the debt. On the other hand, the debtor nations have a responsibility to continue sound economic policies to hold down inflation, improve their balance of payments, and restructure key aspects of their economies. Certain authorities believe that these conditions and others are not likely to be met; thus, periodic renegotiations and restructuring will probably take place. But somehow, the international financial system will muddle through.

Others believe that substantial amounts of the external debt cannot be repaid or serviced, and the international banks will have to write off large amounts. More pessimistic scenarios exist: that the substantial debt of developing nations threatens to bring about a major collapse of the international monetary system and worldwide economic disaster which will have severe consequences on multinational business. While the future is unclear, this important problem will have to be monitored carefully and widespread international cooperation is required to deal with it.

Other Key Changes

Since the early 1970s with 2 major global recessions, there has been a major resurgence of protectionism. Despite the progress made in the Tokyo round, the continued imposition of voluntary export restraints, various subtle nontariff barriers, the politicalization of East-West trade, the rise in other trade conflicts involving Japan and other major industrial nations, disagreements over the future of GATT—these and many other developments—threaten the liberal trading system developed in the post-World War II period. The continued resurgence of protectionism also poses major difficulties to the large developing countries to service their substantial debt. Further, the European Economic Community has encountered major problems in moving ahead with its economic integration, and the member nations have been experiencing record levels of unemployment.

In the 1970s and 1980s the global economy has become more competitive because of increased competition not only from Japan but also from the newly industrialized nations such as South Korea, Brazil, Taiwan, Hong Kong, and Mexico, in products such as textiles, apparel, steel, metallurgical products, and electronics. Further, rapid developments in high technology are on the way in new generations of computers, data processing, robotics, satellite communications, biological industries, and other industries.

Recently, the power of the OPEC cartel has seriously weakened and oil prices have been falling; nevertheless, the energy crisis may reemerge within the next decade with growth of demand and limitations in supply. After a period of considerable weakness in 1978–1979, the U.S. dollar has been exceptionally strong during the last few years and is considered to be over-valued. Partly as a result, substantial short-term funds have flowed into the United States; the trade deficit in this country was about $123 billion in 1984, and U.S. MNCs have suffered substantial translation foreign exchange losses. When the U.S. dollar declines, it may overshoot "purchasing power parity" value and have major effects upon investment, money, and trade flows.

Rapid population growth, including urbanization, continues in some developing nations while population has largely peaked in a number of developed countries. The People's Republic of China, while continuing its socialism, has been adapting certain capitalistic measures to spur its economic development and modernization. In the future, we may see further moves toward convergence of Western mixed capitalism and state socialism, following the patterns of Hungary and China, particularly in view of the economic difficulties of communist nations. Widespread hunger in many African nations has been a very serious problem during recent years. Major differences continue to exist between the Group of 77, representing developing nations, and the Western industrial countries. The major actors involved in the North-South dialogue are making slow progress in reaching accommodations. These are simply a few of the recent developments, among many, that will have significant impacts on multinational business.

Managerial Responses of Multinationals _____

Multinational companies have been responding to the multi-actor setting, the demands of host and home countries, the increased political and other uncertainties, and rapidly changing international environments by more effective strategic and operational planning, organizational adaptation, computerized information systems, strategic and operational controls, and management development. The conclusion of this article will concentrate briefly on recent developments in strategic planning and organizational development by MNCs.

International Strategic Planning

Faced with these rapid changes in environments, including increased political risk and more global competition, many MNCs have responded by fine-tuning their strategic planning systems [Dymsza 1984]. They have developed more integrative planning to rationalize resources more effectively on a global basis. They have granted primary responsibility for strategic planning to line managers at national, regional, product, and other levels while also fully involving staff officers in the process. MNCs have increasingly utilized computerized forecasting models with alternative assumptions, expanded use of more sophisticated portfolio planning in resource allocation, engaged in more rigorous competitive assessment, and developed strategies aimed at productivity improvement, cost reduction, new product development, increased market penetration, and management development. International strategic planning has become more hardheaded as MNCs have striven to increase their profitability by concentrating on their more promising global product lines and divesting country and product operations that do not achieve their earnings goal or do not fit with their longer-term missions. Further, MNCs have been concentrating on international risk management and exploiting their unique advantages.

Even so, some evidence indicates that U.S. companies still place major emphasis on bottom line profitability from year to year rather than on longer-term strategic management. Further, American companies reward managers with bonuses and advancement in the corporate hierarchy based upon short-term profitability achievements rather than effective strategic planning and implementations. In order to emphasize strategic management, many MNCs need more positive incentives to reward managers for effective long-range planning and its implementation.

Organization Change

Building on the major contribution of Chandler that the underlying strategy of a firm determines its structure, Stopford, through his own empirical research, developed a model of the evolution of organization of the U.S. MNCs in response to changes in their international strategy [Stopford and Wells 1972].

U.S. MNCs established the international divisions structure mainly after they expanded through direct investments in manufacturing overseas. However, in view of difficulties of integrating international divisions and domestic product divisions and the inherent conflicts in this organization, U.S. MNCs changed to more global structures: companies that formulated strategies to diversify by products overseas established global product divisions; firms that developed strategies to expand globally by geographic areas with few products (and that emphasized marketing) established global regional divisions. Companies that developed strategies to expand overseas, with a mix of products into a number of regions and encountered greater complexity in their business established mixed or matrix structures. Many U.S. MNCs have followed the pattern of this model developed by Stopford; yet, numerous U.S. companies have continued to have international divisions in some form and have followed organizational patterns that vary from the model. In fact, a number of U.S. and Western MNCs have frequently revised their structures in ways that cannot be attributed to their changes in fundamental international strategy.

The proposition that international strategy determines structure remains an intriguing proposition, but it has not been supported by recent research and experience. For example, in my interviews of close to 100 executives of U.S. and Western European MNCs from 1978–1983, I did not find conclusive evidence that international strategy determined structure; rather, there was an interdependent relationship between international strategy and organization with each influencing the other. Many other factors, such as a company's history, its international experience, its availability of international managers, its expansion through acquisitions, the role of dynamic chief executives, and its corporate culture and style of management, all have significant influence on the organization of MNCs.

Further, the change to more global structures does not necessarily make an MNC more geocentric in practice. For example, Davidson and Haspeslagh showed in a recent study that many corporations that adopt global product divisions often do not achieve the advantages of global rationalization of production that they anticipated, and in certain cases they fail to develop the integrated strategies that would make the companies more effective global competitors. [Davidson and Haspeslagh 1982]. The global product structure may lead managers to become more risk aversive in their strategic perspective and may further lead them to emphasize domestic business.

Actually, because of the complexity and changing character of their international business, many MNCs have adopted various mixed structures. Some MNCs have established a mixture of product and geographic organizations, using aspects of a matrix, and retaining some elements of the international division to manage part of their international business or to act as service units.

Bartlett in a recent article emphasizes that many companies have been misdirecting their efforts in persistent reorganizations from international divisions to more global structures in the search for the ideal organizations [Bartlett 1983]. The diverse and highly successful MNCs he studied, all of which retained international divisions, have focused particularly on developing new management perspectives and decision-making processes to deal with the complex demands of international business. Among other aspects, these companies have encouraged product and functional personnel to participate more actively in international decision making with the line division, regional, and country managers. They have developed supplementary and informal lines of information and communication through headquarters, regional and country meetings, training courses, conferences, task forces, interdepartmental teams on particular problems, and project groups. These MNCs have particularly emphasized a supportive corporate culture that encourages cooperation, negotiation, and compromise, that rewards improved interpersonal relations and communication, and that fits with the articulated company strategies, goals, and values [Bartlett 1983].

Western European MNCs that established centralized functional and mother-daughter structures in the postwar period have moved to more global division types of organizations—often mixed types—as they have become more multinational. In a number of cases they have changed to global georgaphic structures or to mixed global functional-product, product-geographic, or matrix structures. Thus, in many respects, there has been some convergence in structures as well as in strategic planning by U.S. and Western European MNCs.

Concluding Remarks

Western MNCs have been responding to the more rapidly changing multi-actor global environments by more realistic, fine-tuned strategic planning, organizational adaptation, computerized information systems that track developments around the world, competitive assessment and opportunity/risk evaluation. They have also been emphasizing strategic and operational controls, management development, and external relations globally. In addition, MNCs have had to make trade-offs of the advantages of global integration of their business against pressures for adaptation to national conditions and the demands of other important actors. As a consequence, many MNCs have been engaging in more joint ventures, various contractual arrangements, and counter-trade. MNCs will continue to face major challenges from rapid changes in global and national environments—including unexpected discontinuities—and from the pressures of other major actors.

References

Agmon, Tamir, and Kindleberger, Charles P., eds. *Multinationals from Small Countries.* Cambridge, MA: MIT Press, 1974.

Akinsaya, Adoye A. *Multinationals in a Changing Environment.* New York: Praeger Publishers, 1984.

Arpan, Jeffrey S.; Flowers, Edward B.; and Ricks, David A. "Foreign Direct Investments in the United States: The State of Knowledge of Research." *Journal of International Business Studies,* Spring/Summer 1981, pp. 137–154.

Bartlett, Christopher A. "MNC's: Getting off the Reorganization Merry-Go-Round." *Harvard Business Review,* March-April 1983.

Behrman, Jack N. *Industrial Policies: International Restructuring and Transnationals.* Lexington, MA: Lexington Books, 1984.

———. "Transnational Corporations in the New International Economic Order." *Journal of International Business Studies,* Spring/Summer 1981, pp. 29–42.

Bergsten, Fred; Horst, Thomas; Moran, Theodore H. *American Multinationals and American Interests.* Washington, DC: Brookings Institution, 1978.

Boarman, Patrick M., and Schollhammer, Hans, eds. *Multinational Corporations and Governments.* New York: Praeger Publishers, 1975.

Calvet, A. L. "A Synthesis of Foreign Direct Investment Theories and Theories of the Multinational Firm." *Journal of International Business Studies,* Spring/Summer 1981, pp. 43–59.

Caves, Richard E. *Multinational Enterprise and Economic Analysis.* Cambridge, UK: Cambridge University Press, 1982.

Contractor, Farok J. *International Technology Licensing.* Lexington, MA: Lexington Books, 1981.

Davidson, William H. *Global Strategic Management.* New York: Ronald Press, 1982.

———, and Haspeslagh, P. "Shaping a Worldwide Organization." *Harvard Business Review,* July-August 1982.

Driscoll, Robert E., and Behrman, Jack N. *National Industrial Policies.* Cambridge, MA: Oelgeschlager, Gunn & Hain, 1984.

Dunning, John H., ed. *Economic Analysis and Multinational Enterprise.* New York: Praeger Publishers, 1973.

———. "Towards an Eclectic Theory of International Production: Some Empirical Tests." *Journal of International Business Studies.* Spring/Summer 1980, pp. 9–31.

Dymsza, William A. *Multinational Business Strategy.* New York: McGraw-Hill, 1972.

———. "Joint Ventures by U.S. Multinational Corporations in Developing Countries." Proceedings of International Meeting of the Academy of International Business. Singapore: University of Singapore, 1974.

———. "Global Strategic Planning: A Model and Recent Developments." *Journal of International Business Studies,* Fall 1984, pp. 169–184.

Frank, Isaiah. *Foreign Enterprises in Developing Countries.* Baltimore: Johns Hopkins Press, 1980.

Franko, Lawrence G. *The European Multinationals.* Stamford, CT: Greylock Publishers, 1976.

Gladwin, Thomas N., and Walter, Ingo. *Multinationals under Fire.* New York: John Wiley & Sons, 1980.

Goldberg, Walter H., ed. *Government and Multinationals.* Cambridge, MA: Oelgeschlager, Gunn & Hain, 1983.

Hood, Neil, and Young, Stephen. *The Economics of Multinational Enterprise.* London: Longman Group Ltd., 1979.

International Monetary Fund. *World Economic Outlook.* Occasional Paper 9. Washington, DC, 1983.

_____. *World Economic Outlook.* Occasional Paper 27. Washington, DC, 1984.

Hawkins, Robert G. "The International Banking System Outlook in a Contest of Crisis." *International Business in the Asia-Pacific Region: Trends and Prospects for the 1980's.* Singapore: National University of Singapore, 1984.

Kindleberger, Charles P., and Audretsch, David B., eds. *The Multinational Corporation in the 1980's.* Cambridge, MA: MIT Press, 1983.

Knickerbocker, F.T. *Oligopolistic Reaction and Multinational Enterprise.* Cambridge, MA: Harvard University Press, 1973.

Kobrin, Stephen J. *Managing Political Risk Assessment.* Berkeley, CA: University of California Press, 1982.

Kujawa, Duane, ed. *International Labor and the Multinational Enterprise.* New York: Praeger Publishers, 1975.

Lall, Sanjaya. *The New Multinationals.* New York: John Wiley & Sons, 1983.

Lombard, Francois. "The Foreign Direct Investment Screening Process." *Journal of International Business Studies,* Winter 1978, pp. 66–80.

Mazzolini, Renato. "European Government-Controlled Enterprises: Explaining International Strategic and Policy Decisions." *Journal of International Business Studies,* Winter 1979, pp. 16–27.

_____. "European Government-Controlled Enterprises: An Organizational Politics View." *Journal of International Business Studies,* Spring/Summer 1980, pp. 48–58.

Moxon, Richard W. "The Motivation for Investment in Offshore Plants: The Case of the U.S. Electronics Industry." *Journal of International Business Studies,* Spring 1975, pp. 51–66.

Negandhi, Anant. "Global Business in the 1980's and Beyond." *International Business in the Asia-Pacific Region: Trends and Prospects for the 1980's.* Singapore: University of Singapore, 1984.

Oman, Charles. *New Forms of International Investment.* Paris: Development Centre, Organization for Economic Co-operation and Development (OECD), 1984.

Reuber, Grant L. *Private Foreign Investments in Development.* Oxford, UK: Clarendon Press, 1973.

Robinson, Richard. *National Control of Foreign Business Entry.* New York: Praeger 1976.

_____. "Background Concepts and Philosophy of International Business from World War II to the Present." *Journal of International Business Studies,* Spring/Summer 1981, pp. 13–22.

_____. *Performance Requirements for Foreign Business.* New York: Praeger Publishers, 1983.

Root, Franklin R., and Ahmed A. "The Influence of Policy Instruments of Manufacturing Direct Foreign Investment in Developing Countries." *Journal of International Business Studies,* Winter 1978, pp. 81–94.

_____. *Foreign Market Entry Strategies.* New York: Amacom, 1982.

_____. *International Trade and Investment.* Cincinnati, OH: Southwestern Publishing Co., 1983, chapters 21 to 24.

Rubin, Seymour J., and Graham, Thomas R., eds. *Managing Trade Relations in the 1980's.* Totowa, NJ: Rowman & Allanheld, 1984.

Rugman, A. M. *Inside the Multinationals: The Economics of Internal Markets.* Totowa, NJ: Croom Helm, Ltd., 1981.

Savary, Julien. *French Multinationals.* New York: St. Martin's Press, 1984.

Stopford, John M., and Wells, Louis T., Jr. *Managing the Multinational Enterprise.* New York: Basic Books, 1972.

Tsurumi, Yoshi. *The Japanese Are Coming.* Cambridge, MA: Ballinger Publishing Co., 1976.

_____. *Multinational Management* (second edition). Cambridge, MA: Ballinger Publishing Co., 1983.

United Nations Centre on Transnational Corporations. *Transnational Corporations in World Development: A Re-Examination.* New York: United Nations, 1978.

_____. *Transnational Corporations in World Development: Third Survey.* New York: United Nations, 1983.

U.S. Department of Commerce. *U.S. Direct Investments Abroad, 1977.* Washington, DC: Government Printing Office, 1981.

Vernon, Raymond. "International Investment and International Trade in the Product Cycle." *Quarterly Journal of Economics,* May 1966, pp. 190–207.

_____. *Sovereignty at Bay.* New York: Basic Books, 1971.

_____. *Storm over the Multinationals.* Cambridge, MA: Harvard University Press, 1977.

_____. "The International Aspects of State-Owned Enterprises." *Journal of International Business Studies,* Winter 1979, pp. 7–15.

Wells, Louis T. Jr. "Social Cost/Benefit Analysis for MNC's." *Harvard Business Review,* March-April 1975.

_____. *Third World Multinationals.* Cambridge, MA: MIT Press, 1983.

Yoshino, Y. *Multinational Enterprises.* Cambridge, MA: Harvard University Press, 1976.

2. THE RELATIONSHIP OF HEADQUARTERS COUNTRY AND INDUSTRY CLASSIFICATION TO FINANCIAL STRUCTURE

J. MARKHAM COLLINS AND WILLIAM S. SEKELY

J. Markham Collins and William S. Sekely teach, respectively, at The University of Tulsa and The University of Dayton.

Introduction

The concept of an optimal capital structure has been a subject of interest and controversy in the finance discipline. While the question is not yet resolved, several conclusions have found wide, if not total, acceptance. First, the tax subsidy on interest makes debt less expensive than equity, even if one holds risk constant. Second, the level of financial leverage a firm can bear is a function of its business risk. Third, beyond some degree of financial leverage, the expected costs of bankruptcy lower the value of the firm.

Studies of U.S. manufacturing firms have used industry classification as a proxy for business risk. Schwartz and Aronson (S&A) first examined the effect of industry classification on the ratio of common equity to total assets [8]. Using one-way analysis of variance, they found capital structure varied within industries less than between industries and concluded industry classification is a significant determinant of capital structure.

Scott attempted to improve upon the work of S&A in four ways [9]. He increased the number of firms and industries by examining 77 firms in 12 industries. He extended the period to ten years (1959-1968), eliminated regulated industries, and included pair-wise comparisons, as well as one-way analysis of variance. His results show significantly more variation between industries than within industries for each of the ten years, thus concurring with S&A. He further demonstrated that this significance could not be attributed to a single industry by testing for pair-wise difference.

Scott and Martin (S&M), updated this study for the 1967-1972 period with a larger sample (159 firms in 1967 to 277 firms in 1972) [10]. Using one-way analysis of variance they found the industry classification to be a significant determinant of capital structure in each year. Considering the possibility that the assumptions of normality and homogeneity of variance might not hold, S&M also used the Kruskal-Wallis non-parametric test. Results using this test were consistent with the analysis of variance in every case, supporting the significant industry effect.

The headquarters country could also be a proxy for business risk. Studies of firms headquartered in different countries indicate there is a country effect which is also a significant determinant of capital structure. The earliest such study, by Stonehill

Reprinted from *Financial Management, 12*, no 3, Autumn 1983, 45–51, by permission of the Financial Management Association.

and Sitzel (S&S), finds no significant industry effect for firms that are in the same industry but headquartered in different countries. They suggest, but do not empirically support, "country norms are probably more important than industry norms" [12, p. 92]. They further suggest economic factors such as tax regulations, inflation, development of national financial institutions, and national attitudes toward risk are responsible for these country effects.

Remmers, Stonehill, Wright, and Beekhuisen (RSW&B) compared industry classification and size as determinants of capital structure in different countries [7]. They argue that one must adjust for profitability and growth and use a large sample in order to accurately capture the industry effect. Their study considered nine manufacturing industries in the U.S. and compared four industries in five countries for two years. Using one-way analysis of variance, they found the industry effect to be significant in Japan and France for both years, while it was not significant in the U.S., Norway, or the Netherlands in either year. They also tested for the effect of size, but found it to be insignificant in each case. They did not compare firms in the same industry that were headquartered in different countries.

Toy, Stonehill, Remmers, Wright, and Beekhuisen (TSRW&B), as part of the same overall study as RSW&B, examined growth, profitability, and risk as determinants of corporate debt ratios [14]. Their regression models were significant for the U.S., Japan, Norway, and the Netherlands, but not significant for France. In spite of this, they argue "there is still considerable unexplained variation in debt ratios within and among countries." [14, p. 875]. Their model explains from 60.7 percent of the variation in debt ratios for Japan to only 2.4 percent for France. Their findings indicate debt ratios are consistent with higher growth of assets, lower earnings rates, and higher variability of earnings rates. Of the three independent variables, only the earnings rate was significant in different countries.

Stonehill *et al.* explicitly examined country norms by interviewing financial executives in four industries and five countries [13]. They found that executives made decisions on the use of debt based on the ability to service fixed financial charges (or the risk of not being able to service these); the availability of capital funds; and international factors relating to financing foreign operations and reaction to foreign exchange and political risks. These factors were considered more important to the executives interviewed than minimizing the cost of capital.

The five hundred largest companies in Europe were examined by Aggarwal [1]. These fell in 13 countries and 38 industries. He used regression and both one-way and two-way analysis of variance to explain equity as a percentage of total assets. Although his two-way analysis of variance ignored the interaction between industry and country, his results seem to support the existence of significant country and industry effects. Furthermore, size, as measured by sales, was not found to be a significant determinant of capital structure.

The international studies mentioned above considered only developed countries. Errunza studied the developing nations of the Central American Common Market (CACM) [2]. His study, along with that of S&S, is one of the few to examine firms in the same industry but headquartered in different countries. It shows a significant industry effect on capital structure, even across national boundaries. He also finds the country effect significant and that interaction between industry and country is also significant. He concludes, "the effect of the country factor is not as strong as the industry classification," and attributes this to the economic integration of the common market [2, p. 76].

The review of the literature indicates that there is disagreement on the significance of the industry and country effects, and on the source of the country effect as well. This paper extends the existing literature dealing with capital structure of firms headquartered in different countries in three ways. First, the use of more current data will allow an updating of some of the earlier works. Toward that end, this study examines the same set of industries and countries as S&S in their study of capital structure across national borders.

Second, the paper examines the country effect and the industry effect using two-way analysis of variance. Errunza found significant interaction between these two effects for the Central American Common Market. Such interaction necessitates an adjustment for the interaction term in order to assess the significance of the independent variables.

Finally, the paper examines the significance of country effects when the influence of other economic variables is considered. Tax rates, firm size, and before-tax rate of return are analyzed along with the industry and headquarters country using two-way analysis of variance. Industry and country are entered as factors. Tax rates, total asset size, and pre-tax returns are entered as covariates, with the debt ratio as the independent variable.

II. Methods of Analysis ————————————————————————

This study employs 1979-1980 data for 411 firms in nine industries headquartered in nine countries (eight plus the Benelux nations). These are the same industries and countries examined by S&S using 1964-1965 data and were selected for comparative purposes. Following S&S, the ten firms in each industry/country cell with the highest level of sales were selected for the sample, with all firms included when there were less than ten.[1] Data were obtained from *Moody's Industrial Manual* for the United States [3], and *Moody's International Manual* for all foreign firms [4]. By using a single source, the problem of inconsistent accounting treatments is thought to be reduced, although not eliminated. The lists of countries and industries are included in Exhibits 1 and 2.

The study attempts to answer the following questions using the analytical and statistical methods discussed below. (1) Has the proportion of debt financing used by multinationals increased since 1964-1965? (2) Is headquarters country a significant determinant of capital structure? (3) Is industry classification a significant determinant of capital structure? (4) Are the industry and country effects related? (5) Do economic variables such as tax rate, rate of return on investment, and/or size affect either the industry or country effect?

Two-way analysis of variance was used on the independent variable, total debt ratio, with fixed industry and country effects entered as factors, and total asset size, pre-tax rate of return, and effective tax rate entered as covariates. The SPSS procedure ANOVA was employed [6, pp. 398–433].

Exhibit 1
DEBT RATIOS IN SELECTED INDUSTRIES AND COUNTRIES, 1964–1965 S & S (p. 92)

	Alcoholic Beverages	Auto- mobiles	Chemicals	Electrical	Foods	Iron and Steel	Non- Ferrous Metals	Paper	Textiles	Total
Benelux	45.7	—	44.6	37.5	56.2	50.0	59.2	35.9	54.2	47.9
France	35.8	36.0	34.3	59.1	24.7	33.7	55.0	35.5	20.9	37.2
West Germany	59.2	55.1	54.8	67.5	42.5	63.8	68.1	71.8	44.9	58.6
Italy	64.9	77.3	68.2	73.6	66.4	77.9	67.5	—	66.6	70.3
Japan	60.9	70.3	73.2	71.1	78.3	74.5	74.5	77.7	72.2	72.5
Sweden	—	76.4	45.6	60.1	46.8	70.0	68.7	60.7	—	61.2
Switzerland	—	—	59.7	50.8	29.3	—	26.3	—	—	41.5
United Kingdom	43.8	56.5	38.7	46.9	47.6	44.9	41.7	46.6	42.4	45.5
United States	31.1	39.2	43.3	50.3	34.2	35.8	36.7	33.9	44.2	38.7
TOTAL	48.8	58.7	51.4	57.4	47.3	56.3	55.3	51.7	49.4	

Exhibit 2
DEBT RATIOS IN SELECTED INDUSTRIES AND COUNTRIES, 1979-1980

	Alcoholic Beverages	Auto- mobiles	Chemicals	Electrical	Foods	Iron and Steel	Non- Ferrous Metals	Paper	Textiles	Total
Benelux	41.4	61.8	60.0	50.8	64.3	66.2	41.4	63.2	54.2	55.9
France	56.3	67.3	72.1	72.5	77.7	74.1	66.3	74.4	73.9	70.5
West Germany	—	57.1	56.2	66.4	48.8	51.6	67.8	69.8	65.0	60.3
Italy	—	21.7	67.7	79.2	83.4	90.2	86.1	77.4	77.7	72.9
Japan	—	71.3	81.2	65.7	76.3	87.5	88.2	76.6	77.6	78.1
Sweden	79.1	75.2	67.5	76.9	62.8	69.3	56.1	55.5	59.7	66.9
Switzerland	—	—	—	63.2	53.7	63.8	—	—	—	60.2
United Kingdom	41.9	72.8	49.8	59.9	55.3	50.7	56.7	55.9	50.7	54.9
United States	51.1	58.0	54.7	53.6	55.4	54.3	57.6	58.2	47.5	54.5
TOTAL	54.0	60.7	63.7	65.4	64.2	67.5	65.0	66.4	63.3	

The debt ratio was defined as total debt to total assets at book value and calculated as one minus the ratio of stockholders' equity to total assets.[2] Pre-tax rate of return was reported earnings before taxes to total assets at book value. The effective tax rate was computed to be the difference between before tax and after tax earnings divided by before tax earnings ((earnings before tax—earnings after tax)/earnings before tax).

Two-way analysis of variance extends the one-way analysis which has been commonly employed by researchers in this area. Since two independent factors (industry and country) are of interest along with three independent covariates, this procedure is more appropriate than the one-way analysis. In particular, the unexplained variance may now be attributed to the other factor, and the effects of the covariates can be explicitly included in the analysis.

Should there be significant interaction between two factors, such that the two are not independent, one-way analysis both for each country, holding industry constant, and for each industry, holding country constant, allows for interpretation of their independent effects. As Errunza points out, the homogeneity of variance assumption is more important in this one-way analysis [2, p. 74]. Using Cochran's-C as an appropriate test [11, p. 208], homogeneity of variance was found to hold in all but two cases of examining industries within a country and all but three cases of examining industries across countries. The fact that homogeneity of variance held in most cases, along with the fact that the F-test, used to test for significance, is robust with respect to the lack of homogeneity of variance, supports the use of one-way analysis of variance on each independent factor.

As Scott has shown, results that support the hypothesis that debt ratio means are significantly different require further, pair-wise comparisons [9, p. 46]. A number of tests exist for comparison of all possible pairs of group means. Scheffe's test is exact for unequal group sizes and is selected here for that quality [5, p. 219] [6, p. 594]. Simple correlation between covariates and factors can be useful in explaining the significance of these other, economic variables to either industry or country effects.

III. Empirical Findings _____

Exhibits 1 and 2 illustrate average debt ratios by industry and country for the S&S study using 1964-1965 data and for the current study using 1979-1980 data. Although no tests of statistical significance are presented, one can observe a clear pattern of increased usage of debt. Every country and every industry average as well as almost every cell of the matrix show a higher debt ratio in 1979-1980. This trend is confirmed by both the Scott and S&M studies which deal with the United States. One explanation for this increase may be the use of book values over a period of high inflation. This allows the market value of equity to rise much faster than its book value with the result that leverage measures based on book value overstate the true, market valued use of leverage.

Exhibit 3 presents the results of the two-way analysis of variance. As the F statistics show, the industry and country effects are significant at the .01 level, but they have a significant interaction (.035) as well. The only significant covariate is the pre-tax return on investment (ROI). Together these three variables, industry, country, and ROI, explain about 51 percent of the variation in corporate debt ratios.

Given the significant interaction between the industry and country factors, one-way analysis of variance for each factor (holding the other factor constant) is required. Exhibit 4 presents those firms in the same industry but headquartered in different countries. Six of the nine F statistics are significant at the .01 level, meaning we reject the hypothesis that the average debt ratios in these six industries are statistically equivalent for the nine countries.

Exhibit 3

TWO-WAY ANOVA FOR DEBT RATIOS IN SELECTED INDUSTRIES AND COUNTRIES

Source of Variation	Sum of Squares	DF	Mean Square	F	Significance of F
Main Effects	4.348	16	.272	20.639	.000
Industry	.341	8	.043	3.242	.001
Country	3.552	8	.444	33.715	.000
Covariates	1.409	3	.470	35.658	.000
Total Assets	.028	1	.028	2.112	.147
Tax Rate	.006	1	.006	.469	.494
Pre-Tax ROI	1.351	1	1.351	102.593	.000
2-Way Interactions	1.025	55	.019	1.415	.035
Industry Country	1.025	55	.019	1.415	.035
Explained	6.782	74	.092	6.960	.000
Residual	4.424	336	.013		
TOTAL	11.206	410	.027		

411 Cases were processed.   Multiple R^2 = .514
   0 Cases (.0 PCT) were missing

Exhibit 4

ANOVA FOR DEBT RATIOS IN SELECTED INDUSTRIES

	Calculated Ratio	F Ratios		Actual Level of Significance
		95% Confidence Level	99% Confidence Level	
Alcoholic Beverages	4.215	2.82	4.31	.01*
Automobile	.787	2.52	3.71	.61
Chemicals	10.198	2.19	3.00	.00*
Electrical	1.854	2.22	3.06	.10*
Foods	5.346	2.12	2.87	.00*
Iron and Steel	9.559	2.14	2.92	.00*
Non-Ferrous Metals	5.09	2.25	3.12	.00*
Paper	1.96	2.28	3.18	.09*
Textiles	5.545	2.29	3.20	.00*

*Found to be significant at the .01 level by Stonehill and Stitzel.

Pair-wise comparisons, using Scheffe's test on these six industries, reveals in Exhibit 5 that no single country accounts for the differences in means between countries.

One-way analysis of variance for firms in the same country, but in different industries, was performed and is presented in Exhibit 6. Only two countries, Japan and the U.K., have statistically significant differences between industry debt ratios.

Exhibit 5
PAIR-WISE COMPARISONS OF COUNTRY MEANS IN SELECTEDINDUSTRIES

Industry	Significantly Different Countries		
Alcoholic Beverages	Sweden	with	Benelux, U.K.
Chemicals	U.K.	with	France, Japan
	Japan	with	U.S., W. Germany, Benelux
Foods	Italy	with	U.S., U.K.
Iron and Steel	U.K., U.S.	with	Italy, Japan
	Japan	with	Benelux
Non-ferrous Metals	Japan	with	Benelux, U.S., U.K.
Textiles	Japan	with	U.K., U.S.

Exhibit 6
ANOVA FOR DEBT RATIOS IN SELECTED COUNTRIES

Country	Calculated Ratio	F Ratios		Actual Level of Significance
		95% Confidence Level	99% Confidence Level	
Benelux	.993	2.18	2.99	.46
France	1.562	2.25	3.12	.18
West Germany	.869	2.32	3.29	.54
Italy	2.451	2.70	4.14	.07
Japan	2.39	2.17	2.95	.03
Sweden	.872	2.36	3.36	.55
Switzerland	48.78	200.00	4,999.00	.10
United Kingdom	2.68	2.08	2.79	.01
United States	.734	2.06	2.74	.66

These findings (for the U.S.) are contradictory to Scott and S&M. The industries in Japan and the U.K. were also examined using the Scheffe test of pair-wise differences but, due to the fact that Scheffe's test is stronger than the F test, no two industries were found significantly different in either country at the .05 level. Thus, it seems clear that the country effect is more important than the industry effect in this data. This contradicts Errunza's findings for the CACM, but is consistent with the conclusions of S&S.

The possibility that the country effect reflects an underlying economic variable such as total asset size, pre-tax rate of return, or effective tax rate was examined through simple correlation analysis in addition to the analysis of variance presented above.

The correlation results found only pre-tax ROI significantly related to the debt ratio at the .01 level. This is consistent with the analysis of variance findings. The negative correlation ($-.5327$) concurs with the findings of TSRW&B for all five countries considered in their study.

IV. Why Country Norms

S&S presented four environmental variables which "undoubtedly play a role" [9, p. 92] in the establishment of country norms. They cited tax regulations, inflation, development of national financial institutions, and national attitudes toward risk. Stonehill *et al.* support the latter two with their emphasis on availability of capital in domestic markets and concern for financial coverage.

While all tax regulations cannot be treated here, the effective tax rate has been examined. *A priori,* one would expect that higher debt ratios would be consistent with higher tax rates, since the value of the tax subsidy on interest would be higher (assuming that interest is tax deductible, as it is in most cases for the countries considered here). However, we found no significant tax rate effect whatsoever. This held true within industries and within countries.

The argument can be made that higher debt ratios serve as inflation hedges. No inflation data were employed, but casual investigation of average country debt ratios cannot support this argument. Japan and W. Germany have two of the higher debt ratios, while historically they have had low relative inflation rates. The U.K., with the second lowest overall debt ratio, and Italy, with the second highest, both have had relatively high rates of inflation. The relationship of national inflation rates and corporate debt ratios is an area that suggests further study.

The national financial institutions in these countries have certainly developed since the S&S study, and access to international financial markets has improved. These factors may still be a determinant of country norms, but one would expect that their significance has been greatly reduced. More important here are the findings of Stonehill *et al.* regarding the availability of capital and local capital markets. Executives in France, Japan, and the Netherlands felt, for example, that domestic capital markets would not accept large issues of equity financing. In the Netherlands, with neither a well-developed stock or bond market, most new financing must come from commercial banks. Thus, capital structure decisions there are greatly influenced by these financial institutions. In the U.S., the availability of capital was not a concern due to the relatively high liquidity of the U.S. markets.

Finally, national attitudes toward risk, and characteristics of national financial arrangements continue to be a factor. In countries such as Japan, wherein banks hold both equity and debt positions in firms, one can argue that the expected costs of bankruptcy are far less for given debt ratios than in countries where this practice does not exist. Such arguments are consistent with Stonehill *et al.*

Thus, we argue that the country norms are institutional or cultural norms rather than the result of economic variables. As such, increases in the level of international economic activity should work to reduce the differences in capital structure between countries as their financial institutions and markets, practices, and attitudes toward risk become more similar.

V. Summary

This study shows there has been a trend toward greater use of debt financing by multinationals over the past 15 years.

The hypothesis that there are statistically significant differences in the capital structures of firms headquartered in different countries could not be rejected. Much less support can be given to the effect of industry classification on capital structure. Economic variables such as effective tax rate or firm size have little impact on debt ratios, but the pre-tax rate of return is significantly related to the use of debt.

The results of this research support the argument that country effects on capital structure result from either differences in financial institutions and markets or in the national attitudes toward risk and that these differences do cause capital structures to be different between countries.

References

1. Raj Aggarwal, "International Differences in Capital Structure Norms: An Empirical Study of Large European Companies." *Management International Review* (1981), pp. 75, 88.
2. Vihang R. Errunza, "Determinants of Financial Structure in the Central American Common Market." *Financial Management* (Autumn 1979), pp. 72–77.
3. *Moody's Industrial Manual.* (New York. Moody's Investor Service, Inc., 1981).
4. *Moody's International Manual.* (New York, Moody's Investor Service, Inc., 1981).
5. John Neter and William Wasserman. *Applied Linear Statistical Models.* Homewood, IL., Richard D. Irwin, 1974.
6. Norman H. Nie, C. Hadlai Hull, Jean G. Jenkins, Karin Stembrenner, and Dale H. Bent. *Statistical Package for the Social Sciences.* New York. McGraw-Hill, 1975.
7. Lee Remmers, Arthur Stonehill, Richard Wright, and Theo Beekhuisen. "Industry and Size as Debt Ratio Determinants in Manufacturing Internationally." *Financial Management* (Summer 1974), pp. 23–32.
8. Eli Schwartz and J. Richard Aronson. "Some Surrogate Evidence in Support of the Concept of Optimal Capital Structure." *Journal of Finance* (March 1967), pp. 10–18.
9. David Scott, "Evidence on the Importance of Financial Structure." *Financial Management* (Summer 1972), pp. 45–50.
10. David F. Scott, Jr., and John D. Martin. "Industry Influence on Financial Structure." *Financial Management* (Spring 1975), pp. 67–73.
11. B. J. Winer, *Statistical Principles in Experimental Design,* Second Edition. New York. McGraw-Hill, 1971.
12. Arthur Stonehill and Thomas Stitzel, "Financial Structure and Multinational Corporations." *California Management Review* (Fall 1969), pp. 91–96.
13. Arthur Stonehill, Theo Beekhuisen, Richard Wright, Lee Remmers, Norman Toy, Antonio Pares, Alan Shapiro, Douglas Egan, and Thomas Bates. "Financial

Goals and Debt Ratio Determinants: A Survey of Practice in Five Countries." *Financial Management* (Autumn, 1975), pp. 27–41.

14. Norman Toy, Arthur Stonehill, Lee Remmers, Richard Wright, and Theo Beekhuisen. "A Comparative International Study of Growth, Profitability, and Risk as Determinants of Corporate Debt Ratios in the Manufacturing Sector," *Journal of Financial and Quantitative Analysis* (November 1974), pp. 875–886.

Notes

1. Several firms had partial or total government ownership. This study made no provision for government ownership. Based on inspection of the data, we feel that none was warranted.

2. Reserve Accounts were not treated as equity, minority interest was treated as equity.

3. RISK ASESSMENT FOR U.S. AFFILIATES BASED IN LESS DEVELOPED COUNTRIES

JOHN WHITCOMB KENNEDY
Mr. Kennedy is a management consultant with Peat, Marwick, Mitchell & Co.

There are significant business opportunities in newly industrialized nations such as Brazil, South Korea, and Taiwan. The chances of succeeding in business in these labor-intensive developing countries increase in direct proportion to the amount of risk assessment and strategic planning that is done. For instance, foreign exchange fluctuations often wreak havoc to the financial statements of multinational corporations. This article focuses on how methods of identifying foreign exchange risks can provide multinationals with opportunities to minimize their economic exposure and capitalize on new growth.

The Devaluation of Brazil's *cruzeiro* early in 1983 resulted in a 30 percent shortfall in the projected profits of US subsidiaries and affiliates there. Indeed, when American multinational corporations (MNCs) tallied up their books at the end of last year, many found themselves reporting hefty foreign exchange losses as a result of foreign currency devaluations in countries around the globe.

Since the beginning of floating foreign currency exchange rates in 1973, MNCs have had a difficult time protecting their worldwide assets and earnings from sharp and incessant currency fluctuations. For example, if a currency appreciates or depreciates, an exchange loss or gain usually occurs when the foreign affiliates' balance sheets are translated into parent company terms. Furthermore, exchange rate gains and losses may result from timing differences when transactions are initiated and when payments are made.

Exchange losses represent just one of the problems that can complicate American business activities abroad. Other problems include diverse tax and accounting structures, fluctuating inflation rates, and a multiplicity of legal and political systems. On the other hand, there are many benefits for the corporation operating and investing internationally.

Foreign investments are profitable because MNCs exploit imperfections in the international markets. For example, MNCs invest abroad to *capitalize on disparities* in the relative cost of factors of production in different countries. Other reasons for investing overseas might be:

- diversifying the risk of suppliers and distributors for the products;
- reducing the costs of distribution and transportation;
- penetrating a market to establish a presence, gain knowledge, and maintain visibility;

- preserving market share by regarding the foreign market as an extension of the domestic market for the products;
- taxation at favorable rates; and
- political considerations

American companies still dominate the list of MNCs worldwide. There are basically two reasons, both of which are due to a generally overvalued dollar dating from the 1920s. One is that American corporations were obliged to invest and operate overseas if they were to be competitive in world markets. The second is that American multinationals have had an advantage in the dollar dominated international capital market.

In light of the benefits and risks that MNCs encounter, it behooves them to focus hard on two issues:

- assessing the foreign exchange risks inherent in overseas investments versus the expected returns; and
- linking the strategic planning of parent companies to that of their foreign affiliates.

The purpose of the following article is to focus on these two issues by emphasizing how methods of identifying foreign exchange risks can provide MNCs with opportunities to minimize their economic exposure and capitalize on perceived market imperfections.

Assessing Foreign Exchange Risks

Although MNCs can circumvent the imperfections in the international markets by gaining control over foreign production or marketing, this does not ensure their ability to compete and become profitable in the international market place. The underlying reason is the foreign exchange rate which always has some impact on an MNCs financial statement.

The degree of the impact—which is often called the economic exposure—can be gauged by looking at the corporation's:

- *financial exposure,*[1] a measure of the extent to which an American MNC has chosen to protect itself from what happens overseas—by doing business in US dollars, using hedges such as debt service on foreign currency loans, adhering to foreign exchange contracts, and so on; and
- *natural exposure,* a measure of the extent to which an American MNC leaves itself vulnerable to economic conditions overseas by doing business in foreign currency. Natural exposure hinges on the structure of the foreign affiliate's balance sheets, and on the degree to which the devaluation (or revaluation) of a foreign currency is commensurate with relative inflation in that country. (In other words, it hinges on how "equally" the "soft" foreign currency can be converted into "hard" US dollars.)

Thus, to put it simplistically, the full economic exposure of an American MNC can be determined by deducting financial exposure (the dollars the MNC preserves through hedges) from natural exposure (the dollars the corporation gains or loses through operating policies and if foreign currency devaluation does not equal inflation).

Managing economic exposure has become a top priority for many US-based companies, in part because they have recently shifted their manufacturing operations to labor- intensive less developed and developing countries in hopes of simultaneously enhancing their worldwide market shares and boosting their profits.

Consequently, these host countries have been rapidly evolving from agricultural cash-based economies into industrial accrual-based economies. What does this mean to the MNC? In times past, the corporation might have sent a representative to Malaysia to purchase raw goods on a cash-and-carry basis. Currency concerns were confined to the dollar value of the goods to be purchased at the time of the transaction. Today, however, the MNC has a manufacturing presence in Malaysia and two sets of books to juggle: those in Malaysia and those in the US home office.

The accrual of income and expenses in depreciating foreign currencies poses problems for MNCs—especially for those treasurers at home offices who are still reluctant to deal with "below-the-line" adjustments explicitly. For example, in December a treasurer may have to report $5,000 worth of accounts receivable in foreign currency as accrued income (and the MNC will be taxed accordingly)—but by the time those receivables are collected, their worth may have depreciated to $4,000. Thus the MNC will have to wait until the next tax year to report this transaction as an exchange loss.

However, since it is highly unlikely that the accounting problems engendered by doing business in and with the new breed of industrialized nations will diminish—in fact, the chances are they will increase—home offices will simply have to learn to deal with them. Especially when an MNC's equity position in a country is large, as is the case in Mexico and Brazil, it is vital that all of the risks of overseas investment be reflected not only on the profit and loss statement, but also in the long-term strategic position of the company.

Financial Formulas ————————————————————————————

Capital budgeting[2] is the process of analyzing the financial benefits and associated costs of an investment in order to determine its profitability to the investor Company. Two key financial criteria for evaluating such opportunities are after-tax earnings[3] and cash flows.

To determine a potential investment's contribution to the value of the firm, a company applies a cost of capital, or discount rate, to its cash flows. However, for the international company that consists of more than one unit, each with its own financing sources, the US home office and the foreign affiliate office should use different discount rates, reflecting their immediate economic environments, to assess the risk of investments.

For example, the effective local borrowing costs in Brazil currently range from 200 percent to 500 percent (depending upon the size of the borrower and the level of reciprocity, such as the level of compensating balances, required by the lender). But how much will that loan actually cost the American MNC and its shareholders in the long run, taking inflation and devaluation into consideration? The standard discount rate formula is:

$$\frac{(1 \ + \ \text{effective local borrowing cost})}{(1 \ + \ \text{expected rate of devaluation})} = (1 \ + \ \text{dollar equivalent discount cost})$$

If the MNC took the loan out at a real rate of 250 percent per annum (p.a.) the projected rate of devaluation is 100 percent p.a., the ratio would look like this:

$$\frac{(1 \ + \ 2.50)}{(1 \ + \ 1.00)} = (1.75) \text{ or a 75 percent dollar equivalent discount cost.}$$

Thus, while it will cost 250 percent p.a. to borrow Brazilian *cruzeiros,* the effective (real) rate for the MNC and its shareholders will be 75 percent p.a. The discount rate is useful, for example, when the Brazilian affiliate has excessive outstanding receivables, and must take out a working-capital loan to cover the unexpected cash shortfall. The standard discount rate formula shows the consequences by discounting the value of the *cruzeiro* receivables, delineating the indirect costs (risks), and showing the actual return on sales.

Using the discount rate provides a means to measure the local dollar equivalent cost for a company conducting business in a foreign country while holding a certain economic exposure. By measuring the cost of the company's country-specific economic exposure, protective mechanisms can be added or disposed of according to corporate exposure management policy.

A successful economic exposure management program is comprised of two principal protective mechanisms. Operational mechanisms include such protective devices as leading and lagging payments, balance sheet management, and a pricing policy that pegs domestic prices to the exchange rate. Financial hedging mechanisms include such devices as forward exchange contracts. Acting together, these mechanisms can be used to control the degree of financial and natural exposure of the MNC.

Many MNCs make it their policy to maintain a balanced foreign exchange position at any cost. This means that regardless of the extent to which a MNC uses operational mechanisms to protect its overseas cash flows, they manage to eliminate completely the residual economic exposure to exchange risk with expensive financial hedges. Moreover, the shareholders never see the actual cost of these specific (hedging) transactions, because all such costs are charged, in one lump sum, against equity in the aggregate statement for the entire MNC. Since the opportunity cost (a maximum profit that could have been earned if the moneys had been used in some other manner) of borrowing in dollars is not stated explicitly, shareholders remain unaware that the high overhead is in part related to the choice of economic exposure management.

In actuality, the opportunity cost of borrowing in US dollars would be far higher than the opportunity cost of borrowing, for example, in depreciating Mexican *pesos.* The reason? The annual rate of depreciation exceeds the rate of inflation in Mexico. For instance, *pesos* may depreciate 200 percent p.a., as compared to a Mexican inflation rate of 150 percent p.a., leaving a real depreciation rate of only 50 percent p.a. This is an example of how MNCs might use foreign currency debt to manage economic exposure—in specific, the MNC would reduce that particular investment's real cost of capital by 50 percent.

Therefore, an MNC may make a foreign investment and pay back a loan in dollars—but the return on that investment will be in foreign currency that has been devalued by at least 200 percent. By contrast, when an MNC takes out a loan in foreign currency, it also pays back the loan in devalued foreign currency, and therefore loses much less.

Failure to use the local-equivalent discount rate to capture the risk or cost of a foreign investment will misrepresent the true value, or expected return, of the investment. Furthermore, the cost of protection can siphon off large amounts of cash. This in turn results in a higher real cost of production—which will be reflected in lower shareholder earnings. Thus, only with "full information" on an investment's risk and return can the MNC manager identify and make optimal financial decisions.

It is only through analysis of its financial statements—both in local and domestic currency—that an MNC can get a feel for how to manage the specific problems and strategies of its foreign affiliates. Otherwise, it is not inconceivable that short-term coverage may be totally inconsistent with the long-term health of the corporation.

Implications ——

Unless an affiliate and its parent company have compatible business goals and share an overall strategic plan, one may end up draining the other financially. The ways in which the home office and its foreign subsidiaries choose to structure their balance sheets can provide a good example of conflicting goals. For example, many treasurers of MNC affiliates abroad are structuring their local currency balance sheets to show a negative working capital position—one in which liabilities exceed assets. Their goal? To turn these affiliates into "cash cows"—siphoning off any earnings and bringing them back to the States.

For example, Brazil's money market has the highest real returns in the world, averaging over 500 percent p.a. Why, then, would a treasurer choose to invest in plants or equipment when he can get a 500 percent return on paper? The treasurer opts to invest all his dollars in short-term assets, not fixed assets or equity. The result: a negative equity position. (See Table 1.) Furthermore, when local currencies depreciate faster than local prices increase, there is always a temptation to show a negative working capital position. After all, cheap debt is preferred to cheap assets; hence, a "net liability position" on the subsidiary's balance sheet.

As a result of this "net liability position," foreign affiliates have generally hedged their natural exposure, while refraining from investment in new fixed assets. Instead, they tend to overleverage themselves, invest in the high yielding local money market, and become cash machines. The XYZ Corporation's balance sheet, seen in Table 1, portrays this type of cash machine. In general, their balance sheets are structured to be (1) *very liquid,* which allows the firm to meet maturing short-term obligations, (2) *highly leveraged,* which provides a cheap local dollar equivalent cost of capital in financing growth, and (3) *negative equity,* which minimizes economic exposure.

Table 1
XYZ CORPORATION SUBSIDIARY
(IN FOREIGN CURRENCY)

Current Assets	90
Fixed Assets	10
Total Assets	100
Current Liabilities	40
Long-term Debt	80
Owners' Equity	−20
Total Liabilities and Owner's Equity	100

The final effect here is to minimize the subsidiary's reduction in earnings and increase its return on investment on the profit and loss statement. This is precisely the wrong kind of financial management, because it is destined to swiftly erode the company's capital base and discourage fixed-capital investment.

The temptation to maintain a net liability position is even greater in view of present American business conditions. A US economic recovery is well under way, and a promise of declining long-term interest rates and steady low prices may also augur an investment boon. An investment-led period of growth would place additional pressure on foreign affiliates to provide cash back to the parent company. Unless the foreign affiliates are part of the parent's overall strategic plans, any foreign expansion proposals would take a back seat to investment opportunities at home.

Furthermore, the restructuring of the US economy presents another good reason why the business plans of foreign affiliates and the home office should be linked. Smokestack industries appear to be leaving the American economy for a long time— if not for good. They are relocating to newly-industrialized countries, such as Brazil, South Korea, Taiwan, and Mexico. Thus, MNCs that are involved in these countries would do well to delegate to their overseas subsidiaries the labor-intensive portion of their business. This would allow the parent to concentrate its US investments in less labor-intensive products, while building a solid long-term capital base overseas.

Several firms are already doing this, to some extent. General Motors produces many parts of its "world car" in Brazil; General Electric's Brazilian operation is the sole manufacturer of the company's "world iron." Such a "world orientation" would enable MNCs to get the most for their money, by contracting in the countries that offer the most advantageous price and production structure.

It seems likely that newly-industrialized nations could grow into even more fertile fields of multinational production. Skilled labor, however, might become scarcer, because worldwide investment in this vital resource has been sorely lacking. Therefore, MNCs must consider methods to prepare their own labor force, including the use of American middle management to train local managers for key positions and an increased emphasis on productivity.

To implement such a strategy, the MNC must take a long-term view. In turn, the MNC must have a sound equity base, even if the bottom line on the profit and loss statement does not look so good in the short run.

Parent company treasurers and shareholders may have to alter the ways in which they manage foreign investment, especially in capital-short developing countries. If foreign currency losses cannot be tolerated, or if the risk of major devaluations is overwhelming, the cost of protection against such losses should be explicitly considered for strategicmanagement purposes. This is where the discount rate comes in.

There is no such thing as an "industrial futures market" to provide MNCs with a hedge against their risks. It is equally important to recognize that the nature of the enterprises emerging in this new breed of industrialized countries is undergoing significant change. Corporate reporting and planning, therefore, must reflect these changes and corporate management must exercise tighter control over the assessment of overseas risks and potential returns.

Notes

1. Business commonly uses two definitions of financial exposure: (1) translation or accounting exposure, which measures the impact of exchange fluctuations on a firm's net worth, and (2) transactions or conversion exposure, which measures the impact of fluctuations on cash flows identified with specific time periods.
2. Capital budgeting is a financial tool that reduces to a single number of certain projects' contribution to the value of the investing company. The project is normally accepted if its net present value is positive or if its internal rate of return exceeds the firm's cost of capital.
3. Foreign income can be taxed on either a *cash basis,* when it is received in the form of cash dividends, royalties, etc. or an *accrual basis,* when sales and associated costs are incurred.

II. ———FOREIGN INVESTMENT DECISIONS—

4. SURVEY AND ANALYSIS OF CAPITAL BUDGETING METHODS USED BY MULTINATIONALS

DAVID J. OBLAK AND ROY J. HELM, JR.

David J. Oblak is an Assistant Professor of Finance at George Mason University. Roy J. Helm is an M.B.A. student at the University of Maryland.

Introduction

The survey results described in this paper report on the capital budgeting techniques that large U.S. multinational corporations use, as well as their procedures to estimate project returns, risk, and the required rate of return. (Survey and response details are available from the authors.) We wanted to see whether significant changes had occurred in foreign project evaluations since Stonehill and Nathanson [11] had surveyed 110 U.S. and foreign-based firms in 1966.

Survey Design and Capital Budgeting Statistics

We sent surveys to the principal financial officers of 226 *Fortune* "500" firms [5] which operated wholly-owned subsidiaries in 12 or more foreign countries, as reported in the *Directory of Corporate Affiliations* [6]. The lower bound of 12 foreign subsidiaries, although arbitrary, was used to ensure that the sample was drawn from a population of firms with a relatively high degree of international activity.

There were 58 completed questionnaires, a 26% response rate. Of the 40 respondents indicating a title, 13 were Treasurers, 11 Vice Presidents of Finance, 8 Chief Financial Officers, and 8 Junior Financial Officers. The median number of foreign countries in which wholly-owned subsidiaries were operated is 19,[1] and foreign sales averaged 31% of total sales.

The capital budgets of the respondent firms range from $10 million to $2 billion annually with a median of $200 million. The median number of projects formally considered in the latest fiscal period was 200—approximately 24% of them generated by foreign subsidiaries. Formally analyzed projects, those for which capital budgeting techniques are applied, constituted about 90% of all projects considered, and the acceptance rates of these projects were high: 35% of the MNCs reported an acceptance rate of at least 90%, while 85% of the MNCs reported an acceptance rate of at least 75%. This indicates that projects are not formally analyzed unless they are expected to meet the MNC's acceptance criteria. These figures are also consistent with the Gitman and Forrester [7, p. 61] findings in a recent survey of 110 U.S. firms.

Reprinted from *Financial Management 9,* no. 4, Winter 1980, 37–41 by permission of the Financial Management Association.

We asked the sample firms to identify the return and risk characteristics of domestic and foreign investments over the last five years. Responses indicated that foreign projects over this period were slightly less profitable and more risky than domestic projects. Specifically, 42% of the MNCs reported less annual return from foreign projects, 27% found more, and the remaining 31% detected no difference. In regard to risk, 55% of the firms indicated that foreign investments exhibited greater variation in annual return, 7% found less variation, and 38% observed similar variation. Nevertheless, the majority of MNCs reported that they use the same capital budgeting procedures for both sets of investments.

Capital Budgeting Techniques

The sample MNCs were asked to rank the capital budgeting techniques that they use most frequently. As Exhibit 1 indicates, the internal rate of return method was the favorite as the primary evaluation method, while the payback period was most frequently mentioned as the secondary criterion. Almost 76% of the respondents indicated that their primary capital budgeting technique is one of the discounted cash flow (DCF) methods, and 94% reported using at least one of the DCF methods. For comparison, Schall, Sundem, and Geijsbek [10, p. 282] in a recent survey of 189 large U.S. firms reported that 86% used DCF methods.

Only three (5%) of the MNCs replied that the capital budgeting techniques applied in evaluating domestic projects are given different weights in evaluating foreign projects. Two of these firms indicated that the payback period is given greater consideration in evaluating foreign investments. Stonehill and Nathanson [11, p. 48] also found that most companies apparently used the same procedures to review domestic and foreign projects.

Previous surveys have documented the increasing use of DCF techniques, and the results of this survey confirm their finding. Although Stonehill and Nathanson [11] did not report the number of their sample firms that used these methods, a 1970 survey by Klammer [9, p. 393] indicated that 67% of a sample of 184 large firms with sizable and continuing capital expenditure programs use discounted cash flow methods. If it can be assumed that Klammer's findings do not understate the

Exhibit 1

CAPITAL BUDGETING TECHNIQUES USED BY MNCs (IN PERCENTAGES)

Technique	Primary Use	Ancillary Use
Accounting Rate of Return	14	33
Internal Rate of Return	60	21
Net Present Value	14	36
Payback Period	10	62
Profitability Index	2	12
	100	

usage rate of Stonehill and Nathanson's sample firms, then a statistically significant increase in usage rates has occurred from 1966 (67%) to 1979 (94%).[2]

Income Measurement

In regard to how MNCs measure potential income from a foreign project (Exhibit 2), 54% of the responses indicated that the investment's expected cash flow is used. Approximately one-half of these firms considered only the after-tax cash flow accruing to the parent firm, while the other half also included reinvested earnings in the subsidiary. All but one of the remaining 46% of the respondents stated that some measure of accounting profitability is used. Expected accounting profits after foreign taxes was the definition most frequently mentioned.

Stonehill and Nathanson [11, p. 48], in answer to a similar question, obtained these responses from U.S.-based MNCs: 45% measure income in terms of cash flow, with most of these including reinvested earnings; 29% use accounting profits; and 23% define income by neither measure. Inspection of the answers in the last group reveals only four responses (payback analysis) that clearly indicate some use

Exhibit 2
DEFINITIONS USED BY MNCs IN MEASURING INCOME FROM FOREIGN INVESTMENTS

Definition	Percentage
Earnings	
Count all expected accounting profits after foreign taxes, regardless of currency	22
Count all expected accounting profits after foreign taxes, except where there are currency restrictions	9
Expected return on book investment	14
Cash Flow	
Count all expected cash flows to the parent after domestic and foreign taxes, regardless of currency	27
Count all expected cash flows to the parent plus reinvested earnings, adjusted for domestic and foreign taxes	24
Count all expected cash flows to the parent plus reinvested earnings, adjusted for foreign taxes only	3
Other	1
Total*	100

*The 58 firms made 70 responses to this question; thus, the figures represent the percentage of times a given definition was mentioned.

of cash flow in measuring project return. Adding these to the 45% of the responses that directly identified cash flow measures of income gives a total of 49% (51 out of 104) of the answers reporting use of cash flow measures. A comparison of this value to the 54% figure recorded in this survey indicates no significant change in the use of cash flow methods between 1966 and 1979. (A chi-square test of the hypothesis of no significant change cannot be rejected at the 0.10 level.)

Determination of the Discount Rate

The firms that use DCF methods were also asked to identify how the discount rate was determined. As Exhibit 3 indicates, 54% of the MNCs use the firm's weighted average cost of capital either exclusively or in combination with another discount rate. Additionally, over 90% of the firms with annual capital budgets greater than $500 million use a weighted average cost of capital. A discount rate arising from the expected growth in dividends was given in 16% of the cases, the cost of debt in 13%, the risk-free rate plus a risk premium in 9%, a measure based on past experience in 5%, and another rate in 3%. Finally, 86% of the firms use an after-tax discount rate, with the average value reported as 12.5%.

These figures are generally comparable with the findings of Schall, Sundem, and Geijsbeck [10, p. 283]. The weighted average cost of capital was used by 46% of their sample firms, and the average after- tax discount rate reported was 11.4%.

Of the 48 MNCs that use a DCF method, 23 (48%) do not vary the discount rate for foreign investments, and 19 out of the 23 employ a weighted average cost of capital. The firms that vary the required rate of return listed the adjustment procedures given in Exhibit 4. The majority of the firms use either a local cost of capital (44%) or subjective assessment (40%) in determining the appropriate discount rate.

Stonehill and Nathanson [11, p. 48] found that 69% of U.S. firms using the cost of capital did not vary this rate for foreign projects. The firms that did vary the cost of capital most frequently (45%) used a local cost of capital. It therefore appears

Exhibit 3
DISCOUNT RATES USED BY MNCs

Discount Rate	Percentage
Cost of debt	13
Measure based on past experience	5
Rate based upon expected growth in earning and dividends	16
Return from a risk-free asset plus risk premium (CAPM)	9
Weighted average cost of capital for firm	54
Another rate	3
Total*	100

*The 48 firms answering this question made 56 responses; thus, the figures represent the percentage of times a given discount rate was mentioned.

Exhibit 4

METHODS USED BY MNCs TO ADJUST THE DISCOUNT RATE FOR FOREIGN PROJECTS

Method	Percentage
Subjectively vary the weighted average cost of capital	40
Use cost of funds applied	4
Use local (foreign) weighted average cost of capital	44
Use local (foreign) prime interest rate	4
Another method	8
Total*	100

*The total number of responses was 25.

that more MNCs today vary the discount rate for foreign investment (52% vs. 31%), although the procedures for adjusting the rate, primarily the use of local cost of capital, have not changed appreciably. A significance test was not performed in this case because of possible selection bias (there were only 25 responses to the question in this survey, 22 in Stonehill and Nathanson's) and the different wording of the question in the two surveys.

Risk Analysis

It was noted previously that 55% of the sample MNCs had experienced greater variation in the return from foreign projects compared to domestic projects over the last five years, while only 7% found less variation. Furthermore, almost 73% of the firms with large capital budgets ($500 million or more annually) observed greater variation in foreign returns.

Over 72% of the respondents reported that they explicitly consider the risk of capital projects. This result is consistent with Gitman and Forrester's [7, p. 69] finding that 71% of a sample of large U.S. firms explicitly consider risk. The majority of the firms in our survey that listed their risk assessment procedures, however, identified subjective evaluation, implying that the risk adjustment was qualitatively determined. A minority of the firms reported use of: sensitivity analysis, examination of the probability distribution of cash flows, and estimation of the risk premium from the CAPM.

The methods that the MNCs employ to incorporate varying degrees of foreign projects risk are given in Exhibit 5. No one method is used more than others. The most frequent response, to borrow funds locally, was reported in 22% of the answers. Adjustment of the required accounting rate of return (19%) and the payback period (17%) were mentioned next; variation of the discount rate was chosen by only 14% of the total responses.

Stonehill and Nathanson [11, p. 50] found that 95% of their sample of U.S. firms allowed for risk, but 41% stated that the allowance was subjective. Variation of the

Exhibit 5

METHODS USED BY MNCs TO ADJUST FOR DIFFERENT LEVELS OF RISK IN FOREIGN PROJECTS

Method	Percentage
Adjust cash flows	7
Adjust cost of capital in present value analysis	14
Adjust payback period	13
Adjust required accounting rate of return on investment	19
Borrow funds locally	22
Insure risks where possible	9
No distinction is made	11
Another method	5
Total*	100

*The 58 firms made 85 responses to this question; thus, the figures represent the percentage of times a given method was mentioned.

required accounting rate of return was given in 31% of the answers while adjustment of the discount rate was listed in only 2% of the responses.

Changes in the risk adjustment procedures used by MNCs as measured by the two surveys are difficult to assess because of differences in the wording of this question. It does appear, however, that more MNCs currently borrow locally (22% versus 5%), and more vary the cost of capital (14% versus 2%) in an attempt to adjust for foreign project risk.

Also, if it can be assumed that the category "subjective evaluation" found in Stonehill and Nathanson's [11, p. 50] question excludes explicit adjustment of capital budgeting techniques to allow for risk, then significantly more MNCs (53% versus 39%) now alter these criteria for foreign projects. (A chi-square test of the hypothesis of no change rejects it at the 0.01 level.) The adjustments made to the capital budgeting criteria, however, are in a majority of the cases subjectively determined.

The sample firms were also asked to indicate if they considered foreign project risk due to changes in exchange rates, inflation rates, or the political environment. The affirmative responses were 67%, 73%, and 73%, respectively. Baker and Beardsley [2, p. 39] similarly found that exchange rate and political uncertainty as well as the prospects for remitting profits to the U.S. were major factors in foreign project analysis.

Finally, Grubel [8] and others have argued that international diversification produces benefits for investors by providing risk reduction that cannot be gained from a well-diversified domestic portfolio. Agmon and Lessard [1], furthermore, have offered empirical support for the motive of international diversification at the corporate level by showing that U.S. investors appear to recognize the extent of international diversification of U.S. firms. Only 17% of our respondents, however, indicate that risk reduction through international diversification is a significant reason for investing in foreign projects.

Summary

The results of this mail survey indicate that MNCs are conducting more detailed analyses of their foreign projects. Compared to the results reported by Stonehill and Nathanson [11] in 1966, we found that a higher percentage of MNCs now use DCF methods and adjust for risk in foreign project evaluations. MNCs, however, have not significantly changed the way in which returns from foreign projects are measured or the determination of the appropriate discount rate.

Because the mail survey data were not confirmed by follow-up interviews, certain caveats about the results are necessary. First, our requirement that the sample firms have a high degree of international activity means we surveyed only large MNCs. Previous surveys have found that larger firms are likely to be more sophisticated in their capital budgeting analyses. Second, previous studies have also observed that respondents tend to be more comprehensive in project evaluation than non-respondents. For these reasons, the reported results of this survey may overstate the capital budgeting sophistication of MNCs.

Finally, we performed cross-sectional tests of the relationships between the systematic risk of the MNCs and measures of: 1) capital budgeting sophistication; and 2) international diversification. (Details of the tests are available from the authors.) The results generally revealed no significant association in either set of tests. Since there is no theoretical foundation linking systematic risk and capital budgeting sophistication, the results in the first case were expected and consistent with those of Schall, Sundem, and Geijsbeck [10, p. 285]. In the second case, our finding of an insignificant relationship differs from Agmon and Lessard's [1]. Possible specification errors, however, impair the reliability of our tests.

References

1. Tamir Agmon and Donald R. Lessard, "Investor Recognition of Corporate International Diversification," *Journal of Finance* (September 1977), pp. 1049–1056.
2. James C. Baker and Laurence Beardsley, "Multinational Companies' Use of Risk Evaluation and Profit Measurement for Capital Budgeting Decisions," *Journal of Business Finance* (Spring 1973), pp. 38–43.
3. W. J. Conover, *Practical Nonparametric Statistics,* New York, John Wiley & Sons, Inc., 1971.
4. "Foreign Business Enhances Prospects of U.S. Firms," Standard & Poor's *The Outlook* (August 14, 1976), pp. 613–614.
5. "Fortune's Directory of the 500 Largest Industrial Corporations," *Fortune* (May 8, 1978), p. 238.
6. *Geographical Index to the Directory of Corporate Affiliations.* Skokie, Ill., National Register Publishing Co., Inc., 1979.
7. Lawrence J. Gitman and John R. Forrester, Jr., "A Survey of Capital Budgeting Techniques used by Major U.S. Firms," *Financial Management* (Fall 1977), pp. 66–71.

8. Herbert G. Grubel, "Internationally Diversified Portfolios: Welfare Gains and Capital Flows," *American Economic Review* (December 1968), pp. 1299–1314.

9. Thomas Klammer, "Empirical Evidence of the Adoption of Sophisticated Capital Budgeting Methods," *Journal of Business* (July 1972), pp. 387–397.

10. Lawrence D. Schall, Gary L. Sundem, and William R. Geijsbeck, Jr., "Survey and Analysis of Capital Budgeting Methods," *Journal of Finance* (March 1978), pp. 281–287.

11. Arthur I. Stonehill and Leonard Nathanson, "Capital Budgeting and the Multinational Corporation," *California Management Review* (Summer 1968), pp. 39–54.

12. *The Value Line Investment Survey.* New York, Arnold Bernhard & Co., Inc., January 5, 1979.

Notes ——

1. Where the sample mean and median differ significantly, the median is presented since it represents a superior measure of the central tendency of the sample. Otherwise, the sample mean is given.

2. Assuming that a selection bias is not present in the current sample, then a chi-square test, Conover [3, p. 142], rejects the hypothesis of no change in usage rates at the 0.001 level.

5. INTERNATIONAL INVESTMENTS: WEIGHING THE INCENTIVES

ROBERT WEIGAND

Mr. Weigand is professor of marketing at the University of Illinois in Chicago. He has written several HBR articles, the most recent being, " 'Buying In' to Market Control" (November-December 1980). This article grew out of his interest in protectionism (see his HBR article, "International Trade Without Money," November- December 1977) and recent research on barter and foreign investments done in Italy, West Germany, the Netherlands, and Japan.

There are certain rules in international business that have stood since commerce began. "Don't second-guess the culture" is one, "Get a good local partner," another. In international investment the rule has been that companies can cope with myriad foreign political situations "as long as the host country explains the rules and points out the players."

Sophisticated business people know, however, that many of these rules are often profitably broken. For example, one honored dictum is that managers making investment decisions should consider investment incentives—that collection of everything from cash grants to lower taxes offered by governments to companies investing in their countries—as insignificant variables. Economic stability, infrastructure, production costs, and nearness to market should always top the list of factors evaluated, with incentives seen as nothing more than a happy windfall. Mr. Weigand argues that shrewd executives have been breaking this rule for some time and benefiting from an intense bidding war conducted by governments eager to attract companies and ready to use whatever incentives they can think of. This article shows how old rules are changing.

Slow economic growth has brought the world close to an international trade war. We are all aware of protectionist moves and threats made by governments and of their negative impact on business. Yet this trend toward economic nationalism has a positive side for corporations looking overseas for investment sites. National, regional, and local development commissions offer a near avalanche of investment incentives to lure corporate capital, skills, and technology.

Incentives have been around in one form or another for years, but never to the degree or in the variety that exists today. A worsening economic climate and growing corporate reluctance to risk over-seas investment have forced governments to offer more inducements. (For a discussion of why governments offer incentives, see the accompanying insert.) Local clamor for politicians to "do something" about unemployment and low economic growth will probably result in their offering foreign companies more incentives in the coming decade.

Subsidies are not equally dispersed throughout the economic landscape; the major donors continue to be countries classified as "newly industrializing." Ireland granted incentives to 70% of its U.S.-owned businesses; South Korea, Israel, Taiwan, and Brazil provided special arrangements for more than 40% of the U.S. companies investing there.

Even so, all countries are in the investment race. Recently, for example:

▪ The Netherlands awarded $3.2 million to Philip Morris to expand its factory at Bergen op Zoom. The European Court of Justice declared the grant illegal because the Dutch assistance program allowed virtually the whole country to be eligible for investment aid. Since the investment would create new jobs and exports, however, the Dutch and Philip Morris looked around and found another incentive program outside the court's jurisdiction.

▪ Asian countries are adding to what can only be termed a cornucopia of aid possibilities. Singapore provides accelerated depreciation, tax holidays, and low-interest government loans; Malaysia waives taxes for up to ten years if the foreign investor locates in the right place and meets export quotas; and India gives out direct capital grants if the investor builds a plant in depressed areas. Motorola elected to build a semiconductor plant in Sri Lanka's investment promotion zone, an area near the Colombo airport, where the government ensures tax-free treatment for up to ten years, negligible taxes on exports, telephone lines, and roads to the airport.

▪ Despite European resistance to encroachment by the Japanese on their home markets, the European Community recently approved a $6.7 million subsidized loan for Sony to build a television tube factory at Bridgend, Wales, where unemployment has been running at about 15%.

▪ Algeria has moved further toward encouraging joint ventures with foreign companies, particularly those in electronics, housing, and consumer goods, and has promised to institute changes in the country's investment regulations and tax holidays.

▪ Canada's new constitution gives each province the freedom to assist industry investment, sometimes at the expense of other provinces. Cuba says it will encourage foreign private investment in tourism to the extent of waiving corporate taxes. France has decided to give $136 million in direct grants and low-interest loans to its electronics industry in the hope of greater exports.

All sophisticated planners realize that they must give incentive programs more weight when analyzing new investment sites. The problem comes in learning how to calculate the value of the subsidies offered in relation to their own corporate cases. This learning process will take time. The often desperate need of host governments for foreign investment in the face of economic chaos means that planners must be extremely careful to analyze the programs that governments offer. For example, the most touted incentives will be those given at the initial stage of a venture. But governments continue to make additional promises that may turn out to be little more than expressions of good intentions.

A planner must learn to judge the probability that government promises are realistic. Governments change, policies change, promises are not kept, and delayed promises are virtually worthless. For example, one multinational was promised major highway and rail improvements that would make its remote plant accessible. After four years of bureaucratic red tape, the company spent its own money on the infrastructure. Also, Jamaica promised Alcoa Minerals that tax rates would not be raised for 25 years. Partly as a result of this promise, Alcoa built a bauxite mining operation including an alumina plant. Six years later, taxes were increased ninefold. Fortunately for Alcoa, the International Center for the Settlement of Investment Disputes—part of the World Bank—agreed to hear the dispute.

Furthermore, a planner must compare costs on an international and interregional basis. Investing in the Estremadura Region of Spain, the Midi in France, the Negev in Israel, or the Mezzogiorno in Italy will mean lower costs for some factors and higher for others. (For an example of an investment analysis considering such variations, see the *Exhibit.*)

Incentives can help companies but they can also cause problems. Their effect can be so profound as to change a company's way of doing business. Only if managers understand the impact of an incentive offered to an overseas unit on their company's entire operating system are they able to decide whether the financial assistance will enhance—or cripple—their organization's effectiveness.

Direct & Indirect Help ———————————————————————————————

By strict definition an investment incentive is any enticement likely to attract new investment, and it is usually limited to specific industries or companies. Straightforward incentives include tax holidays, accelerated depreciation, rent-free land and buildings, outright grants, low-interest loans, loan guarantees, subsidized energy or transportation rates, construction of rail spurs or access roads, and free worker training.

There also are less direct incentives that make a particular country attractive for investment. These disguised subsidies include low public utility rates, lax enforcement of pollution laws, controlled raw material prices, "buy local" laws, money kept cheap by a central bank, and a tranquil work force trained at public expense.

Europeans sometimes argue that Americans subsidize their industries in more subtle ways. For example, in one recent confrontation the British argued that American companies were selling synthetic textile products in Western Europe at unfairly low prices. U.S. industry spokesmen countered that a fair look at the books would show that companies were selling synthetic textiles at full markup. The British parried with the point that the U.S. industry's access to low-priced natural gas—a major raw material in the synthetic textile industry—gave it an unfair advantage. An in-

Governments use direct incentives, often with other strategies that promote local business growth, for six good reasons:

1. "Look what we did for you."

Incentives are politically attractive because they are a conspicuous way of doing something with meaning for voters. Investments bring jobs, jobs beget money, and money buys food for the table. Politicians, whether they gained their positions via the ballot box or a coup d'état, enjoy reading newspaper headlines that say, "New Plant to Be Built Here: Will Bring 600 Jobs."

2. "If it's so wrong, where are the police?"

There is no widely supported international group that monitors and regulates the legality or fairness of international investment subsidies. The General Agreement on Tariffs and Trade has made great progress at reducing or eliminating tariffs and quotas, and at minimizing a variety of nontariff barriers to trade. But it devotes little time or attention to investment subsidies. The European Commission's mandate to monitor state aid is, of course, limited to EC member states. There is no legitimate police force to stop the beggar-thy-neighbor practice of investment subsidies.

3. "Who, us?"

Investment subsidies are easier to disguise than other discriminatory practices. There is no agreement on what constitutes an investment subsidy. Moreover, subsidies are doled out by so many different, often obscure, government bodies that monitoring and measuring them may not be possible. Some subsidies come from national governments, but others come from regional and local authorities whose decisions can have a significant impact on an investor's profitability. Indeed, benefits may come simultaneously from half a dozen different sources.

4. "It's just like the Welcome Wagon."

Investment incentives can be selective. Just as the Welcome Wagon has gifts only for the new folks on the block, investment incentives can be limited to selected industries or companies that a government favors in its growth plan, such as sunrise or high-technology industries. Furthermore, they can be limited to new projects. They need not be extended to long-established businesses in a country.

This may seem unfair, but pragmatism and equity don't always make good partners.

5. "We're just helping the free market system move faster."

Investment incentives are sometimes seen as a way of achieving sooner the same goals that would be reached eventually under free market forces. It may take years for capitalists to realize, say, that machine tools can be built as well in the Philippines or Portugal as in West Germany or the United States. But when government negotiators show up on the corporate doorstep with a 2 (or 10 or 50) million dollar incentive package, it wonderfully focuses the managerial mind.

6. "Everyone does it."

This defense pretty well describes just how pervasive the practice has become. Virtually every country provides incentives designed to encourage investment that would otherwise go to another country. Some do so on a grander scale and more conspicuously than others.

vestment incentive? Perhaps. Another indirect incentive is a tacit promise by government that companies—particularly those with many employees—will be put on a life-support system during economic difficulties.[1]

Incentives are the happy side of the coin. On the reverse are the disincentives or conditions the host country imposes on corporate beneficiaries. These "performance requirements" include job creation quotas, export minimums that generate foreign exchange, local value-added minimums, domestic market share maximums, and obligatory local participation in ownership. One of the most threatening is a provision, variously called a give-back, claw-back, or the other-edge-of-the-knife clause, that calls for penalties if the entry contract conditions are not met.

An analysis of the impact of both incentives and disincentives will determine whether a company should turn thumbs up or down on a foreign investment proposal.

In a country where the number of jobs created or the volume of output determines the size of incentives, companies may have to undertake activities themselves that they might otherwise shift to outside specialists. Incentives will often tip the scales in a make-or-buy decision. The government will nudge a company to make the product in-house; this pressure will be effective when available subsidies offset the cost of inefficiency.

A decision to produce in-house means that the subsidized foreign plant cannot buy from its U.S. parent company. For the global management team, the problem is tough. In this case, a foreign operation cannot be treated as a major captive customer for the output of domestic plants.

The host government can force a guest company to produce in-house by erecting trade barriers against foreign suppliers; even intracorporate transactions can be stopped this way. A government's most blatant method of forcing in-house job creation is increased tariffs; protracted customs procedures or tough value-added conditions are a less obvious—but equally effective—means.

A current dispute that illustrates this issue of in-house production is Nissan's discussions with the British government over its plan to build a $700 million Datsun factory in Britain. It seems that the British government will provide $282 million only if Nissan makes at least 60% of the Datsun car in Britain. Nissan wants a smaller local content percentage, thus reducing the number of jobs created for British workers. The Japanese company believes that it can produce many parts more efficiently elsewhere and airfreight them to Britain for assembly.

A Marketing Windfall? _____

Investment incentives can have a profound impact on a corporation's marketing program. For example, if the subsidy is large, the company can afford a low selling price that could open new markets or enlarge existing ones. In turn, of course, the marketing manager would have to devise promotional campaigns that appeal to different cultures and select local distribution channels to reach prospective customers.

Pricing can be difficult. A company may be tempted to practice dumping in some markets if its entry contract requires a large volume of exports. Part of Ford's agreement with the Spanish government, for example, called for the export of two-thirds of its automobile production. Sometimes a contract calls for a level of production that exceeds the domestic market's needs. The company involved will have to export part of its production and may feel that it is necessary to lower its prices sharply to do so.

If an entry contract encourages dumping, the marketing manager must pick target markets with care. Governments can retaliate, and dumping charges are often easy to prove. An offended government can levy a countervailing tariff or embargo to prevent dumped imports from destroying its own industry.

A country with no local industry to protect would be a better export market. In this case, lower priced goods can be seen as a form of transfer payment from the producing country.

An example of the intricacies of the dumping issue is a processing plant for turkeys recently built in Brittany with the financial assistance of the French government. Private capital accounts for only about two-thirds of the investment; the balance comes from France's special area development fund. The French company can sell turkeys in Britain at about three-quarters the price of British-raised turkeys, while still earning a satisfactory return on investment. Alarmed British turkey growers have sought relief from their farm ministry. Last Christmas, the British ate subsidized British turkeys. By Christmas 1983, the bureaucratic foot-dragging may have stopped; the British will be eating subsidized French turkeys.

Companies can expect intracorporate warfare when an aggressive, subsidized overseas manager decides to invade a territory historically belonging to another unit of the company. Fortunately, U.S. anti-trust laws give companies the right to allocate territories among their wholly- or majority-owned subsidiaries.

Top management must also face the difficult problem of evaluating the overseas manager of a subsidized operation in a way considered fair by other company managers. Otherwise, domestic management may feel victimized by the company's decision to invest abroad, arguing that the rules of the game are rigged. Division managers may feel that they are unfairly evaluated in annual reviews because they must slug it out in the marketplace while overseas managers enjoy the protection and subsidies of a host government.

Labor may also resent overseas operations, believing that jobs created abroad are jobs lost by the domestic work force. The work force may call for the company to show more national allegiance and invest its funds at home, a higher return from foreign subsidized investments notwithstanding. Top management needs to deal with such expressions of value systems, and "facts" may not help much.

The Unholy but Necessary Partnership

Subsidies can be tantamount to an alliance between government and business, but the friendship often proves bittersweet. The more companies ask from governments, the more governments expect to dictate to companies. In a sense, the guests become hostages to the policies and practices of the hosts.

U.S. managers can face severe difficulties when trying to go out of business abroad. Closing up shop overseas is often difficult, slow, and expensive. For example, the Badger Company, a subsidiary of Raytheon Company, began operations in Belgium in 1965. It operated at a loss every year until 1977, when it terminated business because management decided there were no prospects for profits. Badger indicated that it would leave all the subsidiary's assets, valued at about $2.8 million, to resolve employee claims. All employees were paid salaries and bonuses up to the date the plant was closed. The union argued that the company owed each employee an additional $25,000 on termination. Since Badger's assets were depleted, the additional sum would have to come from other Raytheon units in other countries, including the United States. The union eventually settled the matter out of court; gossip holds that Raytheon had to pay for the Belgian terminations with funds transferred from other units.

By way of contrast, a recent decision by the U.S. Supreme Court (*First National Maintenance* vs. *National Labor Relations Board*) held that a U.S. company has the right to close down a business, or a unit of a business, without bargaining with its union. In this case, First National Maintenance, a cleaning and maintenance company, terminated a contract with Greenpark Care Center in Brooklyn and let off 36 employees who worked at the center. Although the National Labor Relations Act obliges employers to bargain over terms and conditions of employment, the Supreme Court held that termination is not covered by the Act. Closing shop is much easier, and cheaper, in the United States than in many other countries.

ECONOMIC TARGETS OF HOST COUNTRIES

Countries that are the home bases and the hosts of multinational enterprise likewise have a specific set of economic objectives—goals that are determined by local political processes which to the outsider are often obscure, and which can differ substantially both in time and in space. To complicate matters further, national economic objectives, being a political product, inevitably fail to satisfy various *group* interests. Farmers, textile workers, environmentalists, pipe-nipple manufacturers, and consumer advocates all have their own "druthers," some of which invariably depart from the official economic policy of the government toward multinationals. So even if bilateral dissonance between the economic objectives of MNEs and government policy-makers can be ironed out, there is still plenty of room for conflict with vocal and often powerful national interest groups.

National economic objectives are usually rather straightforward in their principal dimensions. . . . Countries have comparable aggregate policy goals, whether codified or not, that spell out the economic stewardship of the government. Politically, the "jobs" issue is almost always the most sensitive. Inflation becomes a political problem above some "threshold" level of tolerance which varies internationally. . . . Governments ignore the growth objective only at their own very distinct peril—nothing foments political change more effectively than the absence of hope for a better life among the masses. The things that contribute to growth, such as the formation of physical capital like buildings and machinery, infrastructure facilities such as schools, telecommunications, roads and hospitals, and technological advancement, are of critical concern in this context. And finally, for many countries the balance of payments represents a central element in the achievement of economic targets as a determinant of real resources from abroad that can be absorbed in the growth process.

From
Thomas N. Gladwin and
  Ingo Walter
Multinationals Under Fire:
Lessons in the Management
  of Conflict
(New York: John Wiley & Sons)
With permission of the publisher

Exhibit
WHERE TO LOCATE—THREE SCENARIOS

Companies making a foreign investment decision have always given great thought to consideration of market opportunity, production, labor and transportation costs, and economic and political stability. In considering incentives, many go to the trouble of constructing hypothetical profit and loss statements for each of the sites considered within a given country. Such statements force planners to pay attention to the details of an investment while providing top management with a "big picture" of the consequences of various proposals. They help planners think about the interaction of variables and permit contingency planning in conjunction with computer modeling.

Hypothetical planning provides the company with the documentation needed during negotiations for benefits with the foreign ministry responsible for economic development in the country under consideration. It encourages the company to do its homework and prepare the best possible case to demonstrate that a subsidy is necessary. It is therefore most important from the point of view of investment incentives.

Let's look at three investment possibilities for a hypothetical company, illustrating how the aggregate costs may be the same but how individual cost items in the profit and loss statement may differ. The company produces a consumer good largely sold in the home country but exports some of the output. For each unit produced, the company charges 50 cents for equipment and plant depreciation, 30 cents for labor (.05 hours labor at $6 per hour), 40 cents for raw materials, and 10 cents profit. Total unit costs, including profit, are $1.30. The company ships the product to a foreign market by sea, incurring a 10 cents per unit charge, and the foreign-specific tariff is 10 cents. Overland trucking charges are 10 cents per unit. Due to the vagaries of shipping such a long distance, the company stores large quantities of the product in a warehouse near customers; the charge is 10 cents per unit.

The company sells the product in the foreign market for $1.70, f.o.b. at the foreign warehouse. This simple scenario is illustrated at the right.

Home country

Production and profit $ 1.30

Foreign country

Sea freight $ .10

Tariff .10
Land freight .10
Storage .10

Target market

Where....

Production costs:	
Equipment	$ .50
Labor (.05 hours at $6.00/hour)	.30
Raw materials	.40
Profit markup	.10
Total production and profit	**$ 1.30**
Sea freight	.10
Tariff	.10
Land freight	.10
Storage at market	.10
Selling price at market	**$ 1.70**

(continued)

The company has two other options. The first possibility is to build the factory in a remote area of the foreign country. In the absence of special grants or other subsidies, factory and equipment costs are 70 cents per unit. Labor is unskilled and takes longer to complete its tasks than the work force in the high rent area or in the United States. However, the hourly rate is less, so wage costs are 25 cents per unit produced. Raw materials are nearby, so unit costs are 35 cents. Profits of 10 cents per unit are added. Thus the production costs, including profit, are $1.40, less than for either of the other alternatives. But trucking the product to market over bad roads costs 15 cents per unit. And since the distribution system from the depressed area is so chaotic, the company would need to store the product in a warehouse near customers. This would cost another 15 cents per unit. Selling price, covering production and distribution costs and a small profit, is $1.70 per unit.

The second is to build a small factory in the foreign market near customers. The company will almost certainly suffer some production diseconomies because (a) the market is too small, so the plant is too small for maximum efficiency, (b) it will be located in the "high rent" area where the company must pay more for land, plant construction, and the work force, and (c) the host country's commercial policies will encourage in-house production.

Since the equipment is somewhat underused, the company must charge 70 cents for plant and equipment depreciation. The foreign work force has the same skills as its domestic counterpart, but the hourly wage rate is higher, so projected labor costs are 40 cents per unit. Because raw materials are purchased in small quantities, they will cost 50 cents per unit. Again, the company asks only 10 cents per unit profit and incurs no sea freight charges, no tariffs, and no land freight charges. Finally, since the new factory can ship directly to customers, it keeps a small inventory at its warehouse. The selling price to customers is $1.70.

These two possibilities are illustrated at the right.

The company can now see the interaction of various cost factors. Hypothetical P L statements can show whether producing abroad will reduce a company's domestic production and therefore raise domestic unit costs. They help the company gauge the impact of incentives (for example, what if a foreign government provides a loan for 12 years at 8% interest?). Most important of all, this information helps a company prepare to negotiate for "hidden" inducements not written up in investment guides but offered to companies at the bargaining table. If a company can demonstrate that, with additional inducements, its costs will be sufficiently low to provide higher profits to benefit a depressed area, a foreign government is more apt to go the extra distance for it.

Location in a depressed area — Depressed area

Location near the market — Target market

Foreign country

Where....		
Production costs:		
Equipment	$ .70	
Labor	.25	
Raw materials	.35	
Profit markup	.10	
Total production and profit	**$ 1.40**	
Sea freight	0	
Tariff	0	
Land freight	.15	
Storage at market	.15	
Selling price at market	**$ 1.70**	

Where....		
Production costs:		
Equipment	$ .70	
Labor	.40	
Raw materials	.50	
Profit markup	.10	
Total production and profit	**$ 1.70**	
Sea freight	0	
Tariff	0	
Land freight	0	
Storage at market	0	
Selling price at market	**$ 1.70**	

Many West European and Latin American countries that subsidize new business also impose heavy payment penalties for employee terminations. For example, in the Netherlands one month's pay for each year of service is obligatory, in West Germany approximately one year's pay is normal, and in Mexico up to two years' pay is routine termination settlement. The Spanish Ministry of Commerce recently reported that negotiated termination settlements—"pacted layoffs," they are called—averaged $15,000 per employee for private companies and $21,850 for state-controlled businesses.

Who Needs Incentives?

A company that can comfortably locate in any one of a score of countries will obviously benefit most from incentives. It can logically choose among, say, Singapore, Spain, Egypt, and Colombia. If a half dozen or more sites are acceptable, the country with the plushest and most enduring incentives is most likely to get the investment, the new jobs, the foreign exchange from exports, and the new technology. Small wonder the bidding is getting so intense, present government budget constraints notwithstanding.

The dramatic increase in the number of qualified countries that should be looked at, and the pervasiveness of incentives, makes the site selection process today far more difficult than it was just a few years ago. Few countries can be dismissed for being too remote, for having too primitive an infrastructure, or for having an untrained work force. To facilitate decisions, companies can construct models that provide insight into the attractiveness of each site. Such models require executive judgment, a large dose of factual information, and the inevitable small dose of guess-work. But we have come a long way from hunch, gut feelings, and the dart board.

Notes

1. For a description of government rescue efforts, see Kenneth D. Walters and R. Joseph Monsen, "State-Owned Business Abroad: New Competitive Threat," HBR March-April 1979, p. 160.

6. POLITICAL RISK ASSESSMENT FOR FOREIGN DIRECT INVESTMENT DECISIONS: BETTER METHODS FOR BETTER RESULTS

THOMAS L. BREWER

Thomas L. Brewer is Professor of Political Science at Eastern Michigan University, Ypsilanti, Michigan.

Recent events have dramatized the importance and the difficulty of political risk assessments for foreign direct investment decision making. The developments in Iran and Afghanistan and the responses to them by the American and other governments will surely reinforce attitudes toward political risk assessment that are prevalent among business managers. Systematic surveys of management personnel and more impressionistic observations reported in the literature indicate a long-standing and widespread recognition of the significance of political risks. Yet it is also frequently and paradoxically noted that assessments of political risks are commonly not very careful or rigorous-if they are undertaken at all.[1]

The purpose of this article is to suggest some guidelines for the improvement of political risk assessments, especially in regard to foreign direct investment decisions. It specifically suggests that present widely used approaches to political risk assessment are deficient in three important respects. First, they are too narrowly focused on expropriations, exchange controls, and government instability in the developing countries of the Third World. Second, their methods of information collection and analysis are either too impressionistic and intuitive, or too mechanistic and formalized. Third, the integration of political risk assessments into capital budgeting analyses tends to be simplistic. In short, foreign direct investment decisions are frequently based on political risk assessments that are conceptually and methodologically constrained.

There are three ways that political risk assessments can be improved. In particular, they can be improved by a more systematic specification of the types and sources of risks, by more eclectic imformation processing methodologies, and by more refined capital budgeting analysis. These three themes will be considered in turn.

Types and Sources of Risk

Political risk assessment tends to focus on expropriations, exchange controls, and government instability, which are based on a narrow notion of political risk. Such a notion is readily evident in many publications. A widely used textbook, for instance, asserts, "There are really only two political risks, both usually associated with

Reprinted from *The Columbia Journal of World Business 16,* no. 1, Spring 1981 5–11, by permission of Columbia University.

investments in developing countries having unstable governments. These risks are related to exchange and expropriation. . . ."[2] These are, of course, important types of risk associated with foreign direct investment, but they hardly provide an exhaustive list of such risks. Nor are they necessarily the most important types of risk. For there is also uncertainty about future tariffs, non-tariff barriers, taxes, export controls, labor relations, and other politically related developments that can affect returns on a foreign direct investment.

The existence of such diverse risks has led to an opposite extreme in some treatments of political risk. Thus, political risk often becomes a catchall term that refers to miscellaneous risks that are not otherwise known by particular names.[3] The extremes of overly narrow or highly unstructured notions of political risk should both be avoided. Instead, what is needed is a comprehensive list of specific types of risks that tend to emerge from political processes.

Once the types of risk of interest are specified, the next step is to specify the potential sources of those risks. Government instability in developing countries is surely one source of risk, but it is not the only one and indeed not even the most important one for many investment decisions. A more encompassing analysis of political sources of risk is necessary—one that takes into account the diverse array of potential political developments that can have significant negative consequences for a foreign direct investment project.

There are fortunately numerous models of politics that can facilitate the analysis of political sources of risk. Each of these models can be though of as a set of assumptions about the nature and determinants of various political processes. Each one represents a distinctive conceptual approach to political analysis. Among the many such models of politics, four that are particularly pertinent are the state-centric model of international politics, the pluralist model of national politics, the bureaucratic politics—organizational behavior model of government policy-making, and the transnational politics model.[4] Although each one includes many explicit and implicit variables to help explain and predict political processes, we can provide only very brief suggestions of their emphases here.

The state-centric model of international politics assumes that national governments seek power and status in relation to one another, that they do so in the context of a competitive, decentralized international political system, and that they utilize whatever internal political resources are available in pusuit of their international objectives. National governments' actions are thus assumed to be functions of officials' desire for international power and status and their reaction to political pressures exerted by other national governments.

The pluralist model of national politics assumes that national governments are responsive to the diverse and conflicting interests and pressures of multiple interest groups within a political system. Group interests and pressures are expressed through electoral processes, but are especially important in legislative and administrative processes, where they take the form of lobbying activities. National governments' actions are thus assumed to be functions of officials' desire to remain in office and/ or their reaction to internal political pressures.

The bureaucratic politics—organizational behavior model assumes that national governments' actions are the results of organizational processes within government bureaucracies. Intra-governmental conflicts are generated, for instance, by the differing policy preferences of individual officials and agencies—which arise from their conflicting organizational interests, differences in their career experiences, differences in their ties to domestic clientele groups, and other factors. This model also suggests that government policies are slow to change because of bureaucratic inertia.

The transnational politics model emphasizes the increasingly important role in world politics being played by organizations other than those of national governments. Thus, not only multinational corporations, but also international organizations and nongovernmental associations such as transnational interest groups are all assuming greater influence, often at the expense of national governments.

Each model is of course much more elaborate than these few sentences suggest. Each one contains numerous variables and propositions about relationships among the variables. Each one is also evident in an abundance of impressionistic cases studies, systematic quantitative studies, and historical narratives, as well as the more conceptual political science literature.

However, even this highly abbreviated discussion suggests the utility of these models in political risk assessment. For they can be used to develop a lengthy and systematic list of potential political sources of risk.

Once the lists of types of risk and sources of risk have been developed, they can be combined into the form of a matrix, as indicated in Figure 1.

Such a matrix can facilitate political risk assessment in two ways. First, it can provide a checklist of possible problems and thereby encourage more systematic scanning of the environment for risk. Second, it can help to focus attention on those few analytic dimensions that bear especially close scrutiny. Thus, it can enhance both the broad surveys and the close looks in a two-phase analytic process.

Even this summary of the combinations of types and sources of risk suggests 40 possible areas of inquiry. Of all those possibilities, "traditional" political risk assessment for foreign direct investment decisions focuses on only a few-particularly those involving expropriations subsequent to changes in national governmental regimes.

Not all of the cells in the matrix are necessarily pertinent to any given decision. However, many of them might be, and only carefully focused analysis can determine which ones are not pertinent.

Such an analysis should help decision makers avoid the common casual assumption that the political risks associated with foreign direct investment are different in kind from those associated with exporting. In assessing FDI related political risk, it should be remembered that much of the output of foreign direct investment facilities is typically exported. Moreover, inputs in FDI production processes are often imported. Thus, accepting foreign direct investment risk does not make a firm immune from trade related risk. Foreign direct investment and trade-and their respective risks-should not be treated as mutually exclusive choices.

Imagine, for instance, a firm that is now producing in country A (its home country) and exporting to countries B and C. It is facing the risk of export barriers being imposed by country A and the risk of import barriers being imposed by countries B and C. If it undertook foreign direct investment in country B and exported to countries A and C, then it would be facing FDI related risks in country B. But it

Exhibit 1:

MATRIX OF SOURCES AND TYPES OF RISK PERTINENT TO FOREIGN DIRECT INVESTMENT

Types of Risk	State-centric international politics	Pluralistic national politics	Bureaucratic—organizational politics	Transnational politics
	Sources of Risk Suggested by Models of Politics			
Destruction of plant and equipment				
Expropriation				
Exchange controls				
Taxes				
Tariffs				
Non-tariff barriers on imports				
Export controls				
Labor relations				
Other				

would also be facing export related risks in country B and import related risks in countries A and C. Finally, if its production process utilizes imported materials as inputs, then it would still be facing import related risks in country B.

It is clear, then, that foreign direct investment not only entails expropriation risks, but also import related and/or export related risks, perhaps in several countries. Furthermore, it is easy to imagine cases in which there is a greater probability of increases in trade barriers than of expropriation. It is also possible that compensation for an expropriation would be sufficiently large that the cash flow losses would be greater from trade barriers than from the expropriation. Moreover, government subsidized insurance against losses from war, expropriation, and inconvertibility is readily available for many foreign direct investment projects, but no insurance is available against trade barrier risks.

Futhermore, the risks associated with exporting and importing are likely to increase over the next several years, and they will probably become increasingly difficult to assess as well. Barriers to trade seem likely to become more problematic as the Western industrialized countries continue to experience more serious income, employment, and price difficulties. The recent shift away from tariffs toward non-tariff barriers as impediments to imports is probably a harbinger of a long term trend; and changes in non-tariff barriers are more difficult to predict than tariff changes because the GATT rules concerning them are more novel and less precise than the tariff agreements.

Moreover, the recent American expansion of export controls may also be a harbinger of growing risks of that nature. Several political and economic indicators suggest such a trend, and there is an increasing interest among foreign policy makers and their advisers in finding economic alternatives to military capabilities as a means of exercising international political influence. Economic warfare may be used in lieu of military warfare to a greater extent in the future. Finally, to the degree that inflation supercedes unemployment as a central concern of economic policymakers, and to the extent that resource scarcity also becomes a more salient concern, export controls become more likely.[5]

Information Processing

Political risk assessment for FDI decisions requires more than a comprehensive and clear conceptualization of political risk problems; it also requires eclectic information collection and analysis procedures.

Until recently, political risk analyses relied on impressionistic observations and intuitive analysis almost exclusively. In the past few years, however, the use of more formalized and quantitative methods has increased. Although this trend will probably result in better political risk assessment, there is a danger that political risk analysis will become overly mechanistic. The desire for more systematic, data based political analyses could lead to overreliance on a few readily available quantitative indicators of political risk. Such a tendency, in combination with the overly narrow conception of political risk noted above, would be particularly unfortunate.

For example, data on domestic political stability are widely and increasingly available. Although such data are potentially useful in political risk assessment, they must be used with caution. As Krobin has demonstrated, it matters a great deal which indicator of domestic instability one uses-coups vs. internal wars, for instance.[6]

However, there are even more basic pitfalls in a preoccupation with quantitative indicators of domestic instability. One is that when applied to a given country it can lead to simpleminded extrapolations from the past to the future. Although there have been some recent dramatic incidents of domestic instability in South Africa and South Korea, for example, their overall levels of domestic violence and other forms of instability have been quite low. The use of simple quantitative indicators of domestic stability for those countries could therefore lead to dubious assessments of their medium term prospects for continued "stability."[7] As the Iranian case illustrates, when authoritarian regimes do finally collapse, the ensuing instability can be very great indeed. The past stability of an authoritarian regime should not be taken as a predictor of future stability.

Nor does the existence of domestic instability necessarily pose risks to individual firms. The level of violence in Northern Ireland, for instance, has been relatively high for many years. Yet individual firms' labor relations have hardly been affected by it, since the war being waged in the streets has rarely been brought into the factories. Protestants and Catholics have generally been in harmony in the workplace in spite of the otherwise severe conflict.[8]

In short, internal stability is not by itself an adequate indicator of a favorable investment climate, but neither does internal instability necessarily pose a serious risk to foreign direct investment. Other political sources of risk and all of the kinds of risk that can be affected by political developments need to be considered.[9]

The analysis of these types and sources of risk will require many kinds of information. Since each type of information and each analytic technique has its own advantages and limitations, the most successful political risk assessments are likely to be those that are highly eclectic. Nor is there likely to be a methodological mix that is uniformly more successful than others. Rather, the specific combinations of information collection and processing methods should be adapted to the needs of individual decision makers.

Since the relative strengths and weaknesses of each approach are so numerous and would require an extensive methodological critique, we can merely list some of the possibilities here.

Initial information collecton processes can include first hand impressionistic observations "in the field," and impressions gained secondhand through periodicals, reference books, news media, commercial information services, and government information sources. In addition, there are numerous sources of systematically collected data sets. These include not only the politically relevant economic and social data published by governmental and international agencies, but also information published by individual scholars and research organizations. The latter include data on conflicts that have resulted in war or may lead to war; trends in public opinion and voting behavior; interest group activities; and legislators' attitudes. All this information can provide the input for a variety of analytic techniques-for instance, computerized simulations, scenario formulations, the use of panels of experts in the Delphi format, or regression modelling.

The result of these analytic procedures can be a mixture of quantitative and verbal estimates of possible political risk developments. These analytic possibilities pose a dilemma, however. On the one hand, sophisticated financial analysts are likely to treat quantitative estimates based on "soft data" with some skepticism. On the other hand, if the conclusions of political risk assessment are perceived as merely vacuous, overly qualified verbal analyses, they are unlikely to be explicitly and fully integrated into the financial analysis for any given decision.

However, even if political analysts can develop methodologically respectable estimates and even if financial analysts are receptive to the possibility of incorporating them directly into the financial decision making process, a difficult problem still remains. That is the problem of how to integrate the results of political risk assessment into standard financial analysis procedures, particularly in the capital budgeting process.

Capital Budgeting Analysis

The several issues of interest in the capital budgeting process are concerned with the appropriate method of adjusting capital budgeting formulas to take into account politically related risks. The alternative adjustment methods can best be understood after a brief exposition of the standard net present value and the internal rate of return formulas.[10]

A key difference between the net present value and the internal rate of return methods of evaluating capital budget proposals lies in their assumptions about the rate of return on reinvested cash flows. The net present value method calculates an estimated return on the initial investment using a return on reinvested cash flows that is assumed to be equal to the marginal cost of capital, as represented by the required rate of return (k) in the standard formula:

$$NPV = \Sigma_{t=1}^{N} \frac{F_t}{(1 + k)_t} - I.$$

The internal rate of return method, on the other hand, assumes a return on reinvested cash flow that is equal to the same rate of return as the initial investment, (r) in the equation:

$$\Sigma N_{t=1} \frac{F_t}{(1 + r)^t} - I = 0.$$

Both of these reinvestment return assumptions are somewhat arbitrary, though they do have the virtues of simplicity and consistency. However, when either method is applied to an international capital budgeting analysis, it suffers from an additional limitation. If earnings that are scheduled to be remitted from a subsidiary to a parent are prevented from being transferred by exchange controls, they may have to be reinvested in the host country.[11] Assumptions concerning the return on reinvested cash flow consequently become particularly important, and they are a function of political risk estimates. In the event of effective exchange controls, therefore, neither of the assumptions concerning reinvestment returns in the normal net present value method or the normal internal rate of return method is likely to be very accurate. Instead the return is likely to be determined by local credit market conditions and government regulations in the host country.

The terminal value refinement of the net present value and internal rate of return methods provides a way to adjust capital budget analyses in the light of estimated reinvestment returns in the event of effective exchange controls in particular host countries. Thus, the refined net present value equation becomes:

$$NPV^* = \Sigma N_{t=1} \frac{TV}{(1 + k)^t} - I.$$

The terminal value (TV) is the sum of the accumulated annual net cash flows plus the compounded interest on the reinvested cash flows.

Thus, the net present value method adjusted for the estimated terminal value of the project is quite similar to the normal net present value method.[12] The difference is that the terminal value method requires that assumptions be made about the reinvestment returns which are specific to the circumstances of individual projects. The use of the terminal value method thereby encourages an explicit consideration of the effect of restrictions on remittances on the net present value of a project. For a given project, a comparison of the results of a terminal value net present value analysis with the results of a normal net present value analysis would indicate the sensitivity of the project to the imposition of exchange controls. The difference in the results of the two analyses would therefore provide a measure of the project's vulnerability to that one type of politically related risk.

However, there are further adjustments that should also be made in the capital budgeting analysis. The use of terminal values is helpful, but it is not sufficient. Other types of politically relevant risks should also be taken into account. In general, there are two additional ways to adjust the basic net present value calculations.

One way to take those risks into account is to adjust the discount factor (k) so that a higher required rate of return is used—k, in the formula:

$$NPV^* = \Sigma^{Nt=1} \frac{F_t}{(1 + k_j)^t} - I.$$

This commonly used adjustment method has the advantages of allowing intuitive judgments of politically related risks to be simply applied to the calculations.

However, this approach also has several implicit assumptions about politically related risk that are frequently inaccurate. In particular, it assumes that risk is a smooth, monotonic, and increasing function of time. Further, it may tend to lead analysts to overestimate politically related risk, because even small upward adjustments in the discount rate have rather large negative effects on the net present value. As a result, a combination of psychological overreaction to political risk together with the mathematical power of small adjustments in the required rate of return can lead to capital budgeting analyses that "discriminate against" politically related risk. Merely adjusting the discount factor, in other words, can easily lead to an exaggeration of the effects of political risk on the rate of return estimates.

Moreover, there are other reasons why the adjustment of the net present value calculations through the use of the certainty equivalent method is preferable to adjusting the discount factor. The certainty equivalent method adjusts the cash flow estimates with a certainty equivalent coefficient—ϕ in the following equation:

$$NPV^{***} = \Sigma^{Nt=1} \phi \frac{F_t}{(1 + i)_t} - I.$$

In that equation, i represents the risk free interest rate, and ϕ is a factor with values such that $0.0 < \phi < 1.0$, which are inversely related to the degree of risk. The coefficient (ϕ) represents the ratio that would make a decision maker indifferent between a certain (riskless) cash flow and a given risky cash flow; thus ϕ = certain cash flow/risky cash flow. Hence it is a function of the decision maker's utility preferences concerning risk, i.e., his attitude toward a particular risk-return tradeoff.

The use of the certainty equivalent method does not eliminate a subjective element in the risk analysis. Nor does it preclude the need for estimates of the probabilities and magnitudes of such politically related risks as exchange controls or expropriations. It merely provides a procedure for adjusting cash flow estimates on the basis of estimates of politically related risk. It is nevertheless preferable to the discount rate adjustment approach because the political risk estimates for each individual time period (year) can be integrated into the analysis. Whereas the use of an adjusted required rate of return implies a regularity in the pattern of the political risks over time, the certainty equivalent method allows for the adjustment of each annual cash flow amount according to the year-specific political risk estimates. The certainty equivalent approach conforms more closely to the realities of the relationship of political risks to time-though of course it also imposes more onerous demands on the political risk assessment process.

Another advantage of adjusting the cash flow estimates rather than the discount rate is that the effects on the project's value of each type of risk can be analyzed separately. Thus, the results of the assessment of the numerous types of risks identified above can be used to adjust cash flow estimates.[13]

There are two reasons why it is preferable to adjust cash flows on the basis of political risk assessment for each of the several types of risk rather than to adjust the discount rate in a single step that implicitly incorporates all types of risk. In the first place, a single adjustment in the discount rate is likely to be based on judgments concerning only one or two types of risk-expropriation and exchange controls in particular—even though they are not necessarily the only or even the most significant pertinent types for a given project. In addition, a single adjustment in the discount rate does not allow the analysis to include sensitivity analyses of the effects of each individual type of risk.

Conclusion

The implications of this discussion can be stated in the form of several aphorisms for management:

- There are many specific types of risk which have their origins in a diverse array of political processes.
- Models of politics can help identify potential political sources of risks.
- The most dramatic political events are not necessarily the most frequent or most costly ones.
- Political risks are everywhere; an alternative that avoids some risks will encounter others.
- Readily available information sources and analytic techniques can improve the quality of political risk assessment.
- Stability in the past and present does not necessarily lead to stability in the future; stability may actually be a harbinger of instability.
- Instability does not necessarily create risk.
- The results of political risk assessment can be integrated into financial analysis through the capital budgeting process.

- Ternimal value calculations can be used in net present value or internal rate of return calculations as a way of including exchange control risk estimates.
- Adjustment of cash flow through the certainty equivalent method is preferable to adjustment of the discount rate, as a way to reflect political risk assessment.
- Finally, and most importantly, since the essence of managerial decision making is coping with uncertainty, complexity, and trade-offs, political risk assessment should be central to any serious international management process.

Notes _____

1. See especially Stephen J. Kobrin, "Political risk: a review and reconsideration," *Journal of International Business Studies*, Vol. 10, No. 1 (Spring/Summer 1979), pp. 67-80; and Stephen J. Kobrin, John Basek, Stephen Blank and Joseph La Palombara, "The assessment and evaluation of non-economic environments by American firms," *Journal of International Business Studies*, Vol. 11, No. 1 (Spring/Summer 1980), pp. 32-47.
2. R. Rodriguez and E. Carter, *International Financial Management*, 2nd ed. (Englewood Cliffs, N.J.: Prentice-Hall, 1976), p. 385.
3. See for example Michael Z. Brooke and Lee H. Remmers, *The Strategy of Multinational Enterprise* (London: Longmans, 1970), ch. 8; David K. Eiteman and Arthur I. Stonehill *Multinational Business Finance*, 2nd ed. (Reading, Mass.: Addison-Wesley, 1979), esp. pp. 168-178, 184-231, and 391-424; and William Hall, "The fashionable world of project finance," *The Banker*, January 1976, pp. 71-82.
4. These and other models of politics are summarized and evaluated in Thomas L. Brewer, *American Foreign Policy: A Contemporary Introduction* (Englewood Cliffs, N.J.: Prentice-Hall, 1980), ch. 2.
5. Although this discussion emphasizes the trade implications of many FDI decisions, it is of course also true that many times direct investment and exporting ar alternative choices for a given strategic decision. In those situations, it should be recognized that there are many political risks associated with the export alternative. Indeed, foreign direct investment, as a strategic alternative to exporting, is not necessarily more vulnerable to political risk. The casual assumption that the expropriation risk associated with direct investment is greater than the trade barrier risk associated with exporting is probably the result of two conditions: The losses associated with the expropriations are normally more conspicuous and dramatic; and those losses involve direct losses of assets and are therefore relatively easily measured. In contrast, the political risks associated with exporting are more likely to involve undramatic developments such as changes in tariffs, and exporting is less likely to involve direct losses of measurable, tangible assests. The cash flow losses, however, may be greater.
6. Stephen J. Kobrin, "When does political instability result in increased investment risk?" *Columbia Journal of World Business*, Vol. 13, No. 3 (Fall 1978), pp. 113-122.

7. The current Prime Minister of South Africa has acknowledged the volatiltiy of the situation there. See *The Economist*, Vol. 275, No. 7138 (June 21, 1980), p. 22.
8. For an analysis of the level of violence in Northern Ireland and its effects on labor relations and foreign direct investment, see *The Economist*, Vol. 275, No. 7139 (June 28, 1980), p. 65.
9. A recent wave of disinvestment in Belgium because of governmental changes may reveal a degree of preoccupation and even skittishness about stability. See *The Economist* Vol. 276, No. 7141 (July 12, 1980), p. 76.
10. This discussion of capital budgeting analysis draws on Alan C. Shapiro, "Capital budgeting for the multinational corporation," *Financial Management*, Spring, 1978, pp. 1-16; J. Fred Weston and Eugene F. Bringham, *Managerial Finance*, 6th ed. (Hinsdale, Illinois: Dryden Press-Holt, Rinehart and Winston, 1987), Part 3; Thomas E. Copeland and John F. Weston, *Financial Theory and Corporate Policy* (Reading, Mass.: Addison-Wesley, 1979); and James C. Van Horne, *Financial Management Policy*, 4th ed. (Englewood Cliffs, N.J.: Prentice-Hall, 1977), Part 2.
11. The effects of exchange controls can often be reduces by changes in transfer pricing, debt repayment, or other forms of funds transfers. The effectiveness of exchange controls on earnings repatriation therefore varies considerably.
12. The terminal value adjustment to the internal rate of return method is analogous. In spite of some interesting and potentially significant differences between the net present value and internal rate of return methods, however, the remainder of this discussion is limited to the net present value method since it is the normal mode of analysis in capital budgeting decisions.
13. It should be noted, however, that a simple cumulative estimate based on the additive effects of the individual types of risks is necessarily based on an assumption that the risks are independent of one another. Alternatively, if the assumption of independence is not plausible, estimates of the marginal or incremental addition of each type of risk to the cumulative total can be used.

The Author is indebted to Gunter Dufey for comments on a draft of this article.

III. ——FINANCING DECISIONS ————————

7. International Financial Planning:

THE USE OF MARKET-BASED FORECASTS

GUNTER DUFEY
IAN H. GIDDY

Corporate planning is an integrated effort by all levels of management to achieve the firm's strategic objectives under future conditions of opportunity, risk, and uncertainty through established forecasting, planning, and budgeting procedures on a regular basis. International corporations face greater risks than domestic ones but also have wider opportunities, and therefore they require a planning system specifically adapted to international market uncertainties.

The formal planning and budgeting process is similar in all large corporations. Based on overall strategic business objectives, operating plans originate from product groups or regional business units. These plans are then coordinated at the corporate level and are adjusted in a process of give and take with financial management, which in turn provides information about the availability of funds at various cost levels. Once an agreement has been reached on the volume of assets to be financed, work can begin on a detailed financing plan.

Planning and Budgeting in International Companies

In multiunit, multijurisdiction organizations such as international corporations, this process is an involved one, since it must be done for every corporate entity. In the end, financial planners in such firms must make decisions about the following issues:

- Should funds be obtained in the form of equity or debt and, if the latter, for which maturity? Alternatively, in which financial instruments should excess funds be invested?
- In which market (and which currency) should funds be raised (invested)?
- What legal entity is to raise (invest) the funds?
- How should funds be transferred from the corporate entity that raises them from third parties to the entity(ies) that need them for investment in productive assets and working capital?

The primary task of international financial management is to minimize the cost of funds and to maximize the return on investment over time, by means of the best combination of currency of denomination and maturity characteristics of financial assets and liabilities. The implementation of these choices, however, requires the formulation and revision of capital structure decisions for various units and budgets for intercompany funds transfers. Only to the extent that financial managers have some influence over these decisions will they be able to take full advantage of the firm's financial planning and forecasting tools described in this article.

Forecasting Requirements of Financial Planning

The international corporate planning process relies heavily on forecasts of prices, availability of supplies, government actions, competitors' responses, labor conditions, technological development, and so forth. We can conveniently identify three categories of forecasts necessary for corporate planning: (1) forecasts of product market and industry conditions: product demand, industrial activity, and so on; (2) forecasts of conditions within the firm: technical changes in production, labor relations, management needs, and so on, and (3) forecasts of conditions in financial markets: interest rates, funds availability, and so on.

In this article we are concerned chiefly with the forecasts necessary for financial planning. How are such forecasts used? We take as given the timing, amount, and currency of cash outflows and the needs of the firm during the planning period. The financial manager's role is that of planning for the transfer of funds within the firm and for international working capital and funding decisions. Undoubtedly, a large part of this task is to devise the legal entities and arrange the form of international transactions so as to maximize flexibility for corporate funding and transfer needs. Yet we take these as given too, focusing specifically on the decisions that remain when institutional and legal opportunities and constraints have been identified.

What decisions are left? Given the anticipated cash needs or surpluses of various operating units at various dates in the future, and given the constraints on how and where funds can be moved, the financial planners have to decide on the timing, maturity, and currency of denomination that will minimize funding costs, and on the timing and maturity of investments in financial assets.

Decisions about when funds should be raised, and at what maturity, depend on anticipated interest rate movements or changes in the availability of funds, as well as the timing of cash needs. Decisions on the currency of debt depend on expected exchange rate changes, as well as the currency of denomination of funds needs and flows. The million-franc needs of a French subsidiary six months from now, for example, could be met by borrowing French francs when the funds are required. Depending on forecasts of credit and currency market conditions, on the other hand, financial planners may recommend the issuance of long-term debt now (if interest rates are lower than expected in the future) instead of later, or borrowing in dollars instead of francs (if the French franc is regarded as a strong currency).

To summarize: financial planning decisions on timing, maturity, and currency of denomination of financial assets and liabilities require interest rate and exchange rate forecasts. In the next section we shall describe the rather wide range of implicit forecasts provided by the financial and currency markets themselves, and how they relate to one another. Later we suggest the use of such forecasts in financial planning.

The Market's Forecasts of Financial Conditions _____

The traditional theory of markets views the price of any good or service (a bicycle or a haircut), and of any financial asset (a bond or a pound sterling), as the outcome of the forces of supply and demand. While few would dispute this basic contention, in recent years the focus of theoretical and empirical research has emphasized the role of *market expectations,* rather than current supply and demand, as the prime determinant of prices and interest rates in financial markets. This fact is of great interest to forecasters, because if present prices and yields embody the market's expectations of future prices and interest rates, it may be possible to determine the market's forecast by looking at competitively determined prices and rates.

Future prices in commodity markets provide the best available information about the market's forecasts of spot prices. For example, market participants who believe that they have better information about future spot prices of soybeans than do other market participants will attempt to make profits by buying or selling futures contracts. The result is that new information is quickly incorporated into the prices of futures contracts, and the pattern of futures prices reflects the best guesses of well-informed market participants about the path of future spot prices.

We can go further: according to the "efficient market" hypothesis, the market's forecast is *rational,* in the sense of being a function of the true determinants of future spot prices, and utilizes all available information in the most efficient way possible. If this is true, the market forecast, and hence the futures price, is the best available estimate of the future prices of a commodity.[1] While many do not accept this argument in its pure form, the bulk of evidence in recent years supports the notion that futures prices are unbiased predictors of subsequent spot prices.

While futures prices exist in some uniform raw materials and agricultural commodity markets, these are too few and far between to be of much use to operating management. The market for labor, for example, is too diverse and inefficient for a futures wage rate (if it existed) to be of much use in forecasting labor costs. In contrast, the markets for many currencies and financial instruments are highly efficient and standardized and numerous traders stand ready to exploit perceived profit opportunities whenever they arise.

In the currency market, the market's forecasts are embodied in the forward exchange rate (futures prices). Of course, the forward exchange rate is not an *accurate* forecast, because traders' buy or sell decisions are only based on information available *now*. Not only will the market-based forecast be continually revised as new information reaches the market, right up to the date of the maturity of the futures contract, but the *actual* future price will also deviate from the predicted price because of new information that reaches the market. In fact, even over long periods the forecasting error of the forward rate is not likely to average out to zero.[2]

Thus, over any given period the actual price will turn out to differ from the futures price. The amount C in Figure 1 will usually be positive or negative. But the chances that the actual price will be above or below the futures price are equal. Because price changes result from new information reaching the market, and because new information is by its nature unpredictable, the deviation C tends to be randomly distributed about zero. In other words, the *expected value* of the forecasting error C is *zero.*

For financial planning purposes, the forecaster should consider three differences (illustrated in Figure 1). Amount A, the difference between today's exchange rate and the actual future rate, is often thought of as the possible exchange risk. However, by calculating amount B, the difference between today's rate and the market-expected future rate, we are usually able to *anticipate* much of the exchange rate change. Hence, what matters to the planner is amount C, the *unanticipated* exchange rate change; and, as we have seen, this can be positive or negative, and has a zero expected value.

If the forward exchange rate equals the expected future spot rate, we may assume that forward rates for various maturities trace the expected movement of the spot exchange rate in the future. By expressing the forward rate as an annualized discount or premium from the spot rate, as in Figure 2, we can estimate the market forecast of the rate of change of the exchange rate for any period in the future.

We have thus far linked the forward premium or discount to exchange rate expectations. But exchange rate expectations themselves are linked to inflationary expectations, or rather, expectations about *relative* inflation rates in the two countries. This so-called purchasing power parity relationship simply states that the rate of change of the exchange rate tends over time to equal the difference between inflation rates in two countries.

Figure 1.

EXCHANGE RATE FORECASTING USING THE FORWARD RATE.

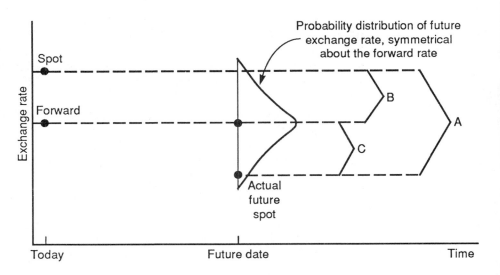

A - Actual exchange rate change: difference between today's and the actual future exchange rate.

B - Anticipated change: difference between today's spot rate and the forward rate.

C - Unanticipated change: difference between the forward rate and the actual future exchange rate.

Figure 2.

MARKET-IMPLIED EXCHANGE RATE EXPECTATIONS, AUGUST 1977.

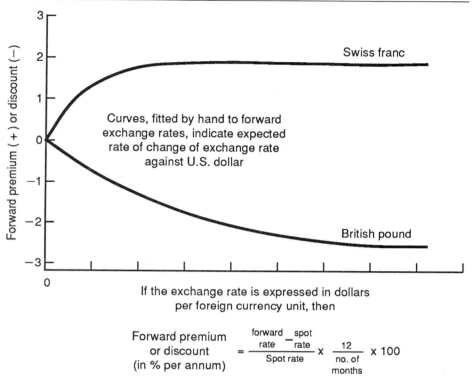

Further, covered interest arbitrage between two currencies creates a linkage between interest rates and the forward premium or discount. That is, the forward premium or discount tends always to equal the interest rate differential between financial assets denominated in different currencies. The relative interest rates are themselves also linked more or less directly to exchange rate and inflation rate expectations, for one would expect that the country with the higher inflation rate and whose currency is expected to depreciate would also have a higher interest rate.

All these relationships are summarized diagrammatically in Figure 3. As the diagram suggests, while market-based forecasts of expected exchange rate changes can be obtained most directly from spot and forward exchange rates, they can also be obtained from the interest rate differential. By subtracting the domestic from the foreign interest rate we obtain the expected rate of change, and hence the expected path, of the foreign currency's value, as Figure 4 illustrates.

So far, we have talked only of market forecasts of exchange rates (and inflation rates) based on the term structure of forward exchange rates.[3] Can interest rates be forecasted in the same way? In principle, the answer is yes, although the technique for discovering the market's interest rate forecast is usually a little more subtle than that for exchange rates. Nevertheless, the market's forecast for interest rates at

Figure 3.
EQUILIBRIUM RELATIONSHIPS AMONG EXCHANGE RATES, INFLATION RATES, AND INTEREST RATES.

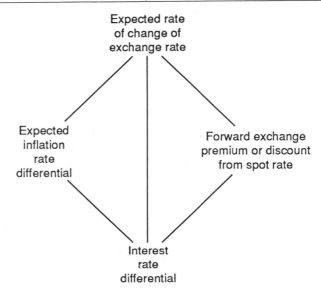

almost any date in the future can be estimated by looking at the yield curve on, say, government bonds. The yield curve is a chart that plots the current yields to maturity of a group of securities of various maturities, but which are all equivalent as to credit quality. This "term structure of interest rates" is often upward-sloping, but can also be flat, downward-sloping, or even humped. Figure 5 illustrates three such curves.

In an efficient market, the shape of the yield curve is determined largely by expectations about future interest rates. An upward-sloping curve means interest rates are likely to rise; a downward-sloping one, that a fall is expected.

Long-term rates tend to equal the average of expected future short-term rates; if that were not the case, investors would take speculative actions tending to bid long-term rates up or down until they fulfilled that condition. For example, if interest rate expectations rise so that the average of expected intervening short-term rates is higher than long-term rates, investors will sell long-term bonds and buy short ones, in the expectation of reinvesting the money in short term securities. This will continue until long rates are bid up to the point of reflecting expected future short-term rates.

More specifically, the rate on a nine-month Treasury bill tends to approximately equal the average of today's rate on a three-month bill and the market-expected rate on a six-month bill issued three months from now. If today's three-month rate is 4 percent and the nine-month rate 6 percent, the implied forecast for the six-month rate three months from now is 7 percent. This is because the weighted average of 4 percent for three months and 7 percent for six months is 6 percent. The general method for calculating the market interest rate forecast is shown in Figure 6 (see appendix for formula).

Figure 4.
MARKET-BASED FORECAST OF EXCHANGE RATE CHANGES, FROM INTEREST RATE DIFFERENTIAL.

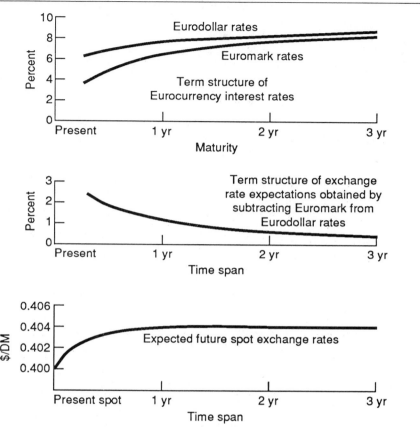

Source: from Gunter Dufey and Ian Giddy. The *International Money Market*, Englewood Cliffs, N.J.: Prentice-Hall, 1978, section on "The Term Structure of Eurocurrency Interest Rates." Used with permission.

The method just described is the traditional approach and will work whenever rates are free to reach their competitive levels. Recently, however, the development of interest rate futures markets has provided a more direct guage of interest rate expectations. The prices of futures contracts for three-month Treasury bills and government securities provide a set of market forecasts of near-term interest rate prospects parallel to those available from yield curves. The two approaches should provide identical forecasts. Since contracting to buy a three-month Treasury bill six months from now is exactly equivalent to borrowing at a fixed rate for six months and investing the proceeds in a nine-month Treasury bill, interest rate expectations have the same effect on financial futures as they do on the term structure of interest

Figure 5.
RECENT YIELD CURVES FOR U.S. GOVERNMENT SECURITIES.

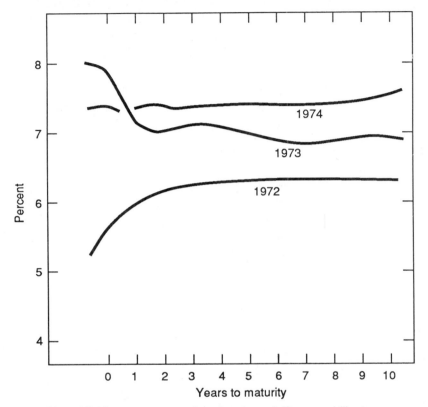

Note: Yield curves are as of each year end. Treasury bill rates
are included on a bond-equivalent basis.

Source: From Morgan Guaranty Trust Co., *The Morgan Guaranty Survey*, July 1977, p. 11.

rates. Futures prices for financial instruments are quoted on a discount basis; hence the interest rate forecast implied by a Treasury bill futures contract priced at 96 is $100 - 96 = 4$ percent.

In conclusion, we find that in reasonably efficient and competitive markets for uniform goods or assets, today's prices and rates are strongly influenced by forecasts of future market conditions, and that the term structures of commodity futures prices, forward exchange rates and interest rates provide good readings of the market's forecasts.

At this point, we must address the possibility that market prices of futures, both interest rate futures or forward exchange rates, may not predict future rates in an unbiased fashion. Put differently, the question is whether there is reason to expect

Figure 6.
THE MARKET FORECAST IMPLIED IN THE YIELD CURVE.

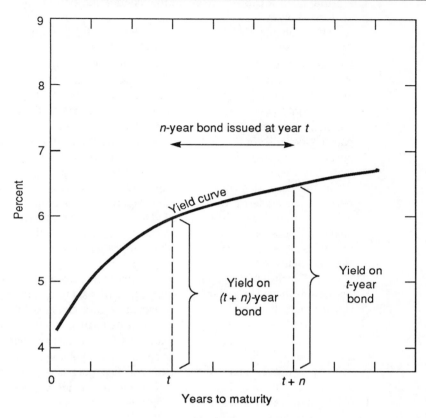

Rule of thumb for calculating market forecast:

$$\text{Yield curve implied market forecast for bond commencing at year } t \text{ and maturing } n \text{ years later} = \frac{(t+n)\left(\begin{array}{c}\text{Present interest rate on a } (t+n)\text{ year bond}\end{array}\right) - (t)\left(\begin{array}{c}\text{Present interest rate on a } t\text{-year bond}\end{array}\right)}{n}$$

that the rate predicted by the forward instrument will be systematically over- or under-estimated. Two possible sources of bias may exist.

First, a bias may result from obvious market imperfections. For example, the existence of extensive credit allocation, heavy-handed administrative barriers to borrowing and lending, and tight exchange controls would provide prima facie evidence for the arguments that forward rates may deviate systematically from the expected future exchange rate. On the other hand, the mere presence of controls does not necessarily imply that forward rates or interest rate differentials are biased, for many and devious are the paths of arbitrage. Only when controls on both the credit and foreign exchange markets are effective is a systematic bias likely to be evident. In such cases, forward rates or interest rate differentials provide a good starting point for forecasting and for the identification of profit opportunities, as we shall see below.

More difficult to deal with is the claim of the existence of systematic ex ante deviations, when no such barriers exist. The best known source of biases of this kind is the presence of a liquidity premium inherent in the prediction of short-term interest rates by long-term rates. According to this view, the yields on long-term instruments overestimate future short-term interest rates, just as yields on financial futures contracts are upward biased estimates of expected future interest rates. The empirical evidence on the existence of liquidity premiums is not altogether clear, partially because of the statistical measurement difficulties. More important for our purposes, however, is the fact that estimates of such liquidity premiums have been quite small when they were found at all.[4]

In the case of foreign exchange rates the issue is a bit more difficult, if only because the evidence of market imperfections is more pervasive. Several strands of reasoning can be distinguished. One hypothesizes that because currencies are financial assets issued by different countries, they differ in terms of "political risk": countries can deprive holders of the use of their money balances, or can otherwise restrict their ultimate use to settle claims.[5]

Another argument supporting systematic forecasting errors has been based on the notion that yield differentials on the same assets denominated in different currencies reflect not only expected exchange rate changes but also a risk premium arising from the possibility that exchange rate changes may be correlated with returns on other assets, creating a systematic risk for speculators that cannot be diversified away.[6] The prevailing conclusion of researchers, however, is that such a "covariance term" is probably small, and that for practical purposes it is virtually impossible to identify any ex ante bias in the absence of specific market imperfections.[7] The equilibrium relationships presented in this section probably provide the most reliable framework for planning purposes.

How Can Financial Planners Use Market-Based Forecasts? ———————

We have argued that, in the absence of a systematic bias, the forecasts of interest rates and exchange rate changes contained in the term structure of interest rates and forward rates represent the most realistic point estimate of market expectations. We shall now show why such forecasts should not be used in isolation, but rather as a *benchmark* against which to judge the firm's own ability to forecast or to exploit market imperfections. Given the market-based forecasts, we can distinguish three situations each with distinct implications for the maturity and currency aspects of financial planning.

■ Situation 1: *When the financial markets in question are reasonably efficient, and financial planners know of no systematic biases or constraints on market rates, then market-based forecasts should be accepted as valid.* Under these conditions, which probably hold for most financial decisions involving the U.S. and major international financial markets, no expected gain will result from manipulating the timing or currency of borrowing or investing, and financial management's energies should be directed toward matching borrowings and investments with the timing and currency of the funds needed or generated by the firm's operations.

Although this is a simple principle, its implementation requires a fairly detailed analysis of the firm's cash flows. The application of the above principle to financial planning must begin with the recognition that it is likely that the market's expected value will seldom be attained; indeed every *actual* interest rate and each *actual* exchange rate will be likely to differ from the value that was predicted by the futures or forward rate, respectively.

The use of market-based forecasts then implies planning for the deviations, or forecasting errors, that we know will occur. The first step in the planning process is to obtain a forecast that indicates how deviations around the expected interest rates or exchange rates will affect the entity for which a financial plan is established. This entity can be the corporation as a whole, or one of its affiliates. In the latter case, however, it is imperative to assess not the effects on the operating unit per se, but rather the effect that the change in the expected rate has on the unit's contribution to the return (or net cash flow) of the firm as a whole. In other words, marginal analysis is required.

Specifically, what we want to know is how cash flows from operations (return on assets) will change for any given deviation of the interest or exchange rate from the value predicted. As long as the return on assets is contractually fixed and denominated in a particular currency, as would be a portfolio of bonds or loans, the analysis is quite straightforward. A rise in interest rates will cause a proportional fall in the value of such as fixed-interest portfolio; and a given fall in the exchange rate will lead to an equal drop in the dollar value of the portfolio. Protecting the value of such assets, therefore, simply requires funding the liabilities of the firm in the same currency and maturity as the assets.

Unfortunately, this simple procedure is not applicable to multiunit international manufacturing operations. In such a firm, unexpected exchange rate and interest rate changes cause changes in prices, volumes, cost of inputs and similar factors in complex ways. Net cash flows and, therefore, return on assets can be affected positively, negatively, or not at all by a given exchange rate, according to its dependence on imports, its volume of export sales, its ability to raise prices and so forth. Similarly, an interest rate change may be associated with a rise or reduction in demand for the firms' products and have other indirect effects on operating cash flows. It is one of the most important functions of the financial planner to identify the specific cash flow effects that unanticipated interest or exchange rate effects may have for his particular firm. This, of course, is not an easy task.

Apart from the complexity of the analysis, there are technical issues of measurements that must be resolved. Should "return on assets" be measured in accounting terms, or in terms of expected future cash flows?

In periods of inflation, the valuation of assets at historical cost distorts accounting results. When foreign exchange rate changes combine with different rates of inflation and valuation principles based on historical cost, the resulting data differ substantially from those obtained by analyzing the impact of an unexpected exchange rate change on the operating results. The cast flow approach is the correct one; but financial planners who have faced the task of recasting data in pro forma accounting statements will recognize the difficulty of doing so. And if management compensation is tied to accounting results ("the bottom line"), the implementation of financial plans founded on market-based forecasts and deviations from expected cash flow becomes a heroic task. Finally, as to whether stock prices are affected by accounting results that do not reflect the cash flow effect of exchange rate changes, the empirical evidence is at present too scanty to draw conclusions one way or another.

Under the assumption that the market forecasts are the best available, no anticipated gain can be had by changing the maturity or currency mix of liabilities. Hence, the only rational purpose of financial planning in an efficient market is *to structure the firm's liabilities in such a way that any unanticipated change in the return on assets is offset, as far as possible, by a change in the effective cost of liabilities.*

Let us examine the basis for this principle more closely. Manufacturing and other nonfinancial enterprises expect a net profit because they have a competitive advantage in providing goods and services by managing real assets. The role of financial management is to protect this expected profit from unexpected fluctuations in financial market conditions. Since the structure of real assets is determined by fundamental business strategy considerations, the adjustment to offset financial risk must, therefore, occur on the liability rather than the asset side of the firm. We can illustrate the general principle with a few simple examples.

1. A firm operating only in one currency, whose operating cash flows fluctuate with inflation, can afford to fund itself largely with short-term debt, assuming that inflation is also the major influence on short-term rates.
2. On the other hand, a corporation whose operating return is uncorrelated or negatively correlated with short-term interest rates is well advised to borrow long-term at fixed interest rates in order to stabilize its funding costs and thereby reduce the impact of unanticipated interest changes on final net cash flows.
3. Since the cost of foreign currency debt is directly correlated with unexpected exchange rate changes, the application of our general principle to foreign cash flows is quite straightforward. When a unit's operating returns are positively correlated with a currency's value, that unit should be funded in the same currency, because any unanticipated depreciation of the currency reduces not only returns from operations, but also the effective cost (interest rate plus/minus exchange rate change) of the liabilities.

It is, of course, very rare that the change in the net cash flow on the asset side will be completely offset by a change on the liability side; hence, a residual risk will always remain. However, it is an essential part of the task of financial planning management to gauge the magnitude of such risks and to communicate it effectively to top management. The function of top management is to decide whether this risk is tolerable, or whether operations must be restructured to reduce the basic sensitivity of the corporation to unanticipated changes in interest and exchange rates. Such operational adjustments often involve far-reaching strategic decisions: a change of markets and marketing (long-term contractual sales), a change in sources of supplies, the degree of in-house production versus purchases from outside suppliers, and perhaps even a change in the choice of technology to be employed in the production process.

The financial planning framework laid out above assumes the market's forecasts are unbiased predictions of future interest and exchange rates. Often, specific market imperfections will not allow this assumption to hold. The next two sections consider the implications of such biases.

■ Situation 2: *When the term structure of interest or exchange rates deviates in a systematic way from the market's actual expectations because of government controls on interest rates and exchange rates, or because of other specific market imperfections, financial management has profit opportunities.* The exploitation of these opportunities requires (a) a flexible legal and operational structure, and (b) an explicit trade-off function that permits management to decide whether the gains are worth the increase in risk that the exploitation of market imperfections may involve.

Government intervention in credit and foreign exchange markets through administrative action, such as interest rate ceilings, quantitative credit allocation, or selection restrictions on international fund transfers tends to keep both interest rates lower and exchange rates higher than market participants think they should be. By the same token, such administrative controls imply that government limits access to credit and foreign exchange markets, thereby deciding who obtains credit and foreign exchange and the profits that are inherent in such favored positions. It is here that international firms as producing, job-creating enterprises with legal entities operating in many countries, centrally coordinated by corporate financial planning, have an advantage in arbitraging between actual rates and expected rates.

Unlike pure financial operators who could exploit profit opportunities only by contravening government laws and regulations, international firms can legally circumvent these restrictions, provided their financial activities are properly coordinated—and this is what financial planning is all about. Government controls tend to be always partial, never comprehensive. The reason is simple: controls on *all* borrowing or lending, and *all* international transfers of funds would cause economic activity to come to a grinding halt. Therefore, with regulations permitting certain transactions, and funds being fungible, international firms with diverse legal structures and a multitude of intercompany links usually are in a privileged position to exploit the financial windfalls that government actions provide by keeping interest rates low and preventing exchange rates from adjusting to market pressures.

Sometimes the maturity and currency of debt that will best capitalize on such market opportunities is close to that which would have been chosen merely in order to offset fluctuations in asset returns. However, decisions become complicated when the financial management must consider a maturity or currency structure that would increase the overall risk of the firm, but whose cost is less than the risk-minimizing alternative because of government controls of the type described above. In this case, top management must provide indications of how much more risk it is willing to accept in return for the lower cost of funds. Again, the task of financial planning is to clearly communicate the dimensions of the choice to top management in order to aid it in this crucial decision.

In many respects, situation 2—where market-based forecasts deviate from forecasted rates because of specific market imperfections—is similar to the situation which we discuss next.

■ Situation 3: *When the market-based forecasts deviate from forecasted rates, not because of market imperfections but because the firm has some proprietary information or unusual forecasting ability, then financial managers should act on their forecasts only when the risks of doing so are offset by the expected gains.* When financial planners can confidently answer the question, "Why do we believe we can predict interest or exchange rates better than the market?" their focus should be on the proper perspective on the risks involved in speculative actions, and on a rapid response to opportunities when action is warranted.

Few financial managers can consistently resist the temptation to base financing decisions on their own judgments rather than those of the market. In most cases little harm is done, for unless the firm really goes out on a limb, positive and negative forecasting errors tend to cancel out over time. But the mark of a good financial manager is not his knack for occasionally outguessing the market's forecasts, but rather his ability to obtain the highest return on invested assets, for a given level of risk, and the best long-run terms and conditions on debt, *irrespective* of the trend of interest rates or exchange rates. It is important for the integrity of the financial management process to keep these aspects of the function strictly separate. Otherwise, the inability of financial management to outperform the markets tends to be hidden in the results of the risk-management function.

Speculative actions in financial markets should be vigorously segregated from the other functions of financial managers, and subjected to separate policy guidelines and scrutiny. A strategy for performance evaluation of the financial forecasting abilities of financial management is suggested in the next section.

Market-based Forecasts as Yardsticks for Budgeting and Performance Evaluation ____

We began this article with a discussion of corporate planning and budgeting; in this last section we shall try to show how market-based forecasts of financial data have applications in operating budgets and management control as well as in financial planning.

For multinational corporations with decentralized operating units, Robbins and Stobaugh have argued cogently that the prime tool for goal-setting and performance evaluation should be the periodic budget that is set jointly by financial planners and operating managers and revised in the light of changing conditions.[8] On the other hand, few dispute the gains to be had from a centralized control of intracompany cash flows in order to respond to changing currency, interest rate, taxation, and exchange control developments. For our purposes, this means that operating units, such as foreign subsidiaries, should not be held responsible for interest rate or exchange rate developments.[9] Yet all budgets must explicitly or implicitly incorporate a cost of funds, and budgets for foreign operations must be translated at some exchange rate. What interest and exchange rates should be used?

Most corporations calculate the cost of funds using a standard interest rate based on past borrowing costs and translate foreign subsidiaries' cash flow projections at the exchange rate prevailing at budget date. That approach would be fine if the firm were somehow guaranteed the same interest rate and exchange rate for the entire budget period. When subsidiary managers are not held responsible for the impact of deviations from the budgeted exchange and interest rates, it surely makes more sense to use projected interest costs and exchange rates for budget preparation and performance evaluation than to use past rates. In the past, firms without access to a reliable exchange rate and interest rate forecasting service may have been reluctant to make such projections. The availability of costless market-based forecasts of interest and exchange rate trends, however, leaves them with no such excuse.

The market's forecasts may not be very accurate, but they will certainly result in fewer errors than the implicit assumption that today's rate is the appropriate projection. In addition, market rates have the virtue of being objective.

If operating managers are not held responsible for deviations of the actual cost of funds and exchange rate from the budget rates, then the financial managers whose task is to manage intercompany cash flows and transactions in the credit and foreign exchange markets must be made accountable for the impact of unanticipated interest rate and exchange rate changes. Here we find an additional virtue to the use of market-based forecasts for budgeting and performance evaluation purposes. We have argued that if financial managers choose to reject the market forecasts as a basis for financing, investment and currency decisions, they are implicitly asserting their own ability to "beat the market."

Can they do so? Only time will tell, but it will tell very explicitly if the consequences of actions based on the financial managers' *own* forecasts are consistently evaluated against the results of actions based on the *market's* forecasts. Either method of forecasting will result in errors, but the financial decision maker is justified in relying on his own forecasts only if doing so results in a superior average track record than would reliance on the market-based forecasts.

No financial manager can reasonably be blamed for being unable to predict unanticipated events in the financial system, but all managers should be evaluated against the dual criteria that (a) the cost of any effort to forecast interest and exchange rates should be justified on the basis of better-than-market performance, and (b) the recognition that forecasting errors are inevitable and that the prime task of financial management is to structure the firm's cash flows in such a way that the impact of such errors is minimized.

Conclusions

The message of this article is as follows: corporate planning and budgeting relies in large part on projections of conditions in various markets, including those for the firm's products and services, labor and other inputs, credit, and foreign currencies.

Management attention, we argue, should be concentrated on those markets in which the firm has a competitive advantage. Since the market's forecasts—implicit in the term structure of interest rates and of forward exchange rates—are readily available in the financial markets, which are both competitive and efficient, and in which the firm is unlikely to have a particular advantage, there is an a priori rationale for making borrowing and investment decisions based on these forecasts.

On the other hand, where financial managers feel they have a peculiar advantage in such financial markets, resulting from the firm's legal structure, geographical locations or because of an unusual forecasting ability, then the timing, maturity, and currency of borrowing and investment decisions should be based on the firm's own forecasts whenever the expected gains justify the risks. However, the risks and ex post performance of the decisions taken should always be compared against the outcomes of decisions based on market-based forecasts. The market's projections constitute the best benchmark for the evaluation of financial management's performance.

Notes _____

1. To be precise, market efficiency need not imply that future prices are unbiased forecasts. For an exposition of the efficient markets argument, see Aldich A. Vasicek and John A. McQuown, "The Efficient Market Model," *Financial Analysts Journal*, September—October 1972, pp. 71–82.
2. See, for example, Robert Ankrom, "Among Their Hedges, Treasurers May Miss the Obvious," *Euromoney*, December 1977, p. 99.
3. The precise formulas for these linkages between interest rates, forward exchange rates, and currency and inflation rate expectations may be found in Ian H. Giddy, "An Integrated Theory of Exchange Rate Equilibrium," *Journal of Financial & Quantitative Analysis*, December 1976.
4. See studies cited in A. E. Burger, R. W. Lang, and R. H. Rasche, "The Treasury Bill Futures Market and Market Expectations of Interest Rates," *Federal Reserve Bank of St. Louis—Monthly Review*, July 1977, p. 5.
5. R. Z. Aliber, "Exchange Risk, Political Risk, and Investor Demand for External Currency Deposits," *Journal of Money, Credit and Banking*, May 1975, pp. 161–179.
6. Versions of this idea can be found in Michael C. Adler and Bernard Dumas, "Portfolio Choice and the Demand for Forward Exchange," *American Economic Review*, May 1976, pp. 332–339, and Bruno H. Solnik, "The International Pricing of Risk: An Empirical Investigation of the World Capital Market Structure," *Journal of Finance*, May 1974, pp. 365–379.
7. See Jeffrey A. Frankel, "On the Mark: A Theory of Floating Exchange Based on Real Interest Differentials," unpublished manuscript, Massachusetts Institute of Technology, October 1977, Appendix A.
8. Sidney M. Robbins and Robert B. Stobaugh, "The Bent Measuring Stick for Foreign Subsidiaries," *Harvard Business Review*, September—October 1973.
9. These issues are discussed in some detail in Donald R. Lessard and Peter Lorange, "Currency Changes and Management Control: Resolving the Centralization/Decentralization Dilemma," *Accounting Review*, July 1977.

Appendix

The exact formula for the term structure implied interest rate forecast is

$$t''_{t+n} = \left[\frac{(1 + {}_oR_{t+n})^{t+n}}{(1 + {}_oR_t)^t} - 1 \frac{1}{n} \right]$$

where ${}_t r_{t+n}$ is the implied interest rate on a bond starting at t and maturing at $t + n$, ${}_oR_{t+n}$ is today's interest rate on a bond of maturity $t + n$, and ${}_oR_t$ is today's interest rate on a bond of maturity t. All interest rates are expressed as decimal fractions rather than as percentages.

8. CAPITAL STRUCTURE AND COST-OF-CAPITAL FOR THE MULTINATIONAL FIRM

MARJORIE THINES STANLEY

Introduction

The objective of this paper is to review recent developments in models dealing with capital structure and cost of capital as these have been extended to the multinational case. The models address a number of issues which bear upon the financing decisions of the multinational firm. The questions relating to capital structure include: Is there an optimal capital structure for the multinational firm? How does multinationality affect this question? Does subsidiary capital structure "matter"? The questions relating to cost of capital include: What is the effect, if any, of multinationality upon parent cost of equity? Is the multinational firm's cost of capital affected by its debt financing decisions? Does currency of denomination exert an influence of its own which is relevant to debt financing decisions? If so, what is the nature of this influence? Is it possible for the multinational firm to benefit from international differentials in nominal interest rates? Do firms attempt to do so? Underlying these specific issues is the basic theoretical and empirical question of the degree of segmentation or integration of international money and capital markets and a related question with regard to the efficiency of the foreign exchange market.

The models employed in research dealing with cost of capital and capital structure for the multinational firm are themselves a subject of controversy. Partially for this reason, the review of the literature has been organized on the basis of the models employed, in each case attempting to point out the specific problems addressed in individual studies, subsequent critiques of the studies, and the nature of the evolution of the theoretical and empirical research. The paper will be concerned not only with the contribution which the individual research studies may make to a resolution of the earlier enumerated questions related to the financial policy of the multinational firm, but will seek to comment also upon the realism and relevance of the models' theoretical assumptions and the practicability of empirical testing of the theoretical constructs.

The scope of the paper has been limited, perhaps somewhat arbitrarily, so as to exclude detailed examination of the issue of the separation/integration of the financing decision and the investment decision, and only tangential consideration will be given to the foreign investment decision itself. Reference to the comprehensive literature on foreign exchange market efficiency and to the extensive literature on international integration of financial markets which has a primarily macro thrust will be limited to conclusions drawn from selected studies which have direct relevance to issues of

Reprinted from *Journal of International Business Studies* 12, no. 1, Spring/Summer 1981, 103–120, by permission of the University of South Carolina College of Business Administration.

capital structure or cost of capital for the multinational firm. In short, the articles reviewed will be selected and evaluated primarily on the basis of their relevance to the financing decisions of the multinational firm, with occasional reference to closely related capital budgeting and international investment decisions.

Because the extension of domestic models to the multinational case has been done within or disputing the Modigliani-Miller framework and within the capital asset pricing model framework, the next section of the paper will examine models within or disputing the Modigliani-Miller framework (3; 34; 44; 45; 59; 66; 85; 98). This will be followed by a section addressing research conducted within or disputing the capital asset pricing model framework (1; 6; 11; 14; 28; 32; 37; 40; 52; 57; 86; 87–91). The paper will conclude with two sections summarizing the current state of knowledge—the first will emphasize current areas of conflict, data problems which hamper resolution of these conflicts, and areas for future research; the final summary will emphasize the financial policy prescribed or suggested for the firm by the current state of knowledge.

Models within or Disputing the Modigliani-Miller Framework _____

Within the Modigliani-Miller framework, Krainer presented an extension analyzing the question of the capital structure and valuation of the multinational firm (44). Abstracting from corporate income taxes and beginning with "a world where firms make physical investments and finance within a single capital market but portfolio investors are free to make investments in different national capital markets." Krainer explored the question of whether a firm can be in the same risk class in two different national capital markets. He concluded that, in a world where currencies are convertible into one another at varying rates and in varying degrees, the claimants to the uncertain earnings stream of foreign firms face currency risks that cause the risk/return relationship to differ as between a firm's foreign and domestic claimants, so "there is no reason to expect the level or structure of capitalization rates appropriate to (a firm's) securities to be the same in two different countries;" that is, arbitrage, though operative, will not completely eliminate a difference in capitalization rates associated with currency rate and repatriation risks. Krainer then arued that this result may enable a firm that invests and finances in several national capital markets to influence the cutoff rate at which it accepts new capital projects by altering its capital structure, given the condition that domestic portfolio investors are not "preferred borrowers" in foreign capital markets; that is, for the M-M results to hold for the multinational firm, portfolio investors must be able to issue personal debt in national capital markets open to the firm. Krainer concluded that financial planners for MNCs should study capital markets in "the larger national capital markets in order to take advantage of possible opportunities to reduce the average cost of capital" (44, p. 563).

Dropping the no-tax assumptions, Krainer concluded that the tax deductibility of interest payments and the associated "rebate" to the shareholders of the levered firm, when capitalized at a favorable foreign rate, provide an incentive for the multinational firm to issue debt up to its maximum debt limit (44, p. 564), imposed by either the firm itself or its creditors. Presumably, the self-imposed limit would be "prudential" in nature or, perhaps, be influenced by finance managers' perceptions of the effect of leverage upon expectations (54, pp. 40–42).

A critique of Krainer by Adler (3) raised several theoretical issues. Basically, these amounted to a criticism of the choice of the M-M model as opposed to a portfolio diversification approach and an emphasis upon default risk rather than foreign exchange risk as the relevant question to ask in extending the M-M model (3, pp. 850–851). Adler reached this conclusion by assuming riskless and costless forward exchange transactions and uniform investor expectations with regard to security returns and exchange rate changes. Krainer found the first assumption unacceptable: "Where there is a real risk, it will not do . . . to ignore the cost of insuring against that risk" (45. p. 861). In part, then, the issue between Krainer and Adler is one of choice of models and realism and relevance of assumptions. [Note that recent foreign exchange market research models have explicitly introduced transaction costs and diverse expectations on the part of market participants (25; 21).]

Krainer stressed (45, pp. 859, 861) that Adler's comment did not note that Krainer had mentioned degrees of currency convertibility, as well as changing exchange rates, as a reason for a possible breakdown of international arbitrage or for redefining of risk classes (44, p. 555). In later literature inconvertibility seems to have been relegated to the category of political risk and thus often excluded from financial models. Potential currency inconvertibility is nevertheless a factor likely to influence financial decisions of the firm and the security investor in ways relevant to the financial structure issue; it enters the literature at the financial management textbook level as a factor influencing planning (18, pp. 413–424). Further empirical study of this issue is needed.

Another point mentioned but not pursued by Adler is that exchange risk affects expected returns on equities differently from the way it affects fixed-income bonds (3, p. 850). This point, assumed away by Krainer (44, p. 556; 45, p. 862), relates to the economic effects of exchange rate risk. The distinction among translation, transactions, and economic effects of exchange risk has been receiving increased attention from financial managers since the advent of floating exchange rates and the adoption in the U.S. of Financial Accounting Standard No. 8 (95). The economic effects of exchange rate fluctuations upon the corporation and its security holders are an area for future research.

Clearly, several issues raised or assumed away by Krainer's pioneering extension of the M-M model to the international case remain to be resolved.

Naumann-Etienne has dismissed "Krainer's findings that exchange rate and repatriation risk are sufficient to invalidate the Modigliani-Miller theorem in an otherwise perfect world capital market," because "the world-wide existence of corporate income taxes . . . achieves the same result" (61, p. 860); however, the many reasons for international validity of the M-M theorem may be of practical importance to the financial policy of the multinational firm.

A critique of Krainer by Severn (81) raised questions relevant to Krainer's original empirical testing of his theoretical constructs. Krainer had attempted to test whether U.S.-based multinational firms had altered the magnitude of their foreign debt financing in response to changes in relative borrowing costs. Three tests were conducted:

the results of these tests tended to support Krainer's hypothesis that multinational firms alter the country source of their debt financing in response to what Krainer perceived to be changes in relative borrowing costs. Severn's criticism was primarily centered on the influence of OFDI regulations on financing decisions during the 1965–1970 period; regressing the ratio of international bond issues of U.S. firms to domestic and international bond issues on the rates of European to U.S. interest rates, he obtained a positive, not negative, relationship over the 1968–1972 period. In response, Krainer took the ratio of foreign currency bond issues of U.S. firms (rather than the formerly employed total international bond issues of U.S. firms) to domestic offerings as it related to the ratio of European interest rates to U.S. A corporate bond yields and concluded that cost minimization was an important consideration in the formation of financial policy of U.S.-based multinational firms (45).

It should be noted that if U.S. multinationals were indeed changing the source and currency mix of their financing in response to what Krainer perceived as changes in borrowing costs, the "fact" that they were doing so does not necessarily make such behavior normative. Apropos of this and of Severn's point with regard to the influence on financing decisions of the U.S. OFDI regulations, a study of U.S. firms that issued international and foreign bonds in the first half of 1968, following the imposition of compulsory regulations, indicated that 60 percent of the issuing firms found cost to be higher than U.S. borrowing would have been (96 p. 58). Of those who found it to be lower, one noted it to be so, "providing foreign exchange risk is contained." With the benefit of hindsight we now know that, for those firms whose financing was denominated in the deutschmark or Swiss franc, relative nominal interest rates prevailing at the time of issue were an inadequate measure of ultimate cost of matured debt in dollar terms. A major data problem, then, for empirical studies relative to multinational cost of capital and financing behavior of the multinational firm is the inability to measure directly expectations with regard to foreign exchange rate changes for relevant currencies over the time periods involved in long-term financing, and the rarity of a spectrum of market conditions which might allow one to infer such expectations from interest rate differentials on differently denominated long-term issues (15, pp. 77–106; 92; 63, pp. 169–171).

Other weaknesses of Krainer's data certainly included such items as: (1) the use of an "average European" nominal interest rate (even if weighted, does it have economic content and significance?—it is easy to imagine funds flowing from the U.S. to a particular European country, and to the U.S. from another European country.); (2) the use of a U.S. vs. Europe dichotomy in the debt categories employed [is lira-denominated debt equivalent to deutschmark-denominated debt?—data presented by Rugman reveal a correlation of Italian with West German long-term interest rates of .5903 for quarterly data, 1954–1973 (77, p. 40)]; (3) the use of heterogeneous debt measures, for example, inclusive of trade credit (adjusted for intracompany debt?); (4) the inclusion of convertible debt with straight debt [perhaps necessitated by the fact that, at a certain time under OFDI, convertible debt was "about the only thing that could be sold" (96, p. 60)]. In short, the use of such data leads to conclusions which fail to convince and satisfy.

An inevitable result of data problems is that researchers are likely to shun a topic. Stevens is one who did otherwise and attempted to develop and test a theoretical model, consistent with maximization of the market value of the firm, with the goal of explaining capital flows associated with the financing of foreign asset accumulations by international firms (98). Relying on the M-M thesis, he stated that "it does not matter how the firm divides the financing of its foreign assets between capital flows from the United States and foreign sources" (98, p. 327),[1] but postulated a secondary goal for the firm in the form of minimization of risk of losses due to exchange rate fluctuations. Stevens' goal in developing the model was to examine the impact of voluntary and mandatory controls on foreign direct investment; his efforts received faint praise from Robbins and Stobaugh, who referred to his "imaginative use of the statistics that are available" and expressed their reservations with regard to the relevance of M-M for the international firm: "in the very real world of the multinational firm, the distribution of the subsidiaries' capital structure has a very real influence on the level of after-tax earnings" (66, p. 356).

Hirshleifer has also challenged the relevance of M-M to the international firm and has provided an analysis which underscores the importance of complete markets (34), as opposed to the market imperfections stressed by other writers. Thus, Hirshleifer noted that the M-M equation depends upon an assumption of complete markets, as well as the absence of taxes, bankruptcy, and transactions costs, so that individuals and firms together form a "closed system, with no losses to the outside" (34, p. 264). With incomplete markets, he argues, the arbitrage opportunities necessary to equate the sum of the market value of the securities issues with the present certainty equivalent value of the income stream are not present, leaving open possibilities at the margin for profitable financing decisions (34, pp. 271–272). Inasmuch as capital markets are not highly developed in many countries which host subsidiaries of MNCs, a major proportion of foreign debt financing is in the form of private placements or bank loans (93), and Hirshleifer's position is particularly relevant.

An examination of financing decisions and the cost of capital to be used in appraising the profitability of foreign investments was the goal of Shapiro in a recent paper (85). He began by extending the weighted cost of capital concept to the multinational firm. While noting the M-M position that leverage is irrelevant in the absence of taxes, Shapiro assumed the marginal cost of capital to be constant and thus equal to the cost of new funds, minimized by choosing an appropriate capital structure and, following Adler (1, p. 120), assumed that suppliers of capital to the MNC would associate the risk of default with the MNC's consolidated worldwide debt ratio. In his conclusions, however, he noted that investor perceptions of the riskiness of MNCs are likely to be affected by the location as well as the percentage of foreign source earnings (85, p. 224). Such a conclusion would appear to be consistent with the possibility that perceived risk of default may be affected by the location of sources as well as uses of funds, in addition to being affected by the ratio of total debt to assets.

Given his assumption to the contrary, Shapiro proceeded with the costing of various sources of funds and provided a formula for the incremental weighted cost of capital. This employs: (1) the parent's marginal cost of capital ("provided that the foreign investments undertaken do not change the overall riskiness of the MNC's operations"); (2) the cost of retained earnings abroad, using the cost of parent equity here unless tax and transfer costs are significant [which they may be (78, p. 671), but potential for misspecification of cost of subsidiary retained earnings also exists (62)]; (3) the cost of depreciation-generated funds, equal to the firm's incremental average cost of capital, and (4) the after-tax dollar cost of borrowing locally, equal to "the sum of interest expense and the exchange gain or loss" (85, p. 214). The incremental weighted cost of capital can then be calculated including a term for over- or under-leveraging abroad which is associated with the opportunity cost of additional equity needed to restore the consolidated target debt ratio. If the foreign investment changes the parent risk characteristics, then the parent's cost of equity must be adjusted.

A major problem in making the formula operational is of course the determination of the after-tax dollar cost of borrowing locally, which, as noted, Shapiro defined as being equal to "the sum of interest expense and the exchange gain or loss" (85, p. 214). Because the exchange gain or loss cannot be known in advance, expectations must be introduced into the cost of capital fomulation. These expectations are not necessarily adequately observable in market-determined prices and/or rates. Thus, excluding such considerations as those associated with inflation-adjusted accounting and legally required indexing—for example, of bond principal and interest payments—the introduction of such expectations represents a fundamental change in the nature of the concept of cost of capital generally associated with single-currency financing.

When foreign-currency financing is employed, exchange rate expectations not only enter into the calculation of the cost of capital, but they do so in a much more complex way than in Shapiro's cost of capital formula, because the direction, amount, and timing of foreign exchange changes are all relevant. Shapiro employed the expected rate at the end of one year. This has the major advantage of being objectively observable in the form of forward market quotations for currencies for which uncontrolled forward markets exist. In fact, for a one-year period forward cover could be purchased and cost of capital could include this actual known cost, rather than the expected one as revealed by the forward rate. Unfortunately, forward markets for many currencies are nonexistent, thin, or subject to intervention or control, and the corporation is thrown back upon its own internally generated forecasts or those of an advisory service. Furthermore, a cost of capital formula which employs expectations of future exchange rates only one year forward is inadequate, while one that employs expectations of future exchange rates and their time path from date of debt issue to date of debt maturity is highly dependent upon forecasting and probability analysis. Unless international financial markets are perfectly integrated, and the expectations theory of the term structure, international interest rate parity, and purchasing power parity, or the international Fisher effect prevail, the extension to the multinational firm of the concept of weighted average cost of capital entails this difficulty of forecasting and quantifying expected changes in the exchange rate over the maturity of long-term debt.

On the other hand, to the extent that the forward premium and, thus, the short-term interest rate differential provide unbiased estimates of the expected rate of change of the exchange rate, the currency of denomination of short-term debt is a matter of indifference to borrowers. To the extent that the international Fisher effect holds, expected changes in exchange rates are reflected in international interest rate differentials, and changes in exchange rates offset differential inflation rates, thereby tending to keep relative purchasing power costs of debt denominated in different currencies constant. Then, the currency of denomination per se is a matter of indifference, and such factors as availability and tax effects become predominant in the debt financing decision; that is, the firm's cost of local-currency borrowing will be equivalent in an expected value sense to the cost of dollar borrowing, provided that the tax system does not discriminate in its treatment of interest costs on the basis of currency of denomination; such as, by virtue of its treatment of foreign exchange gain or loss. [Shapiro explicitly noted the importance of the latter factor (85, p. 214)].

The work of a number of researchers is relevant to the question of foreign exchange rate behavior and forecasting. First, about the international Fisher effect, Dufey and Giddy not that "by comparing the term structure of interest rates in two Eurocurrency markets, one may readily derive the term structure of exchange-rate expectations" (15, p. 79). However, a number of studies show poor correlations between exchange rate changes and relative interest rates in the short run (26; 48). Giddy found that the relationship held better over a three-year period than over three-month periods (26, p. 28). He also observed that there were persistent small deviations from the international Fisher effect in long as well as short periods but noted that deviations might stem from errors in expectations rather than from interest rates incorrectly reflecting the expectations (26, p. 30).

In a test of forecasting models, Levich (48) found that Fisher external outperformed other forecasting models, judging "performance" on the basis of the mean squared error of forecasts for one-month, three-month, and six-month forecasting horizons for nine currencies in the period 1967–1975. For 27 country-horizon episodes, the Fisher external model had the lowest mean squared error on 13 episodes, followed closely by a lagged-spot model which was lowest on 12 episodes (48, pp. 134–137). Forecast errors tended to be smaller during pegged rate periods, except when there was a discrete change in the rate; forecast errors became larger and more volatile during the manager-float period, with some evidence that they are becoming smaller as the managed float continues (48, pp. 146–147). As in Levich's study, most empirical tests of foreign exchange rate forecasting models have stressed relatively short forecasting horizons.

Solnik and Grall have suggested that market-implied expectations of exchange rate fluctuations are revealed by the currency structure of yield differentials in the new-issue Eurobound market (92, p. 225). From end-of-quarter variables from October 1967 to March 1973, the data implied on average annual rate of devaluation of .7 percent for the dollar vis-à-vis the Deutschmark (92, pp. 219, 227); in the period March 1973 through December 1978, the actual average annual rate of devaluation was in excess of 5.5 percent (38). Thus, the actual rate of change far exceeded the expected rate of change implied by Eurobond yield differentials.

Similarly, Quinn has cited the segmented secondary-market price behavior of Deutschmark- and dollar-denominated Eurobond issues as indicators of expectations of devaluation, although emphasizing a relatively short time horizon (63, pp. 169–172); expected dollar devaluation was imminent; large differentials in yield to maturity in dollar versus Deutschmark bonds appeared: "In terms of the immediate exchange rate changes that transpired the market overreacted" (63, p. 171). The practical import of this particular market overreaction for cost of capital expectations was probably small, however, because, given the market conditions studied, new-issue activity by foreign borrowers tended to dry up.

Note that these researchers focused upon the Euromarkets, not the domestic markets, as being likely to reflect, in interest differentials on like maturities, expected foreign exchange rate changes. The studies indicate that neither new-issue nor secondary-market Eurobond yield and price behavior would have proved very useful as a means of correctly quantifying future exchange rates. The studies were, how-ever, quite limited in scope. Other studies have noted that a risk factor may be embodied in the term structure of exchange rate expectations (15, p. 105). This is an area for future research.

Miller and Whitman, working with macroeconomic models concerned with mon-etary and fiscal policy and the balance of payments, reported that no statistically significant proxy for expected spot exchange rates had been found (58, p. 276). Financial managers report a short-term emphasis in foreign exchange risk manage-ment because "it is too difficult to predict beyond one year" (95). Perhaps even a year is too long: "advisors who were offering year-long forecasts were doing so because clients were asking for it, rather than because such forecasts were worth giving" (7, p. 38).

Tests of foreign exchange forecasting models, even for short periods, show conflicting results. The managed-float "system" of foreign exchange has displayed increased volatility of exchange rates and concomitant decrease in the forecasting accuracy of the forward rate (49, pp. 244–245, 262–271). Studies by Levich of the period 1967–1978 indicated that the model stating that the forward rate is an unbiased predictor of future exchange rate change could not be rejected, but that the prediction power of the relationship, measured by R^2, was very low (49, p. 271). Other research by Levich on foreign exchange forecasting models, noted earlier, had indicated that the international Fisher effect regularly outperformed the forward rate, but the difference was "generally small enough to be explained by transaction costs or sampling errors" (48, p. 137).

Giddy and Dufey, testing models for predicting future spot rates, found that the forward rate was consistently the poorest predictor (27); but Aliber concluded that the forward rate was a somewhat better predictor of the subsequent spot rate over the long run than either relative interest rates or purchasing power parity (42, p. 28); and Kohlhagen concluded that "in the long run, even with floating and volatile markets, the forward rate has in general been an unbiased predictor of the future spot rate" (42, p. 29).

With regard to purchasing power parity, characterized as "the ideological ante-cedent of the current monetary approach" (35, p. 98), there is an extensive body of literature (42). This literature indicates that purchasing power parity seems to hold in the long run (42, pp. 3, 43), and there is some evidence that it held quite well during the pegged rate period, 1959–1970 (42, p. 3). However, there have been short-run deviations from purchasing power parity in both fixed and floating rate periods (42, pp. 3–4, 43), and a number of recent research studies indicate that it has not prevailed during the period of dirty floating exchange rates (42, p. 3).

One empirical study covering six countries during the period 1920–1924 and Canada during 1953–1957 indicates that freely floating foreign exchange markets respond almost if not immediately to changes in relative inflation rates, but it also notes that central bank intervention appears to reduce the impact of differential rates of inflation and to introduce inefficiencies into the foreign exchange markets (70). Central bank foreign exchange market intervention is then a possible channel of influence upon equity and debt costs of the multinational firm.[2]

In summary, tests of foreign exchange forecasting models, even for short periods, show conflicting results, and the research suggests that a satisfactory proxy for long-term exchange rate expectations remains to be discovered. Given such conditions, the borrowing source decision appears to be an important one for the multinational firm, and the use of external local-currency long-term debt financing by foreign subsidiares seemingly leads to possibilities for foreign exchange gain/loss in real terms for the multinational firm and to possible wealth transfers between bondholders and parent-company stockholders.

Despite the lack of a satisfactory proxy for long-term exchange rate expectations, which constitutes a major problem in making Shapiro's formula operational, he claimed that a simplified version of the formula—ignoring the possibility that the optimal D/E ratio may itself be dependent upon the relative costs of debt and equity—makes it possible to settle "one controversy in the literature," that between Zenoff and Zwick, who argued for the use of the company-wide marginal cost-of-capital as the discount factor to be used in multinational capital budgeting (102, pp. 186–190), and Stonehill and Stitzel, who argued for the use of the cost-of-capital appropriate to local firms operating in the same industry (100). Shapiro characterized both as incorrect, because they "ignore the factor of multinationality" (85, p. 216). Zenoff and Zwick defined the company-wide cost-of-capital as

> a normative cost measure which reflects what overall financing costs would be if the firm obtained its debt and equity capital in the least expensive markets in ideal proportions. It is . . . used as the discount rate for capital budgeting decisions unless the proposed project under consideration is expected to change the business risk complexion of the firm as a whole, (102, pp. 188–189).

Zenoff and Zwick went on to consider the possibility that financing for particular foreign affiliates might be more expensive than the company-wide cost-of-capital; they would consider such cost premia as part of project outflows and would base debt policy on a consideration of cash flow characteristics in each local environment. Why? Because "the financial markets are segmented, precluding the selection of an optimal mix for the firm as a whole" (102, p. 189). Thus, they took a partially negative view of the effects of market segmentation, in contrast to the possible oligopsonistic advantages posited by Shapiro.

The Stonehill and Stitzel recommendation was based upon consideration of environmental factors, including concern over misallocation of resources in the host country, not upon a shareholder wealth maximization goal (100, pp. 92–95). Eiteman and Stonehill, referring to the Stonehill and Stitzel recommendation, argued that optimal global financial structure would be different for all multinational firms because of their geographical diversity and that optimal structure from a cost-of-capital point of view can best be decided upon when comparisons can be made among firms in the same country, industry, and risk class (18, p. 225).

Turning to the question of appropriate subsidiary financial structure, Shapiro concluded that this should vary, so as to take advantage of opportunities to minimize the cost of capital (85, p. 216); this assumed explicitly that capital markets are at least partially segmented and that the subsidiary's capital structure is relevant only insofar as it affects the consolidated worldwide debt ratio (85, pp. 217–218). Shapiro then considered the related issues of company guarantees and nonconsolidation and decided that they are largely false issues (85, pp. 218–219, 224). Shapiro also briefly mentioned taxes and regulatory factors, riskiness of foreign operations, political risk, inflation and exchange risk, diversification, investor perceptions, and joint ventures, concluding that a great deal of empirical testing remains to be done (85, p. 226). The multiplicity of issues raised is in itself evidence of the complexities and data problems involved, and of some directions which further research might take in an effort to provide more definitive answers as a guide to policy and action.

International Capital Asset Pricing Models

The extension of the capital asset pricing model to the international case has been advanced by several researchers; here, we shall be concerned primarily with the implications of this work for multinational financing decisions and cost of capital, including both equity and debt capital, but with emphasis upon cost of equity.

Imperfections in international financial markets and their theoretical implications for risk permia and the cost of capital to firms were explored by Cohn and Pringle (11). Their analysis emphasized that to the extent that economic activity in different economies is less than perfectly correlated, a lessening of restrictions on international portfolio diversification would affect risk-return relationships and security prices in two ways. The broadening of the market portfolio to include more (internationally traded) securities would reduce the nondiversifiable risk of each security and, given logarithmic or exponential utility functions, the slope of the capital market line—that is, the marginal rate of substitution of risk for return—would decline (11, pp. 60–62). These two effects would act to reduce the risk-premium component of the cost of capital for firms (11, p. 63) and thereby to improve the efficiency of real capital allocation.

Solnik (88: 89) tested empirically an international market structure consistent with the International Asset Pricing Model and found that "national factors are quite important . . . violating the simple international market structure postulated in the single index market model" (88, p. 552). After diversifying away the domestic factors in international portfolios, it was possible to show a strong relation between realized returns and international systematic risk. Solnik concluded that the true meaning of risk should be the international risk of an investment, not its national "beta," and that "the international capital market seems to be sufficiently integrated and efficient to induce an international pricing of risk for common stocks" (88, pp. 552–553).

Citing statistical problems in Solnik's procedures, Stehle provided an alternative approach, testing both a segmented markets hypothesis and an integrated markets hypothesis and concluding that neither could be rejected in a favor of the other but finding some empirical support for the international model (97).

The question of the extent or degree of international market integration is an important one and other researchers have also addressed it (37; 57). Noting that, if capital markets are perfect, the multinational firm does nothing for investors that they could not do for themselves, but that, if markets are not internationally integrated and the domestic market is efficient, multinational firms are performing a valuable function for investors which should be reflected in the pricing of equities of multinational firms, Hughes, Logue, and Sweeney studied 46 multinational and 50 domestic firms, characterized by them as roughly comparable in size and diversity of product lines,[3] for the period January 1970 through December 1973. They found that the "average returns for (the) multinational firms were higher than the average returns on (the) domestic firms," although "their betas were considerably lower," suggesting "some economies achieved by international diversification. . . . The distribution of measures of unsystematic risk (were) significantly lower for multinational firms than for domestic firms," supporting "the view that investors perceive multinational firms as providing substantial diversification benefits" (37, p. 633). When the domestic market index was used, the performance of multinational firms was significantly superior to that of domestic firms, but when the world index was used the difference in performance was not statistically significant; the authors interpreted this as lending "some support albeit marginal to the view that assets are priced internationally rather than domestically and that international financial markets are indeed integrated" (37, p. 633). Further, they concluded that multinational firms assist in this process and that "investors correctly perceive the diversification benefits of shares of multinational firms and that such firms do something for investors" (37, p. 636).

These conclusions are consistent with those of Agmon and Lessard whose empirical results supported their hypothesis that "U.S. investors recognize the international composition of the activities of U.S.-based corporations" when geographical diversification of these activities is represented by percentage of foreign sales (6, p. 1055). Coupling this conclusion with the observation that capital flows forming part of direct investment by the multinational corporation may have lower cost or barriers than portfolio flows of individual investors, Agmon and Lessard suggested that the diversification motive, while difficult to isolate empiricially, should be given more consideration than has been the case, because it appears to be relevant at the corporate as well as the investor level (6, pp. 1049, 1055).

Rugman has also emphasized diversification through foreign direct investment rather than portfolio investment. Because statistical tests show that international goods and factor markets are less correlated than international financial markets, Rugman suggested that the individual risk averter should purchase shares of the multinational firm as an indirect route to the risk reduction effects of international diversification (77, p. 33).

Lee and Sachdeva have provided a theoretical proof of this for home country investors under conditions of perfect competition and assumptions of equal risk-free rates in the home and host country, a nonstochastic foreign exchange rate, and a constant market price of risk (46, pp. 482–484, 490–491).

In a related empirical study, however, Jacquillat and Solnik found that investing in U.S. multinational firms could not be regarded as a good direct substitute for international portfolio diversification; foreign influence on stock prices was "unexpectedly limited" compared to the extent of the firm's foreign investment (39).

Hughes, Logue, and Sweeney suggested that a fruitful area for further research would be why the appearance and actuality of international market integration diverge. They posited that the higher (risk-adjusted) returns available in countries other than the U.S. may be illusory because they may merely compensate for higher transaction costs. If netting these out were to result in similar risk/return tradeoffs among countries, markets would be shown to be highly integrated internationally (37, p. 636).

Hughes, Logue, and Sweeney repeatedly suggested that one source of advantage for the multinational firm may be higher debt capacity, reflected in stock-market-assigned measures of risk (37, pp. 628, 630) and owed to the diversifications of the MNC's activities among semi-independent economies (37, pp. 631, 633).[4]

Rugman has tested risk reduction by international diversification, using earnings variance as a proxy for risk, and foreign sales/total sales as a measure of international diversification, with earnings defined as net income/net worth. His empirical results showed that the foreign operations variable (foreign sales/total sales) was statistically significant and inversely related to variance of profits (77, pp. 11–13, 16–17). Thus, Rugman's results would tend to support the suggestion of Hughes, Logue, and Sweeney with regard to investor perceptions of higher debt capacity for multinational firms. However, Rugman was specifically interested in examining the risk reduction attendant upon diversification via foreign direct investment and regarded the CAPM (used by Hughes, Logue, and Sweeney) as inappropriate for such tests because of the CAPM's perfect-markets assumptions that are inconsistent with direct investment motivated at the level of the firm by market imperfections (76; 77, p. 12).

Mehra, examining the influence of exchange risk on both the investment and financing decisions of multinational firms within the CAPM framework (and with its perfect markets assumptions) concluded that alterations of the firm's capital structure do not change its value, even in the presence of exchange risk (57, p. 240). Mehra employed a two-country model and assumed nonsegmented capital markets with individuals free to invest in the stock and bond markets of both countries. He showed that in this case a firm's beta consists of two terms, involving covariance of the security with the world market portfolio and with a position in foreign exchange (57, pp. 227, 235). For country A firms, risk was shown to be understated (overstated) by the Sharpe-Lintner-Mossin CAPM depending, for example, upon whether their returns were likely to increase (decrease) due to devaluation (revaluation) by country A and whether country A was a surplus (deficit) country in terms of its net investment position (57, pp. 235–237).

There are capital budgeting implications here; that is, "if the effects of exchange risk are not considered explicitly in capital budgeting decisions, a systematic bias will develop" (57, p. 239). The effect upon cost of capital of project covariance with the exchange rate will depend upon the net investment position of the country; in a country with a surplus investment position, a project whose returns decrease due to a devaluation of that country's currency will have a lower cost of capital, ceteris paribus; in a deficit country the project favored by a devaluation will have a lower cost of capital. Acceptance criteria for a project were shown to be the same for both countries' firms (57, pp. 238–239).

It should be emphasized, however, that all of these "normative implications" of Mehra's model for the "value-maximizing firm" ultimately depend upon the model's assumptions of nonsegmented markets in which individuals are free to borrow and invest.

A main issue, then, is whether the degree of market segmentation is sufficient to make segmented markets models the relevant ones for decision-makers, or whether the degree of market integration is sufficient to make integrated markets models the relevant ones. In the absence of governmental controls, growing individual investor sophistication and evolving financial institutions would be expected to contribute to greater market integration. How much is "enough" seems to underlie much of the disagreement in the literature. The multinational firm itself may tend to reduce the practical managerial importance of this issue, achieving through its use of intra-company funds transfers and transfer pricing many of the effects of market integration (67, pp. 161–171; 61, pp. 863–864).

A propos of the multinational firm's financing decisions, Jucker and deFaro have considered the problem of selecting a foreign borrowing source within a portfolio diversification framework, assuming a one-year time period, no use of forward markets, spot exchange always available when needed, and a pure financing problem, without consideration of other changes that a firm may face as a result of currency devaluations. Jucker and deFaro concluded that: "The principal difference between the (borrowing) source selection problem and the portfolio selection problem is the source of uncertainty" (40, p. 406); namely, currency fluctuations. They therefore presented a model to aid in estimating characteristics of the random variables that express his uncertainty, making it possible to assess the necessary probability distributions. The exposition was developed assuming conditions prevailing under the Smithsonian Agreement, but the basic model is applicable to a managed floating rate system. The paper is useful by virtue of its emphasis upon the applicability of portfolio selection techniques to the borrowing source problem.

In an earlier related paper deFaro and Jucker dealt with both inflation and exchange risk, concluded that only exchange risk matters, and presented a decision criterion calling for comparison of interest differentials and expected foreign exchange rate changes over the duration of the loan (14, pp. 97–104), a conceptually obvious criterion with the previously noted operational problems associated with quantifying the direction, magnitude, and timing of expected foreign exchange rate changes.

Folks, noting (23, p. 246) that he was building upon work of Jucker and deFaro (40), developed an approach applicable to the selection of an optimal currency source for a short-term loan when it is possible for the borrowing unit to enter the forward exchange market for a term equivalent to the maturity of the loan. His approach emphasizes not only that the relevant cost of funds is the cost of covered borrowing in each currency but also emphasizes the tight relationship between the money market and the foreign exchange market, by showing that the optimal sourcing problem may be transmuted into an optimal forward exchange purchase problem (23, p. 252). Folks himself notes that this probably has limited practical application because of the "currency speculation" label that would likely be attached to the prescribed actions (23, pp. 252–253), but the point undoubtedly had educational shock value for financial policy. It also serves to emphasize again the exchange risk aspects of the long-term foreign borrowing source problem.

Current State of Knowledge: Conflicts, Data Problems, Areas for Future Research ___

The review of recent literature which extends to the multinational case financial theory relevant to capital structure and cost-of-capital for the domestic firm reveals the substantially greater complexity of the international case and various areas of conflict in the literature. Data problems contribute to the continuation of the conflict, because definitive empirical testing of certain theoretical constructs is, at best, difficult.

There has been, for example, substantial testing of equity pricing and risk/return relationships in international extensions of the capital asset pricing model, but there is still disagreement on the basic ICAPM to be employed; controversy surrounds "the" world market model, and there is no commonly accepted definition of the world market factor. There is a basic questioning of the applicability of the CAPM, with its assumption of perfect markets and market participants able to borrow or lend at the pure rate, to the question of international diversification of risk, particularly to the case of diversification effects of foreign direct investment which rest upon market imperfections (89; 80; 77). There is also detailed questioning of statistical methodology and judgment solutions to problems involved (76; 77, p. 44; 97).

Conflict over Modigliani-Miller varies from that over the best reason for declaring it invalid at the international level [for example, exchange risk, repatriation risk, taxes and tax differentials (44; 45; 61)], to a thesis extending it to the borrowing source decision (98), implicitly disputed by researchers concerned with the substance of that decision (83; 85; 23; 40).

There is basic disagreement as to how foreign exchange risk should be treated: is it a real factor stemming from (nationally differentiated) consumption preferences, or a monetary factor? (89; 29; 26) Related to this issue is the fact that empirical evidence with regard to the international Fisher effect, purchasing power parity, and forward rate bias and predictive power is mixed (15; 42; 70; 26; 27; 48; 49).

Conflict over the degree and relevance of international market segmentation versus market integration is unresolved (98; 66; 67; 8; 11; 87–91; 55; 37; 46; 47). The main problem is the lack or inadequacy of data, particularly with regard to the testing of M-M models and related financing policies and decisions. The problem is well illustrated by the nature and criticism of the data employed by Krainer and Stevens (44; 45; 98; 3; 81; 66). The available data are inadequate at both the macro and micro levels. Flow of funds and international financial statistics simply do not provide desired detail by country, currency of denomination, or type of financial instrument; data that do exist are often not homogeneous (for example, with reference to default risk characteristics, marketability, tax status), and/or are flawed proxies for desired data (such as, discount and bank rates in lieu of bond market rates) (15, pp. 90, 96; 77, pp. 38, 41).

At the level of the firm, disclosure requirements are not such that information on amount, denomination, and maturity of foreign currency debt is available from corporate financial statements. Indeed, Robbins and Stobough have stated that "the parent firm, itself, may not be fully aware of the total amount of over-all system borrowing" (66, p. 355). Data problems, then, include not only those facing the researcher, but those facing the security market participant whose perception of risk and response to perceived risk/return relationships is fundamental to financial market theory.

The measurement of multinationality itself presents problems. In the absence of data on foreign investment by individual firms, the most frequently used measure is that of foreign sales/total sales; this measure includes both foreign production and home-produced exports and thus mixes international trade (including final sales of export goods as well as intracompany transactions) with international investment.

Data problems make us aware of the fact that empirical research results must be greeted with caution. Can the CAPM and M-M theorems be applied realistically and relevantly to multinational enterprise? The financial theory in question has been developed by theorists in industrialized countries with highly developed financial infrastructures, and empirical testing has been limited largely to such countries. The applicability of such work to the multinational enterprise operating in less developed countries is questionable, because the requisite characteristics of capital, money, and foreign exchange markets may not obtain. Thus, the case of the multinational firm operating in less developed countries is one open to both theoretical development and empirical research.

The financial models reviewed here have thus far largely explicitly or implicitly excluded the joint venture case. Both developed and developing countries may seek to control foreign direct investment by requiring that it be done in the form of a joint venture with a local partner, perhaps a controlling partner; this raises related questions about dividend policy and the interaction between real and financial investment decisions. The interrelationship between the investment decision and the financing decision, still much disputed in the literature with regard to the domestic firm (56; 10; 65), is more complex at the multinational level. Thus, both the joint venture case and the interrelationship between the investment decision and the financing decision in the general multinational case are top candidates for future research.

Another important area for future research is the question of the degree to which the multinational corporation itself serves as an instrument for market integration and greater market efficiency; for example, through intracompany transactions. Further foreign exchange market research is needed to guide multinational corporations' decisions with regard to capital structure, borrowing sources, denominating currencies, and hedging policy. Specific research might be directed to central bank foreign exchange market intervention as a potential channel of influence upon equity and debt costs of the multinational firm. This is part of the broader question of the economic effects of exchange rate fluctuations upon the multinational enterprise and its security holders.

Current State of Knowledge: Financial Policy Prescribed for the Firm _____

What policy is prescribed for the firm by the international extensions of theoretical financial models? The basic question to be answered concerns the effect of multinationality upon cost of capital. Several studies of equity pricing employing an international extension of the capital asset pricing model indicate that the common stock of the multinational firm is priced so as to reflect international diversification of risk. The domestic firm if it goes multinational can do so without adverse effect upon its cost of equity; indeed, it may expect a reduction in its cost of equity, ceteris paribus. Although both theoretical and empirical difficulties exist, and none of the studies is without critics, none presents evidence indicating that cost of equity capital is higher for the multinational than for the purely domestic firm, ceteris parabus.[5]

The international extensions of the Modigliani-Miller theorem tend to emphasize reasons for its inapplicability to the multinational firm and lend support to analyses employing the traditional approach that there is an optimal debt/equity ratio or range thereof for the multinational firm. The subject is more complex for the multinational firm than for the domestic firm because of the influence of such factors as international diversification of risk, foreign exchange risk, inconvertibility risk, subsidiary capital structures, tax differentials, and multiple market environments. Existing research does not provide a definitive answer to the question of optimum capital structure for the multinational firm, nor to how it is determined.

Whereas financial markets are more highly internationally integrated than are product and factor markets (77, pp. 33 42), various researchers (34; 66, pp. 356; 102, p. 189) characterize them as incomplete and imperfect, and several researchers believe them to be sufficiently so as to offer possibilities for reduction of cost of debt capital by appropriate choice of borrowing source and currency (14; 40; 66, p. 356; 34, pp. 271–272). Whether this is approached in a portfolio context (40) or in a weighted cost of capital context (85), the operational problem involved in quantifying expected changes in exchange rates is a major one.

Although quantification of expected foreign exchange risk is important for the determination of ex ante cost of debt, it may be argued that the currency in which debt is denominated is irrelevant if, for example, the international Fisher effect holds. Given imperfect foreign exchange markets, the parent is faced with both translation exposure on long-term debt and economic exposure of interest payments and ultimate repayment of principal if local-currency denominated debt is used. Evidence on this question of foreign exchange risk is mixed.

One policy alternative would be that of using short-term local-currency borrowing to hedge current assets, while financing foreign fixed assets with parent equity and/or intracompany debt. This would avoid translation exposure for the parent under FAS No. 8, while the economic exposure accompanying the equity in fixed assets could be regarded as hedged by an assumed long-run tendency toward purchasing power parity, the receptivity of multinational firms to this policy prescription might well depend upon the ratio of fixed assets to total assets in their industry and their evaluation of their degree of exposure to political risk. An alternative policy would be the use of local-currency-denominated long-term debt within a portfolio diversification approach to foreign exchange risk (18, p. 359; 93). This alternative has the advantage of retaining for the firm the greater capital availability associated with use of local borrowing sources. However, the advisability of use of local-currency-denominated long-term debt in the financial structure of the multinational firm remains a controversial question.

References

1. Adler, Michael. "The Cost of Capital and Valuation of a Two-Country Firm." *Journal of Finance,* March 1974, pp. 119–132.
2. _____. "The Cost of Capital and Valuation of a Two-Country Firm: Reply." *Journal of Finance,* September 1977, pp. 1354–1357.
3. _____. "The Valuation of Financing of the Multi-National Firm: Comment." *Kyklos,* Vol. 26, no. 4 (1973), pp. 849–851.
4. _____, and Bernard Dumas. "Optimal International Acquisitions." *Journal of Finance,* March 1975, pp. 1–19.
5. Agmon, Tamir. "The Relations among Equity Markets: A Study of Share Price Co-Movements in the U.S., U.K., Germany and Japan." *Journal of Finance,* September 1972, pp. 839–855.
6. _____, and Donald R. Lessard. "Investor Recognition of Corporate International Diversification." *Journal of Finance,* September 1977, pp. 1049–1055.
7. "A Guide to the Banks and Firms in the Foreign Exchange Advisory Business." *Euromoney,* August 1978, pp. 25–41.
8. Black, F. "International Capital Market Equilibrium with Investment Barriers." *Journal of Financial Economics,* Vol. 1 (1971), pp. 337–352.
9. Chen, Andrew H. "Recent Developments in the Cost of Debt Capital." *Journal of Finance,* June 1978, pp. 863–877.
10. Ciccolo, John, and Gary Fromm. " 'Q' and the Theory of Investment." *Journal of Finance,* May 1979, pp. 535–547.
11. Cohn, Richard A., and John J. Pringle. "Imperfections in International Financial Markets: Implications for Risk Premia and the Cost of Capital to Firms." *Journal of Finance,* March 1973, pp. 59–66.
12. Cooley, Philip L., Rodney L. Roenfeldt, and It-Keong, Chew. "Capital Budgeting Procedures Under Inflation." *Financial Management,* Winter, 1975, pp. 18–35.
13. Dawson, Steven M. "Eurobond Currency Selection: Hindsight." *Financial Executive,* November 1973, pp. 72–73.
14. deFaro, Clovis, and J. V. Jucker. "The Impact of Inflation and Devaluation on the Selection of an International Borrowing Source." *Journal of International Business Studies,* Fall 1973, pp. 97–104.
15. Dufey, Gunter, and Ian H. Giddy. *The International Money Market.* Englewood Cliffs, N.J.: Prentice-Hall, 1978.
16. Dukes, Roland E. *An Empirical Investigation of the Effects of Statement of Accounting Standards No. 8 on Security Return Behavior.* Stamford, Conn.: Financial Accounting Standards Board, 1978.

17. Dumas, Bernard "The Theory of the Trading Firm Revisited." *Journal of Finance,* June 1978, pp. 1019–1030.
18. Eiteman, David K., and Arthur I. Stonehill. *Multinational Business Finance,* 2nd ed. Reading, Mass.: Addison-Wesley, 1979.
19. Elliott, J. Walter. "The Cost of Capital and U.S. Capital Investment: A Test of Alternative Concepts." *Journal of Finance,* September 1980, pp. 981–999.
20. Fama, Eugene F. "The Effects of a Firm's Investment and Financing Decisions on the Welfare of Its Security Holders." *American Economic Review,* June 1978, pp. 27–284.
21. Figlewski, Stephen. "Market 'Efficiency' in a Market with Heterogeneous Information." *Journal of Political Economy,* August 1978, pp. 581–597.
22. Findlay, M. Chapman, ILL; Alan W. Frankle, et al. "Capital Budgeting Procedures under Inflation: Cooley, Roenfeldt and Chew vs. Findlay and Frankle." *Financial Management,* Autumn 1976, pp. 83–90.
23. Folks, William R., Jr. "Optimal Foreign Borrowing Strategies with Operations in Forward Exchange Markets." *Journal of Financial and Quantitative Analysis,* June 1978, pp. 245–254.
24. Fremgen, James M. "Capital Budgeting Practices: A Survey." *Management Accounting,* May 1973, pp. 19–25.
25. Frenkel, Jacob A., and Richard M. Levich. "Transactions Costs and Interest Arbitrage: Tranquil versus Turbulent Periods." *Journal of Political Economy,* November/December 1977, pp. 1209–1226.
26. Giddy, Ian H. "Exchange Risk: Whose View." *Financial Management,* Summer 1977, pp. 23–33.
27. _____, and Gunter Dufey. "The Random Behavior of Flexible Exchange Rates: Implications for Forecasting." *Journal of International Business Studies,* Spring 1975, pp. 1–32.
28. Goldberg, Michael A., and Wayne Y. Lee. "The Cost of Capital and Valuation of a Two-Country Firm: Comment." *Journal of Finance,* September 1977, pp. 1348–1353.
29. Grauer, F. L. A., R. H. Litzenberger, and R. H. Stehle. "Sharing Rules and Equilibrium in an International Capital Market under Uncertainty." *Journal of Financial Economics,* Vol. 3 (1976), pp. 233–256.
30. Grubel, H. G. "Internationally Diversified Portfolios: Welfare Gains and Capital Flows." *American Economic Review,* December 1968, pp. 1299–1314.
31. _____., and K. Fadner. "The Interdependence of International Equity Markets." *Journal of Finance,* March 1971, pp. 89–94.
32. Hamada, Robert S. "Portfolio Analysis, Market Equilibrium, and Corporation Finance." *Journal of Finance,* March 1969, pp. 13–31.
33. Hartman, David G. "Foreign Investment and Finance with Risk." *Quarterly Journal of Economics,* May 1979, pp. 213–232.
34. Hirshleifer, J. *Investment, Interest and Capital,* Englewood Cliffs, N.J.: Prentice-Hall, 1970.
35. Hodrick, Robert J. "An Empirical Analysis of the Monetary Approach to the Determination of the Exchange Rate." In *The Economics of Exchange Rates,* ed. Jacob A. Frenkel and Harry G. Johnson, Reading, Mass.: Addison-Wesley, pp. 97–116.

36. Hufbauer, G. C. "The Multinational Corporation and Direct Investment." In *International Trade and Finance,* ed. Peter B. Kenen. Cambridge: Cambridge University Press, 1975, pp. 253–319.

37. Hughes, John S., Dennis E. Logue, and Richard James Sweeney. "Corporate International Diversification and Market Assigned Measures of Risk and Diversification." *Journal of Financial and Quantitative Analysis,* November 1975, pp. 627–637.

38. *International Letter.* Federal Reserve Bank of Chicago.

39. Jacquillat, Bertrand, and Bruno Solnik. "Multinationals Are Poor Tools for Diversification." *Journal of Portfolio Management,* Winter 1978, pp. 8–12.

40. Jucker, James V., and Clovis deFaro. "The Selection of International Borrowing Sources." *Journal of Financial and Quantitative Analysis,* September 1975, pp. 381–407.

41. Kohers, Theodor. "The Effect of Multinational Operations on the Cost of Equity Capital of U.S. Corporations: An Empirical Study." *Management International Review,* nos. 2–3 (1975), pp. 121–124.

42. Kohlhagen, Steven W. *The Behavior of Foreign Exchange Markets: A Critical Survey of the Empirical Literature.* Monograph 1978–3, New York University Graduate School of Business Administration, Salomon Brothers Center for the Study of Financial Institutions.

43. Kornbluth, J. S. H., and Joseph D. Vinso. "Financial Planning for the Multinational Corporation: A Fractional Multiobjective Approach." Working Paper No. 5, Graduate School of Business Administration, University of Southern California, October 1979.

44. Krainer, Robert E. "The Valuation and Financing of the Multi-National Firm." *Kyklos,* Vol. 25 (1972), pp. 553–573.

45. ———. "The Valuation and Financing of the Multi-National Firm: Reply." *Kyklos.* Vol. 26 (1973), pp. 857–865.

46. Lee, Wayne Y., and Kanwal S. Sachdeva. "The Role of the Multi-National Firm in the Integration of Segmented Capital Markets." *Journal of Finance,* May 1977, pp. 479–492.

47. Lessard, Donald R. "World, Country, and Industry Relationships in Equity Returns: Implications for Risk Reduction through International Diversification." *Financial Analysts' Journal,* January–February 1976, pp. 2–8.

48. Levich, Richard M. "Tests of Forecasting Models and Market Efficiency in the International Money Market." In *The Economics of Exchange Rates,* edited by Jacob A. Frenkel and Harry G. Johnson. Reading, Mass.: Addison-Wesley, 1978, pp. 129–158.

49. ———. "The Efficiency of Markets for Foreign Exchange: A Review and Extension." In *International Financial Management,* ed. Donald R. Lessard. Boston and New York: Warren, Gorham and Lamont, 1979, pp. 243–276.

50. Levy, H., and M. Sarnat. "International Diversification of Investment Portfolios." *American Economic Review,* September 1970, pp. 668–692.

51. Lewellen, Wilbur G. "A Conceptual Reappraisal of Cost of Capital." *Financial Management,* Winter 1974, pp. 63–70.

52. Lintner, John. "Security Prices, Risk, and Maximal Gains from Diversification." *Journal of Finance,* December 1965, pp. 587–615.

53. _____. "The Valuation of Risk Assets and the Selection of Risky Investments in Stock Portfolios and Capital Budgets." *Review of Economics and Statistics,* February 1965, pp. 13–37.

54. Logue, Dennis E., and Larry J. Merville. "Financial Policy and Market Expectations." *Financial M7anagement,* Summer 1972, pp. 37–44.

55. Logue, Dennis E., Michael A. Salant, and Richard James Sweeney. "International Integration of Financial Markets: Survey, Synthesis, and Results." In *Eurocurrencies and the International Monetary System,* ed. Carl H. Stem, John H. Makin, and Dennis E. Logue. Washington, D.C.: American Enterprise Institute for Public Policy Research, 1976, pp. 91–137.

56. McCabe, George M. "The Empirical Relationship Between Investment and Financing: A New Look." *Journal of Financial and Quantitative Analysis,* March 1979, pp. 119–135.

57. Mehra, Rajnish. "On the Financing and Investment Decisions of Multinational Firms in the Presence of Exchange Risk." *Journal of Financial and Quantitative Analysis,* June 1978, pp. 227–244.

58. Miller, Norman C., and Marina V. N. Whitman. "The Outflow of Short-Term Funds from the United States: Adjustments of Stocks and Flows." In *International Mobility and Movement of Capital,* ed. Fritz Machlup, Walter Salant, and Lorie Tarshis. New York and London: Columbia University Press for National Bureau of Economic Research, 1972, pp. 253–286.

59. Modigliani, Franco, and Merton H. Miller. "The Cost of Capital, Corporation Finance, and the Theory of Investment." *American Economic Review,* June 1958, pp. 261–297.

60. Myers, Stewart C. "Interactions of Corporate Financing and Investment Decisions: Implications for Capital Budgeting." *Journal of Finance,* March 1974, pp. 1–25.

61. Naumann-Etienne, Ruediger. "A Framework for Financial Decisions in Multi-National Corporations: A Summary of Recent Research." *Journal of Financial and Quantitative Analysis,* November 1974, pp. 859–874.

62. Ness, Walter L. "A Linear Programming Approach to Financing the Multinational Corporation." *Financial Management,* Winter 1972, pp. 88–100.

63. Quinn, Brian Scott. *The New Euromarkets.* New York: Halsted Press, 1975.

64. Rendleman, Richard J., Jr., "The Effects of Default Risk on the Firm's Investment and Financing Decisions." *Financial Management,* Spring 1978, pp 45–53.

65. Reinhart, Walter J. "Discussion of 'The Channels of Influence of Tobin-Brainard's Q on Investment,' " *Journal of Finance,* May 1979, pp. 561–564.

66. Robbins, Sidney, and Robert B. Stobaugh. "Comments." In *International Mobility and Movement of Capital,* ed. Fritz Machlup, Walter Salant, and Lorie Tarshis. New York and London: Columbia University Press for National Bureau of Economic Research, 1972, pp. 354–357.

67. _____. *Money in the Multinational Enterprise.* New York: Basic Books, 1973.

68. Robicheck, Alexander A., and Mark R. Eaker, "Debt Denomination and Ex-

change Risk in International Capital Markets," *Financial Management,* Autumn 1976, pp. 11–18.

69. _____. "Foreign Exchange Hedging and the Capital Asset Pricing Model." *Journal of Finance,* June 1978, pp. 1011–1018.

70. Rogalski, Richard J., and Joseph D. Vinso. "Price Level Variations as Predictors of Flexible Exchange Rates." *Journal of International Business Studies,* Spring-Summer 1977, pp. 71–81.

71. Roll, Richard. "A Critique of the Asset Pricing Theory's Tests." *Journal of Financial Economics,* March 1977, pp. 129–176.

72. _____, and B. H. Solnik. "A Pure Foreign Exchange Asset Pricing Model." *Journal of International Economics,* Vol. 7 (1977), pp. 161–179.

73. Ross, Stephen A. "The Current Status of the Capital Asset Pricing Model (CAPM)." *Journal of Finance,* June 1978, pp. 885–901.

74. Rudd, Andrew, and Wilson Chung. "Implementation of International Portfolio Diversification: A Survey." Mimeographed. September 1978.

75. Rugman, Alan M. "A Note on Internationally Diversified Firms and Risk Reduction." *Journal of Business Administration,* Fall 1975, pp. 182–184.

76. _____. "Discussion: Corporate International Diversification and Market Assigned Measures of Risk and Diversification." *Journal of Financial and Quantitative Analysis,* November 1975, pp. 651–652.

77. _____. *International Diversification and the Multinational Enterprise.* Lexington, Mass.: D.C. Heath, 1979.

78. Rutenberg, David P. "Maneuvering Liquid Assets in a Multinational Company: Formulation and Deterministic Solution Procedures." *Management Science,* June 1970, pp. 45–49.

79. Scott, Davis F., Jr. "Evidence on the Importance of Financial Structure." *Financial Management,* Summer 1972, pp. 45–50.

80. Severn, Alan K. "Investor Evaluation of Foreign and Domestic Risk." *Journal of Finance,* May 1974, pp. 545–550.

81. _____. "The Financing of the Multi-National Firm: Comment." *Kyklos.* vol. 26, no. 4 (1973), pp. 852–856.

82. Shapiro, Alan C. "Capital Budgeting for the Multinational Corporation." *Financial Management,* Spring, 1978, pp. 7–16.

83. _____. "Evaluating Financing Costs for Multinational Subsidiaries." *Journal of International Business Studies,* Fall 1975, pp. 25–32.

84. _____. "Exchange Rate Changes, Inflation and the Value of the Multinational Corporation." *Journal of Finance,* May 1975, pp. 485–502.

85. _____. "Financial Structure and the Cost of Capital in the Multinational Corporation." *Journal of Financial and Quantitative Analysis.* June 1978, pp. 211–226.

86. Sharpe, William F. "Capital Asset Prices: A Theory of Market Equilibrium under Conditions of Risk." *Journal of Finance,* September 1964, pp. 425–442.

87. Solnik, Bruno H. "An Equilibrium Model of the International Capital Market." *Journal of Economic Theory* Vol. 8 (1974), pp. 500–524.

88. _____. "An International Market Model of Security Price Behavior." *Journal of Financial and Quantitative Analysis,* September 1974, pp. 537–554.

89. _____. *European Capital Markets.* Lexington, Mass.: D. C. Heath, 1973.

90. _____. "Testing International Asset Pricing: Some Pessimistic Views." *Journal of Finance,* May 1977, pp. 503–512.
91. _____. "The International Pricing of Risk: An Empirical Investigation of the World Capital Market Structure." *Journal of Finance,* May 1974, pp. 365–378.
92. _____, and Jean Grall. "Eurobonds: Determinants of the Demand for Capital and the International Interest Rate Structure." *Journal of Banking Research,* Winter 1975, pp. 218–230.
93. Stanley, Marjorie Thines. "Local-Currency Long-Term Debt in the Multinational's Financial Structure." *Atlantic Economic Review,* December 1979, p. 80.
94. _____, and Stanley B. Block. "Portfolio Diversification of Foreign Exchange Risk: An Empirical Study." *Management International Review,* Vol. 20 (1980/1), pp. 83–92.
95. _____. "Response by United States Financial Managers to Financial Accounting Standard No. 8." *Journal of International Business Studies.* Fall 1978, pp. 85–99.
96. Stanley, Marjorie Thines, and John D. Stanley. "The Impact of U.S. Regulation of Foreign Investment." *California Management Review,* Winter 1972, pp. 56–64.
97. Stehle, Richard. "An Empirical Test of the Alternative Hypothesis of National and International Pricing of Risky Assets." *Journal of Finance,* May 1977, pp. 493–502.
98. Stevens, Guy V. G. "Capital Mobility and the International Firm." In *International Mobility and Movement of Capital,* ed. Fritz Machlup, Walter Salant, and Lorie Tarshis. New York and London: Columbia University Press for National Bureau of Economic Research, 1972, pp. 323–353.
99. Stonehill, Arthur, Theo Beekhuisen, Richard Wright, Lee Remmers, Norman Toy, Antonio Pares, Alan Shapiro, Douglas Egan and Thomas Bates. "Financial Goals and Debt Ratio Determinants: A Survey of Practice in Five Countries." *Financial Management,* Autumn 1975, pp. 27–41.
100. Stonehill, Arthur, and Thomas Stitzel. "Financial Structure and Multinational Corporations." *California Management Review,* Fall 1969, pp. 91–96.
101. Vickers, D. "The Cost of Capital and the Structure of the Firm." *Journal of Finance,* March 1970, pp. 35–46.
102. Zenoff, David B., and Jack Zwick. *International Financial Management.* Englewood Cliffs, N.J.: Prentice-Hall, 1969.

Notes _____

1. A comparable statement might be made with regard to debt financing, relying not on the M-M thesis but on the international Fisher effect in foreign exchange rate determination. This will be discussed later in the paper.
2. Here, a recent suggestion by Elliott is of interest. In an empirical study of the relationship between cost of capital and aggregate investment. Elliott found that 75 percent of the fluctuation in his weighted average cost of capital measure was due to the fluctuations in tax-adjusted equity costs while only 25 percent was due to fluctuations in debt costs (19, p. 994). Accordingly, he suggested that "monetary policy efforts to influence investment by changing the cost of capital will have a much greater impact if they succeed in influencing equity costs than if they are primarily confined to debt markets influences" (19, p. 994).

3. This characterization was disputed by Rugman (76; 77, p. 44).

4. There is an extensive literature concerned with the effect of conglomerate diversification upon valuation and debt capacity of the domestic firm; it has been excluded from consideration here.

5. However, in a study of the effects of statement of Financial Accounting Standard No. 8 on security return behavior, multinationals with relatively large investments in foreign assets were shown to have had lower returns than multinationals with relatively low investments in foreign assets in the period 1975–1977 (16, pp. 99–102).

9. THE FINANCING MUST COME—
BUT FROM WHERE?

BENJAMIN M. FRIEDMAN

Benjamin M. Friedman is a professor of economics at Harvard and director of financial market research, National Bureau of Economic Research. His article is based in part on an address to the Second International Seminar on Saving and Financial Markets sponsored by Caisse des Depots et Consignations, Paris, in March 1980.

What is in store for the bond and other securities markets in the United States and elsewhere in the world in the 1980s? They will, of course, be subject to wide fluctuations; and some of these may well be as traumatic as those occurring in the United States in the first half of 1980.

In contradiction to the dire forebodings of the bond and stock market's demise that dominated the business press a short time ago, these gyrations turn out to be temporary—in this case even fleeting—when viewed from a longer perspective. There is every reason to expect that the markets can continue to function normally. But in the 1980s functioning normally will not be enough.

The prinicpal financial markets of the Western world (including Japan) face three critical challenges in this decade:

- To finance increased domestic capital formation in the major industrialized economies, including not only the huge special requirements for energy exploration and development but also, in many countries, even larger investments to build an expanded and more productive industrial base.
- To finance growing and more unstable international payments imbalances, especially the large and quickly shifting surpluses and deficits associated with rising oil prices.
- To accomplish these tasks during severe and volatile inflation.

Borrowers in most countries will seek to meet their needs, in the first instance, by turning to the banking system and the securities markets in some combination. During the 1970s, bank credit and securities issues bulked large as sources of funds in the six largest OECD countries (see *Exhibit I*). Whether these sources can rise to the challenges of the 1980s is highly questionable.

Limits on the Banks

Can the Western economies rely on the banking system not only to enhance the financing of domestic capital formation but also to repeat its success in coping (almost single-handedly) with the petrodollar recycling problem?

Exhibit I
TWO SOURCES OF FUNDS RAISED IN NATIONAL FINANCIAL MARKETS (IN PERCENT)

	France	Germany	Italy	Japan	U.K.	U.S.A.
Share supplied by banks						
1969–73 average	43.8%	60.6%	49.9%	41.9%	57.4%	32.2%
1974–78 average	33.6	66.1	52.4	32.0	37.0	24.1
Share supplied in securities markets						
1969–73 average	23.7	21.1	30.2	22.4	12.0	31.7
1974–78 average	20.3	26.7	30.5	34.2	22.3	39.5

Source: OECD, *Financial Statistics.*
Note: Data are averages of yearly percentage shares.

Unfortunately, the banks probably cannot deal adequately with a new surge of recycling needs, much less with financing stepped-up capital formation. In 1979 the deficits of the non-oil developing countries totaled about $50 billion, and the recent sharp increase in the cost of their oil imports is no doubt inflating them further this year.

In contrast to the situation in 1974, however, when the first wave of masssive oil surpluses and deficits came, many major banks now begin from a position of substantial portfolio commitment to the non-oil developing countries. Although most of these countries have rebuilt their international reserves, their interest-payment and total debt-service burdens are now significantly greater than they were in 1974, not only absolutely but also relative to their exports.

According to nearly every study of the creditworthiness of these borrowers, the heterogeneity within the group is far too great to permit ready generalizations. For example, newly industrialized countries differ sharply from primary extraction economies. Thus, each country's situation must be considered individually. But the fact of great differences among them is all the more reason to sense potential danger in some countries.

A major factor limiting the banks' ability to lend internationally as well as domestically will be the likely inadequacy of their capital bases. For many U.S. banks, exposure to non-oil developing countries is already large in comparison with capital. And, although exposure data in meaningful form are scarce for other countries, major banks abroad probably are also heavily committed. Even for domestic lending operations, for many banks capital is becoming an ever more pressing restraint on credit expansion.

In sum, the banking system alone cannot reliably meet the challenges of the 1980s.

Limits on Securities Markets _____

Can the securities markets fill the vacuum? Here, too, there is cause for great concern. In recent years the volume of securities issues has indeed expanded in the six largest OECD countries (see *Exhibit II*). But on balance the average rate of expansion among the six has barely kept pace with inflation.

Because the markets can sell securities only to the extent that investors are prepared to buy them, one clue to the modest growth of new-issue volume in the 1970s (and to prospects for growth in the 1980s) may lie in the total-return performance of securities. *Exhibit III* summarizes the performance of equities, long-term bonds, and money market instruments in the 1970-1978 period. For each security the table shows:

>The average total return.

>The volatility of the total return, measured by the annual standard deviation. (A simple rule of thumb is that in two out of three years the return will fall in a range indicated by the mean, plus or minus one standard deviation.)

>The exposure of the total return to inflation risk, measured by the annual correlation with the rate of change of consumer prices. (A positive correlation signals

Exhibit II
NEW-ISSUE VOLUME IN NATIONAL SECURITIES MARKETS (IN BILLIONS OF DOLLARS EXCEPT WHERE INDICATED IN PERCENT)

		France	Germany	Italy	Japan	U.K.	U.S.A.
All securities							
1978	$ amount	13.3	24.9	34.2	105.1	11.0	137.1
1974–78	Average $ amount	9.6	21.5	21.3	73.5	12.8	120.8
1974–78	Growth rate of $ amount	9.5%	19.1%	10.4%	29.1%	19.8%	4.6%
1974–78	Growth rate of home currency amount	8.5%	12.2%	18.0%	21.7%	24.3%	4.6%
Bonds							
1978	$ amount	10.1	22.1	30.2	98.9	9.2	126.4
1974–78	Average	7.2	19.3	18.7	67.9	11.1	110.7
Equities							
1978	$ amount	3.2	2.8	4.0	29.1	1.8	10.7
1974–78	Average	2.4	2.2	2.6	21.7	1.7	10.1

Source: OECD, *Financial Statistics*.
Note: Data converted to dollar equivalent using yearly average exchange rates.
Detail may not add to total because of rounding.

Exhibit III

NOMINAL AND REAL PERFORMANCE OF TOTAL INVESTMENT RATES OF RETURN, 1970–78
(IN PERCENT PER ANNUM, EXCEPT CORRELATIONS)

		France	Germany	Italy	Japan	U.K.	U.S.A.
Return on equities							
Mean	Nominal	7.5	3.4	− 4.6	16.2	12.3	4.6
	Real	− 1.1	− 1.5	−16.6	6.6	− 0.2	− 2.0
Standard Deviation	Nominal	16.7	10.3	16.4	19.8	23.4	13.6
	Real	17.9	10.4	18.7	23.9	22.9	15.3
Inflation Correlation	Nominal	− .36	− .04	− .26	− .60	− .20	− .65
	Real	− .49	− .19	− .53	− .75	− .06	− .73
Return on bonds							
Mean	Nominal	7.5	11.6	2.4	10.8	8.7	4.2
	Real	− 1.1	6.6	− 9.7	1.1	− 3.8	− 2.5
Standard Deviation	Nominal	7.6	14.0	14.0	13.6	10.4	7.9
	Real	9.0	14.6	17.0	18.6	10.5	9.4
Inflation Correlation	Nominal	− .33	− .31	− .39	− .78	.27	− .52
	Real	− .60	− .41	− .66	− .89	− .30	− .69
Return on money market instruments							
Mean	Nominal	8.5	4.3	10.3	5.3	8.5	3.9
	Real	− 0.2	− 0.6	− 1.7	− 4.3	− 4.1	− 0.8
Standard Deviation	Nominal	2.1	1.5	4.3	1.0	2.2	2.3
	Real	2.0	1.8	2.8	5.2	4.8	1.5
Inflation Correlation	Nominal	.70	.35	.88	.77	.64	.77
	Real	− .67	− .60	− .70	− .99	− .94	− .85

Note: Total return on equities equals dividend yield plus capital gain or minus capital loss.
  Total return on bonds equals coupon yield plus capital gain or minus captial loss.

that, over time, the return is higher when inflation rises; a negative correlation suggests a lower return when inflation increases. A correlation near one, or minus one, implies a nearly perfect relationship between the return and inflation, while a correlation near zero implies a weak relationship or none at all.)

The most important feature of the table is that the calculations treat separately the nominal returns realized in the six markets and the corresponding real returns that allow for the six countries' respective inflation rates. The results are hardly encouraging. Although most of these securities show at least a modest return before inflation, almost all betray a negative after-inflation return. During those years, only equities in Japan and bonds in Germany and Japan show average positive returns, adjusted for inflation. As should be expected, the yields from bonds and especially equities were very volatile on either a real or a nominal basis.

Moreover, none of these securities has given investors a systematic hedge against inflation. The inflation correlation line in *Exhibit III* indicates the extent to which the nominal or real return on each class of security varied as inflation fluctuated. The negative correlations for equities and bonds in each country—except bonds in the United Kingdom—indicate that the emergence of rapid inflation produced, on average, lower returns on both nominal and real bases.

While the positive nominal correlations for short-term money market instruments show that the nominal returns on these securities rose on average to offset part of the effect of inflation, the negative real correlations show that the nominal gains failed to keep pace with inflation In other words, higher inflation brought lower returns on these securities too. In not a single case, out of the three securities considered for each country, has the total return warranted considering the security a good inflation hedge.

In view of the poor performance of the securities markets in providing an attractive return to investors on an afterinflation basis—not to mention on an aftertax basis—the ability of these markets to raise sufficient funds to meet the challenges of financing greater domestic capital formation and wider international imbalances also remains questionable.

Innovations for The 1980s _____

If strained capital adequacy and other limitations cast doubt on the banking system's ability to meet these objectives and if poor returns in an inflationary era cast doubt on the securities markets' ability to do so, what then are the prospects for the Western world's financial markets to meet the challenges they face?

Although some unforeseen force may emerge to ease the path (and the major international institutions certainly have much room for an expanded role), it is more likely that the markets themselves will have to make their own way—in some cases with an assist, or a prod, from their regulators. In the end, the markets' success will depend on their capacity to devise and implement innovations that remove the main impediments to their expansion.

Potentially successful innovations are always difficult to identify, but several candidates appear to have sufficient promise to warrant investigation:

- ▪ Underwriting price-indexed securities—in some cases by packaging the debt of different borrowers, each of whom issues debt indexed to the price of a particular product or commodity (presumably the one representing the borrower's principal line of business).
- ▪ Restructuring the conventional bond call provisions which, through the extreme asymmetry of the risk structure that they impose on the holders, make today's long-term corporate debt instrument especially unattractive for investors in a world dominated by volatile inflation.[1]
- ▪ Packaging the bonded indebtedness or even the bank debt of non-oil developing countries in a form that, by diversifying country risk, could attract direct investment by either domestic participants in major securities markets or the oil producers.
- ▪ Realigning regulatory arrangements to facilitate more efficient deployment of bank capital and to enhance banks' prospects for attracting new capital. In the United States, for example, authorities could eliminate unit banking laws and reduce prohibitions on interstate deposit taking.

If the financial markets cannot finance an increase in capital formation and accommodate growing international imbalances, the Western economies must either sacrifice their aim for renewed growth in living standards or accept ever-greater fragility in their international financial arrangements. It is in everyone's interest that the financial markets vigorously investigate the kinds of innovations that offer the possibility of averting either of these outcomes.

Notes _____

1. See Benjamin M. Friedman and Zvi Bodie, "Interest Rate Uncertainty and the Value of Bond Call Protection," *Journal of Political Economy,* February 1978, p. 19.

10. COUNTERTRADE: FORMS, MOTIVES, PITFALLS, AND NEGOTIATION REQUISITES

SARKIS J. KHOURY

The impressive growth in countertrade necessitates a careful look at this trade financing mechanism and a new attitude by American policy makers and businessmen toward it. This study looks at the various forms of countertrade, at the motivating forces behind it, at the pitfalls that countertrade could engender, and at some imperatives in the negotiation of countertrade deals. The issues are examined from the perspective of a policy maker and that of a businessman. The two persppectives are distinct but overlap sufficiently to merit a joint examination. It is the conclusion of this study that countertrade is here to stay, and that American businessmen better learn to cope with it if they are to maintain and improve their competitiveness in the world markets.

The increasing interdependence among the economies of the world requires close scrutiny of the financing methods that facilitate the movement of resources across national borders. The evidence on interdependence abounds. U.S. direct investment in foreign countries reached $227.3 billion by the end of 1981. Foreign investment in the United States was $89.76 billion for the same period. These investments generate trade and capital flows helping make trade and trade financing truly world issues with considerable impact on the welfare of nations and the profitability and stability of business firms. U.S. exports in 1982 amounted to $212.2 billion or 7% of GNP. Japanese and West German exports accounted for 21.5 and 32% of their GNPs, respectively. International competition is increasing across markets and across products with serious implications for the balance of payments account and for domestic employment. In 1982 the United States had a record $42.7 billion trade deficit, $3 billion larger than in 1981, with exports to nearly every area of the world declining. The Department of Commerce estimates that one out of eight jobs depends in one way or another on exports, making trade a significant public issue particularly in a period of high unemployment.

The instruments of international competition include financing methods and their costs. So potent have these methods become in gaining access to markets and improving market share that OECD countries meet occasionally to set standards for international trade financing. The latest revision of the *Arrangement on Guidelines for Officially Supported Export Credits* by OECD countries was made in July 1982. The subject of this study is one method of trade financing: countertrade.

The traditional methods of trade financing are supplier credits and borrowings from private and official sources. Countertrade adds another dimension of particular benefit to countries with mounting debt burdens (primarily East European and Latin American). In a countertrade imports are financed by deferred exports (at an implied financing cost) without significantly altering the level of indebtedness of the countries involved. Additionally, a countertrade transaction may involve the utilitzation of the traditional methods of financing. Trade financed by countertrade has grown considerably. It is estimated that one-fifth to one-fourth of the $2 trillion of world trade estimate for 1982 will be financed through various countertrade arrangements, principally of the buy-back type [1]. The percentage of countertrade financing in East-West trade is estimated to be 40%. Today the Soviet Union requests a countertrade arrangement for any import transaction exceeding $1 million, and 10% of Swiss and West German exports to East European countries are financed by countertrade. However, trade in general and countertrade in particular still receive limited attention from U.S. corporations. Only 10% of U.S. manufacturing firms export and fewer than 10% of these firms account for 80% of U.S. exports. Medium-sized and smaller U.S. firms are predominantly not involved in trade and are consequently not involved in the complex forms of trade financing. In addition, countertrade is still in its infancy even among those U.S. firms with a long history of substantial trade activity. The Department of Commerce estimated U.S. imports of chemicals, minerals, metals, and other products obtained through countertrade in 1980 at $278.6 million, up from $98.3 million in 1974. With U.S. imports in 1980 equal to $244.9 billion, imports from countertrade accounted for about 0.12 percent of total U.S. imports. The dominant portion of this countertrade consisted of buy-back agreements. Recent estimates suggest that the size of countertrade imports in 1982 could be twice that of 1980.

Definition of Countertrade

Countertrade is a generic name for a trade financing method that covers bilateral agreements, counterpurchases, buy-back agreements, switch, and barter trades.

Simply defined, countertrade is an international sale which is conditional on a sale in the opposite direction. An example of this is the countertrade agreement between Pepsico and the Soviet Union, where Pepsico supplied the bottling plant and cola syrup in exchange for Soviet vodka to be delivered over a period of time to Pepsico.

Countertrade can be viewed generally as a modern version of barter trade. Two separate contracts are involved: one for the delivery of and payment for (currency and length of payment period) the goods supplied by a Western company, and the other for the purchase of and the payment for the goods imported from (typically) the East European country.

The link between the two contracts is not a legal one. The performance of one contract is not contingent on the performance of the other, although the seller from the Western country is in effect accepting products and services from the importing country in partial or total settlement for his exports.

Countertrade (CT) also can be viewed as a substitute for foreign direct investment (FDI). In an FDI, Alcoa, say, would export capital equipment, managerial talent, and financial resources to mine bauxite in a foreign country. The bauxite is then shipped to the U.S. for processing and manufacturing. CT allows for the same results without actual ownership of the means of production in the bauxite-rich country, eliminating in the process the risks of expropriation and blockage of profit transfers. CT is, therefore, a mechanism for circumventing the state ownership requirement in East European and other countries.

Countertrade is also a mechanism for circumventing restrictions on trade. East European countries, for example, divide their import requirements into priority and normal, planned imports. Any unplanned imports and some of the planned imports may be done only through CT arrangements because the state will not allocate foreign exchange for the purchase. CT also can be used to circumvent import quotas, for it does not cause a drain on foreign exchange reserves. CT does not fall under the General Agreement on Tariffs and Trade (GATT). This perspective becomes more clear with the explanations below.

Types of Countertrade _____

Countertrades can be classified by different general categories:

1. Classification by the time factor
   a. One-time delivery contracts
   b. Long-term contracts calling for deliveries over several years
2. Classification by financing requirements
   a. No financing is needed—pure barter
   b. Some form of financing is required on either or both sides of the transaction
3. Classification by size of compensation
   a. Partial compensation is required
   b. Full compensation is required—the value of goods imported would equal the value of the exported goods
4. Classification by need for compensation product
   a. The exporting country (company) has a legitimate in-house need for the compensating product
   b. The exporting country (company) has no need for the compensating product and must, therefore, sell it directly or through third parties

The last classification is most appealing for it allows for a better framework for focusing policy concerns (trade policy, efficiency of the international financial system, etc.) and those of businessmen actually or prospectively involved in trade and trade financing.

Under the classification by need for the compensating product several types of CT can be distinguished. The main ones are barter, counterpurchase or commercial compensation deals, buy-back arrangements, and switch trades.

Barter

A barter is a short-term contractual agreement between two parties calling for the direct exchange of goods and services. A classical barter involves no currencies, although a currency may be used as a numeraire in the determination of the exchange ratio. Barter is currently a rarely used form of countertrade.

Some barters are done indirectly and involve the use of currency. A cooperation and classical barter involves, for example, two Western companies selling to and buying from a third party (usually an Eastern bloc country) in order to save on transaction costs which would be incurred in the event of a direct sale. An example of this would be a sale of machinery to an East European trade organization by a U.S. company and the sale of raw materials by the East European Trade Company to a French firm. The French firm pays the U.S. firm for the price of the machinery, which is equivalent to the value of the imported raw materials.

Goods received in barter are acquired on the basis of a genuine need for or ability to sell the product. The nonutilization of money is not a source of economic inefficiency. The acquired raw materials are used in the production process and not as "currency" for the further acquisition of goods and services. The determination of the price of one good in terms of another can be easily arrived at based on the prices of the goods in money, assuming the existence of a market price.

Barters also take place between countries. Any imbalance between the value of goods received and those exported is settled at the end of the year using the clearing account created by a bilateral clearing arrangement. An example is the annual exchange of $200 million of frozen lambs from New Zealand for Iranian crude oil.

Counterpurchase (Swap)—Commercial Compensation Deal

A counterpurchase consists of two legally separate contracts, one calling typically for the sale of Western goods, and the other for the purchase of goods (services) from the importer of Western goods. Payments against each of the contracts is made separately and in an agreed-upon hard currency. A clause covering the transfer of the goods received to a third party is ordinarily included in the contract. Examples of counterpurchases abound. The Soviet Union purchased construction machinery from Japan's Komatsu in return for the sale of Siberian timber. Colombia sold coffee to pay for buses build by ENESA of Spain. Another interesting example involved the sale of a computer by Control Data to the Hermitage Museum in Leningrad in return for an agreement by the Museum to lend some of its masterpieces to Control Data for a two-year tour in the United States. Control Data received exculsive rights to sell Hermitage reproduction and art books. The most interesting of the counterpurchase proposal that did not materialize was the offer of a 150-year-old Mongolian dinosaur skeleton to West Germany in return for $100,000 in cash and 100 Volkswagens. The full counterpurchase cycle is shown in Figure 1.

One of the key concerns in a counterpurchase is the usefulness of the products received in exchange for Western goods and services. This and other related matters will be discussed later in this study.

Figure 1.
MODEL OF A COUNTERPURCHASE/COMPENSATION TRANSACTION.[a]

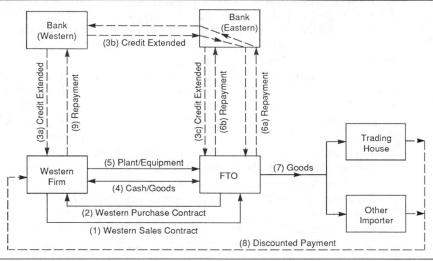

Note --- Indicates payment and credit lines

1. The Western firm contracts for the sale of plane and equipment with the Communist importing enterprise, e.g., an FTO (or in China an FTC), against full or partial payment in goods:
2. The FTO contracts to sell goods to the Western firm, generally under a separate contract from the original Western export contract;
3a. The Western bank extends credit to the Western firm supplier, e.g. *à forfait credit*,[1] for the hard currency necessary against promissory notes from the FTO with guarantees from the Communist state bank; or
3b. The Western bank extends bank-to-bank credit to the state bank to finance the hard currency portion of the transaction on behalf of the FTO; or
3c. For projects which are only partially funded under the five-year plans (FYP), the state bank itself provides the budgeted hard currency funds to the FTO for the downpayment and a percentage of the transaction. For these projects, CT exports are expected to provide the balance of the cost;
4. The FTO may provide the Western firm with a cash down-payment in hard currency for the Western export. CT goods will also be provided by the FTO, in accordance with the provisions of the CT contract, for which the Western firm pays the FTO in hard currency;
5. The Western firm provides the FTO with the plant and equipment contracted;
6a. The FTO remits payment of the outstanding credit to the state bank which in turn repays the Western bank; or
6b. The FTO repays the credit received from the state bank;
7. If the Western firm cannot use internally or sell on its own account the counter-deliveries, it may transfer its rights to these goods to a third party (e.g., a trading house or other importer) at a discount;
8. The Western firm receives payment for the goods transferred to the third party;
9. The Western firm, if it received supplier credit from the Western bank, repays the outstanding credit to the bank (alternatively the Western bank receives payment directly from the FTO or its bank).

_____

[1] *A forfait* financing denotes the buying of trade drafts or promissory notes by a financial institution, without further recourse on the seller. The notes, bearing an interest rate which today is in excess of 10 percent, mature in one to seven years are bought by the financial institute at discount. They provide immediate cash payment for the Western supplier who has accepted them for his exports. *A forfait* financing has not been practiced yet in trade with China.
[a]Source: Pompiliu Verzariu [2, pp. 9-11].

Buy-Back Agreements

Buy-back agreements also involve two separate contracts. They are typically large and long in duration (five to ten years). Here a Western company supplies plant, equipment, technology, and technical assistance in return for shipment of resultant products from the goods and services supplied. The recipients of Western technology are ordinarily East European countries (EE).

The purchase by EE countries is partially financed through long-term Western credit covering the buy-back period. The purchase of resultant products is paid for in hard currency.

The shipments from the plant under the buy-back agreements usually account for 20 to 30% of the plant output, and the financing (government + supplier + bank) ordinarily covers about 40% of the value of Western goods and services.

Ordinarily, the value of the resultant products received exceeds the value of the goods and services supplied by the Western company. The time lag between exports and the import of resultant products is usually between three and five years.

Examples of buy-back agreements are many. The most recent and most controversial is that of the Soviet pipeline. As of September 1982, Germany, France, Italy, and Britain had committed $3.8 billion to the construction of the gas pipeline. The financing of the pipeline was primarily by Western governments at subsidized rates. In return for their commitment the Western countries involved in the project would receive Soviet gas. The Soviet Union would receive about $8 billion annually from the sale of this gas. Europe's dependence on the Soviet Union for energy supply and the questionable ability of the Soviet ultimately to make good on their commitments are the concerns of U.S. policy makers.

Another outstanding example involves the Soviet Union and Occidental Petroleum Corp. Under this $20 billion agreement Occidental will help build chemical plants in the Soviet Union and agrees to buy the ammonia (among other things) they produce for sale in the West.

Once again, the usefulness of the resultant products received by Western firms and the difficulties they may create in Western markets are of great concern.

Switch Trades

Switch refers to a switch in the country of destination of the exported product or in the currency used for settlement.

Bilateral payment agreements among countries call for settlements of trade transactions in one of the participating countries' currencies, in a third country's currency (typically U.S. dollars), or in another agreed-upon unit of account. A switch converts a bilateral clearing currency into a freely convertible currency payable to a third party. The conversion process involves a discount that can be considerable. An example of a switch trade: Colombia buying oil from Libya and paying for it in dollars (required by Libya) made available by Hungary (who needs Colombian coffee) with whom Colombia has a bilateral clearing agreement and accumulated surplus clearing funds. Colombia would get Libyan oil and Hungary Colombian coffee. Colombia would simply credit Hungary's clearing account for the price of oil plus any additional costs charged by Hungary for the service.

Switch trades are ordinarily handled by switch traders who offer technical advice and assistance in obtaining proper documentation, take positions (long or short) in clearing funds, and extend credit and offer guarantees on switch transactions. A simple, but typical, switch transactions appear in Figure 2.

Motives for Countertrade _____

The motives for countertrade can be looked upon from the perspective of the East European and developing countries and from the perspective of the Western firms.

EE/LDC Perspective

Serious trade deficits and heavy debt burdens by the EE/LDC have left them scurrying for alternative vehicles to redress balance of payments problems and to deal with a shortage of financing and with high interest rates. Industrial country bank claims on foreign countries totaled $1.542 trillion in 1981, of which $332.1 billion or 21.5% belonged to U.S. banks. The total debt owed by developing countries at the end of 1982 was $790 billion. During 1982, 25 countries were in arrears or in process of rescheduling bank debts, with the latest, Mexico, jolting the international financial system with its $85 billion foreign debt.

Nearly shut off from traditional sources of financing because of excessive debt burdens and low export revenues (actual and expected), the EE/LDC had to seek a new method of financing; countertrade offered just the right vehicle.

Countertrade is a means of circumventing a structural trade imbalance. EE countries with technologically inferior products have limited access to Western markets. Countertrade allows them to finance their imports with exports of raw materials and inferior products. These exports are paid for by hard currency which the EE countries use to pay for imports which otherwise would have to be foregone. Whatever credit is associated with countertrade does not increase the credit risk of the EE countries for it is self liquidating, assuming the contract is carried out.

The limited availability of hard currency reserves to EE countries and the nonconvertibility of their currency in world markets necessitate CT financing. Similarly, developing countries whose central banks maintain artificial prices for the national currency occasionally have had to resort to countertrade as a measure to balance the trade account. LDCs are further aggravated by the nonconvertibility of their currency.

The importance of countertrade as a trade balancing device has long been acknowledged by EE and LDC countries. Romania effectively legislated countertrade through Law No. 12, which was approved by the Romanian Parliament on December 19, 1980. The law encourages balance between exports and imports. The favored mechanism is countertrade. Indonesia enacted a law requiring bidders on government contracts to export Indonesian products equal in value to the required Indonesian imports for the project.

EE countries with centrally planned economies find countertrade a logical extension of planned systems for it allows for planning exports and imports over time. In so doing the cyclical effects of Western economies are partially avoided as are

Figure 2.
MODEL OF A SWITCH TRANSACTION.[a]

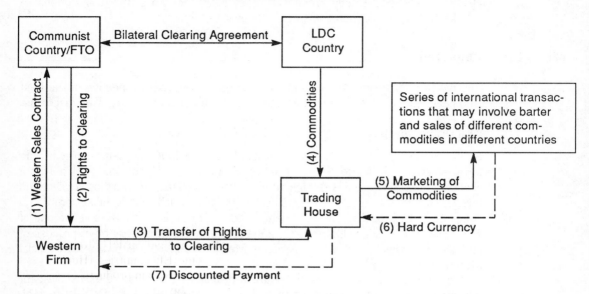

Note --- Indicates payment lines
1. The Western firm contracts for the sale of goods with the FTO of the Communist country;
2. To pay for the Western goods, the FTO receives authorization to transfer the Communist country's clearing account surplus with the LDC to the account of the Western firm;
3. On the basis of the authorization and an appropriate clause in its contract with the FTO, the Western firm transfers its purchasing rights to a trading house specializing in switch transactions;
4. The trading house imports commodities from the LDC for a value equivalent to the FTO's obligation to the Western firm;
5. The trading house, through a series of linked international transactions, often involving the transfer of several types of goods, sells to a buyer willing to purchase for hard currency;
6. The trading house or its designee sells to this buyer at discounted prices and receives hard currency as payment;
7. The cash payment of the final buyer, discounted for the trading house's fees and costs, is remitted to the Western firm.

[a]Source: Pompiliu Verzariu [2, pp. 13-14].

inflationary effects since prices of goods are fixed over a designated time period. While price and cycle uncertainties are diminished, EE countries in the process upgrade their productive assets through the importation of Western technology. Additionally EE countries succeed in shifting the marketing and distribution problems of their products to Western purchasers.

Western Firms' Perspectives

The foremost value of countertrade to a Western firm is the creation of an export opportunity where none existed before. In this regard, countertrade in not an alternative to trade routed, financed, and paid for through traditional channels and means, but rather a supplement to traditonal trade. This export opportunity could prove traumatic, however, if the goods offered in compensation are not needed and have to be marketed through third parties. The ways to reducing this burden are many. The simplest way, of course is to avoid countertrade whenever possible and to reduce that portion of trade financed by CT, but there are other ways.

The Western exporter must insist on two separate contracts in any countertrade. He should specify the nature and quality of goods of interest to him and should keep careful records of every negotiation session. He should also expect that the EE negotiator will insist on a clause covering the transfer of countertrade goods to third parties and occasionally on having the rights of marketing the product (in the event of transfer to a third party) assigned to a company of the EE negotiator's choice. The latter case usually occurs when an East European FTO jointly owns a trade company in the West with a Western partner. The Western exporter should resist these pressures to whatever extent possible.

The Western exporter should expect a good number of surprises. Product lists may be shortened or withdrawn without notice. Quality guarantees by EE countries are never offered, although the Western exporter may get an FTO to agree to a quality inspection by an independent surveyor. Some EE countries (Hungary, for example), however, maintain high quality standards for certain products as a matter of policy designed to improve their image and competitiveness with Western firms. A penalty clause for noncompliance should be included in the contract. A bank guarantee for the penalty payment should also be negotiated.

The central issue in a countertrade transaction remains the countertrade ratio. Costing one product in terms of another is not always easy. It depends on whether a true market price exists for the products received in counertrade, on the need of the FTO for the product from the West, on the extent of the financing involved in the transaction, and certainly on the skills of the negotiators. When competitive market prices do not exist the situation is often similar to bilateral monopoly. Whatever the ratio, it must incorporate the finance charges on the financing done by the Western firms, the cost of technical assistance and spare parts where capital goods are exported, the commission costs of a specialized trading company if one is used, and the expected discount on the goods received from the EE country when sold in the open market or even through a trading company.

The expansion of export markets through CT allows Western firms to cover portions of the large fixed costs committed to research and development and to secure raw materials and intermediate products over the long term. The latter aspect is beneficial only if the goods received as compensation are usable in the Western company's production process. Japan, a resource-poor country, has long used countertrade as a means to secure raw materials supplies. Japan consummated deals with the Soviet Union where it received guarantees of raw materials deliveries in return for filling the industrial requirements of the Soviet Union.

The risks associated with the marketability of the products received in countertrade can be eliminated for a fee through in-house or independent specialized trading companies. These trading companies provide varied trade-related services to include marketing, transportation (including warehousing and insurance), financing (including inventory management and credit extension), and some manufacturing. For a fee ranging between 1 and 5% of the value of the transaction, specialized trading companies make up for the lack of in-house expertise in countertrade. The Export Trading Company Act of 1982 should help in the proliferation of export trading companies in the United States. Several have already appeared on the American scene buoyed by the success of the Japanese trading companies. Many of America's corporate giants are involved. General Electric Trading Co., a subsidiary of General Electric Co., was set up to handle countertrade and not exclusively for GE products. Combustion Engineering Inc., Rockwell International Corp., Sears Roebuck & Co., and Citibank have also set up trading companies which can handle countertrades expertly.

The growth of countertrade was stimulated by other factors. Countertrade may well produce a relationship among the parties extending far beyond the original period and the original products, allowing Western firms to better schedule their production runs and to better cope with the effects of the economic cycles, with the attending benefits of a more stable labor force and a more stable cash flow.

Pitfalls of Countertrade

The pitfalls of countertrade differ considerably, although with a substantial overlap when viewed from the eyes of a policy maker or those of a businessman.

Policy Considerations

As the trade sanctions imposed by the United States on U.S. firms and West European firms shipping American-licensed technology to the Soviet Union for the construction of the gas pipeline illustrate, the separation of the political considerations from the economic ones, at least as far as the United States is concerned, is practically impossible. Long-term strategic interests frequently override legitimate economic interests, confusing in the process the key issues associated with countertrade. The critical policy issue deals with whether the United States should actively oppose, actively support, or be passive to countertrade developments. The current U.S. policy is hostile to cuntertrade, although limited policy options are available to the U.S. government to limit countertrade. No legal action can be taken by the U.S. government to limit countertrade despite the distorting effects countertrade may be having on trade flows. Careful scrutiny of financing applications is applied by official U.S. lending agencies like the Export-Import Bank when countertrade is involved. The EXIM Bank has financed (minimally) countertrade deals but is most critical where the U.S. political and strategic interests are involved. These interests dominate the economic considerations as a matter of policy, although tight domestic (U.S.) economic conditions have frequently shifted the balance in favor of economics.

Countertrade is looked upon as a form of trade barrier which contravenes U.S. commitment to an open international economy and monetary system. CT is viewed as a method for circumventing the GATT provisions, particularly those dealing with nondiscrimination and the methods for protecting domestic industry.

Countertrade, which in some of its forms represents a return to days of barter, reintroduces the inefficiencies associated with this form of trade. The nonutilization of money as a medium of exchange increases the transaction costs of trading and, therefore, economic inefficiency. Prices are further distorted as deliveries are made over time without reference to changes in technology, market structure, taste, and quality of the products delivered and of competing products. The problem with this analysis, however, lies in the fact that countertrade is being compared with a system of free international trade within the context of an internationally agreed-upon monetary system. Countertrade is best understood when it is compared with the no-trade option. The goods acquired in countertrade are acquired for the purpose of immediate consumption or sale to third party for cash. Countertrade goods are not used as "currency." American firms whose products are technologically superior and whose international market position is secure can insist (and always do) on cash settlements. Countertrade fundamentally remains a means to increase world trade, and not simply a means for alternative financing. Thus, it is a means to improve opportunities, those in the labor market in particular, although it introduces price distortions in the process because the agreed-upon prices may not be market-clearing prices.

Other concerns of policy makers are: the technology transfer from the West to the East brought about by countertrade; the escape avenue countertrade provides to countries in serious financial difficulties, thus postponing their day of reckoning; and the disruption countertrade can bring to local and international markets. A U.S. producer of heavy equipment, for example, may accept chemicals from the Soviet Union in a countertrade transaction. With little or no expertise in marketing chemicals, it may end up dumping chemicals in the U.S. or in other markets. The U.S. Commerce Department, after extensive investigation of anhydrous ammonia (from the U.S.S.R.) and truck trailer axles (from Hungary) found those imports to have been indeed disruptive of U.S. markets under section 406 of the Trade Act of 1974.

The above concerns are somewhat exaggerated. Technology transfer occurs in cash deals as well as in countertrade deals. The issue, therefore, is a certain level of trade or a reduced level of trade with EE countries. As to dumping, the emergence of strong, well-financed, and experienced trading companies reduces this likelihood.

The pitfalls we have just discussed are seen from the perspective of Western policy makers. The EE countries look very favorably upon countertrade or it has well served the interest of the centrally planned economies. The impact on world trade and the efficiency of the international economic system are not of significance to EE policy makers.

The Businessman's Point of View

The Western exporter quite often settles for second best in a countertrade transaction. The list of goods offered against the exports is typically short, consists of lower-quality finished goods that are not very competitive in the world markets (EE countries are offering fewer and fewer raw materials in exchange for Western exports), and does not offer goods that can be easily incorporated in the production process of the Western firms.

EE countries, while committed to delivering a certain portion of their production to the Western exporter, are free to do whatever they please with the rest of the production (typically 70% of total production). The Western exporter is thus inviting competition against the products it will be receiving in the countertrade and/or against the products it or one of its main clients produces.

Another problem for Western exporters stems from the higher level of uncertainty associated with countertrade. Cash deals carry much less uncertainty than buy-back agreements, which may stretch up to ten years with considerable uncertainty about product quality, availability, marketability, and price. Furthermore, even if a certain quality level is assured, its constancy may represent a problem in the future as the dynamic environment in which it is produced and sold continues to evolve. This problem has been addressed by Hungary in a very constructive way. Hungarian trade authorities insist on countertrade deals that guarantee updating of production technology so as to insure a competitive end product over time.

Another problem inherent in long-term contracts is pricing of products. To quote prices on products that will be available only after several years could be counterproductive to at least one of the parties if not both. Because of this and other uncertainties, buy-back arrangements force up the sales price of plant and equipment and lower the price of products received in countertrade. The price discount reflects the various costs associated with the sale of inferior products in Western markets. As marketing costs increase, the incentive for specialized trading houses increases. The substantial rise in the number of trading houses is illustrative of the nature and the size of this new market.

One other significant problem faces the Western exporter: negotiation with the EE bureaucracy. The western exporter typically is not as experienced and a lot more delicate than its EE counterparts. The Western exporter, as a competitor in the world market, negotiates with EE organizations that have legal monopolies on the products they trade and are run by bureaucrats who have little incentive to adapt to a changing world and who possess proven skills in wrenching out favorable deals. These bureaucrats typically give minimal, if any, information on product quality and characteristics and are apt to negotiate ad nauseam until the Western businessman is worn down.

Conclusion

Countertrade when used responsibly can be an effective tool for increasing the exports and the employment levels in Western countries, and for penetrating the EE markets. Much uncertainty and confusion can be reduced if not eliminated by careful internalization of the countertrade process or by careful selection of specialized trading companies. The spread of international trading companies (ITCs) owned and operated by major U.S. companies and of reduced forms of ITCs, which have been successfully incorporated in the daily operations of many U.S. firms, are steps in the right direction. American firms have much to do to become more competitive in international trade. They can no longer afford to have Mitsubishi Corp. and Mitsui Corp., both Japanese, handle 10% of U.S. exports.

References

1. *Journal of Commerce*. (August 13, 1982):
2. Verzariu Pompiliu. *Countertrade Practices in East Europe, the Soviet Union and China: An Introductory Guide to Business*. Washington, D.C.: U.S. Department of Commerce (1980).

Notes

The author gratefully acknowledges the valuable comments made by two anonymous referees.

11. EVALUATION AND CONTROL OF FOREIGN OPERATIONS

ALAN C. SHAPIRO

Introduction

A major responsibility faced by the financial executives of multinational corporations (MNCs) is to design and implement an evaluation and control system for overseas operations. This system must incorporate the influence of numerous factors which are rarely, if ever, encountered by purely domestic corporations. These factors include exchange-rate changes, differing rates of inflation, currency controls, foreign tax regulations, cross-border transfer pricing, and the differences between subsidiary and parent-company cash flows.

Unfortunately, developing an evaluation and control system is still an art, relying on judgment more than theory. No universal principles have yet appeared to use in designing such a system for domestic operations, much less for foreign operations. Therefore, this article has the modest goal of suggesting a set of reasonable guidelines, based on a mixture of economic theory, behavioral science and empirical evidence, to use in accounting for a variety of international elements while measuring, evaluating, and controlling the performance of foreign operations and their managers.

Measurement and Evaluation

Designing an evaluation system involves four stages. The critical first stage must be to specify its purpose(s). While trivial perhaps, many companies have gotten into trouble by failing to distinguish, for example, between the evaluation of subsidiary performance and managerial performance. As we will see, it is possible for a manager to do an excellent job while his subsidiary is doing very poorly and vice versa.

The next stage involves determining what decisions will be made on the basis of these evaluations and the information necessary to support such decisions. For example, when evaluating managerial performance, it is necessary to separate the effects of uncontrollable variables, such as inflation, from those which are controllable, such as credit extension. Furthermore, capital allocation decisions require very different measures of subsidiary performance than does ensuring the smooth functioning of current operations.

The third stage is the design of a reporting or information system to provide the necessary information or at least a reasonable approximation. Many companies will probably find that their reporting system is inadequate for the purposes specified.

Reprinted from *International Journal of Accounting Education and Research 14*, no. 1, Fall 1978, 83–104.

The final stage involves conducting a cost/benefit analysis of the evaluation system. *This analysis does not have to be quantitative but it should be comprehensive.* Some benefits might be (1) greater control over current operations, (2) more rigorous capital budgeting decisions, and (3) greater awareness of managerial effectiveness. Against these benefits must be weighed the costs which might arise including (1) time and money involved in redesigning the information system, and (2) behavioral problems which might be associated with the new evaluation system. The latter cost might include reduced initiative on the part of local managers who feel they are being overly controlled. This need not occur since one of the goals of an evaluation system should be to provide the information necessary to reward managers for their performance. An evaluation system which does not motivate a manager to work in the company's best interest will not be an effective one, regardless of its other attributes.

Exhibit 1 shows the design of an evaluation system diagrammatically. It is all too evident, however, that many multinational, as well as domestic, corporations have not fully considered this design process. Complaints by subsidiary managers that too much information is being demanded while management at headquarters complains that too much data, but too little good information, are being supplied by the subsidiaries is evidence enough of dissonance between system design and goals.

The main purposes of the evaluation discussed in this paper include

1. To provide a rational basis for global resource allocation;
2. To have an early warning system if something is wrong with current operations;
3. To evaluate the performance of individual managers, and
4. To provide a set of standards that will motivate managers.

Exhibit 1.

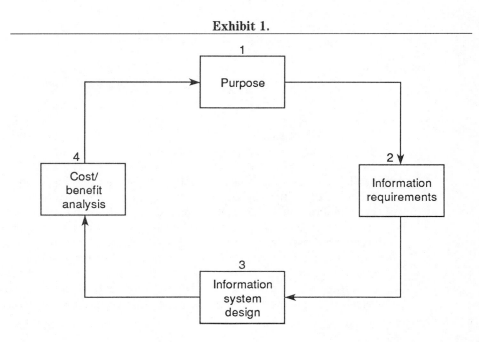

We will now explore each of these purposes in turn and comment on some of the methods currently used by MNCs in achieving these goals.

Resource Allocation

A key decision problem continually faced by multinationals is allocation of capital among their various subsidiaries on a worldwide basis. To aid in this process, companies often use the return on existing investments as a guide. This approach is fine if returns on past investments are *indicative* of *future returns*. There may be problems, though, if proposed investments are not comparable to existing ones or if the relevant returns on past investments are incorrectly measured. Obviously, to the extent that new investments are unrelated to previous ones, using historical subsidiary returns to allocate capital globally will be successful only by chance.

The more interesting, and probably more likely, occurrence in multinational capital budgeting is where potential investments are comparable to past ones, for example, replacement of depreciated assets, but it is difficult to decide on the *relevant selection criteria*. For example, a number of nonfinancial criteria such as market share, sales growth, and stability of production, are often used in comparing investments. Ultimately, though, most firms are interested in the return on their capital employed. A 1970 Conference Board study indicated that some version of *return on investment* (ROI) is the most typical means of measuring the long-run profit performance of foreign subsidiaries.[1] However, there are a number of pitfalls involved in allowing return on past investments to guide this process. These problems fall into two areas: first, problems associated with measuring the correct investment base, and second, difficulties in determining the relevant returns.

The investment base can include:

1. Parent's equity
2. Fixed assets
   a. Gross
   b. Net of depreciation.
3. Working capital
   a. Total
   b. Net of supplier credits
   c. Net of intracompany accounts

In addition, these assets can be valued on an historical or current cost basis.

Fortunately, financial theory pinpoints the *relevant investment* base. It equals the incremental value of all capital required. Thus, the investment must be measured on a *current or replacement cost,* rather than historical cost, basis and should include gross fixed assets as well as total working capital requirements net of external supplier credits. Using historical rather than replacement costs in a period of inflation will understate true capital requirements leading to an unrealized increase in the projected return on investment. The working capital figure should include inventory valued on a current cost basis. Intracompany receivables should be excluded since these accounts cancel on a corporate-wide basis; for instance, increasing one subsidiary's intracompany receivables by a dollar will lead to a dollar reduction in another unit's working capital requirements. Furthermore, these accounts are arbitrary and subject to corporate manipulation.

Measuring the *relevant returns* on foreign operations is a more difficult task. Substantial differences can arise between subsidiary cash flows and cash flows back to the parent firm due to tax regulations and exchange controls, for example. Further, adjustments in transfer prices and intersubsidiary credit arrangements can distort the true profitability of a given investment or subsidiary by shifting profits and liquidity from one unit to another. In addition, fees and royalties are costs to a subsidiary but benefits to the parent company.

Studies by the Conference Board and Business International revealed considerable variation among firms in measuring returns.[2] Measured returns included different combinations of foreign earnings, royalties, fees, dividends, rentals, interest, commissions, and export profits. Some firms included only repatriated profits while others included most or all of these return elements. Some measured only before-tax returns, others only returns after foreign taxes, and still others took into account both U.S. and foreign taxes paid.

The correct approach again relies on economic theory. According to this theory, *the value of an investment is determined by the net present value of incremental cash flows back to the investor*. The key concept here is incremental cash flow. Determining incremental cash flows for a MNC involves taking the difference between worldwide cash flows with the investment and worldwide cash flows in the investment's absence. Thus, all royalties, fees, and overhead allocations paid by a subsidiary should be included in its profit calculation as would be all profits earned by other units due to the subsidiary's existence. This would include profits arising from the adjustment of transfer prices on goods bought from or sold to the subsidiary, as well as all profits on exports to the subsidiary which would not have occurred in the subsidiary's absence. However, any profits on sales or any licensing fees and royalties which would have been earned by another unit of the MNC are not economically attributable to the subsidiary. Further, *the parent MNC should value only those cash flows which are or can be repatriated* since only funds accessible to the parent can be used to pay dividends and interest, amortize the firm's debt, and be reinvested. In addition, since only after-tax cash flows are relevant, it is necessary to determine the taxes that must be paid on foreign-source income and when such payment will occur.

The actual tax on remitted funds will depend on the transfer mechanism used, as well as on the tax regulations involved. These transfer mechanisms include adjustments in transfer prices, dividend flows, fee and royalty charges, overhead allocation, and intracompany loan and credit arrangements.[3] For example, repaying a parent company loan would normally entail no additional withholding taxes.

The cost of carrying intracompany receivables should be excluded from the subsidiary's profit and loss calculation since this cost is offset elsewhere in the corporation by a corresponding reduction in working capital requirements. By the same logic, the subsidiary should be charged for the cost of any intracorporate payables on its balance sheet.

Return on Investment Criteria

A variety of comparisons are possible with a subsidiary's return on investment (ROI) figure. These include comparisons with local competitors, with the firm's subsidiaries and/or competitors on a regional or global basis, and with parent-company operations. In addition, comparisons can be made with the firm's original investment plans. We will now examine the information content of these comparisons to see what decisions are likely to be affected, and how, by the data generated.

Even if caution is exercised, comparisons with local or regional competitors can be meaningless. Different accounting and disclosure requirements leading to different depreciation and earnings reports under similar operating circumstances may not permit comparisons to be made with any degree of certainty. Some foreign firms, for example, do not separate non-recurring income arising out of the sale of assets from operating income. Even if comparisons were limited to home-country competitors, it is usually impossible to determine the actual profitability of local operations because of the high degree of integration and the less-than-arm's length dealings between units of a multinational corporation.

Cross-country comparisons with other affiliates of the multinational corporation are possible, but to what purpose? Ex post, some investments will always be more profitable than others. Thus, in evaluating new investments, *a comparison of historical returns is useful only if these returns are indicative of the relative returns to be expected on future investments in these countries*. Even if expected ROIs differ across countries, it is necessary to consider the element of risk as well. Certain low risk-low return investments may well be preferable to some high risk-high return investments.

Furthermore, as Robbins and Stobaugh point out, multinationals have many *strategic motivations* for going abroad which are not necessarily expressed in ROI calculations.[4] For example, a firm may willingly forego economies of scale in production to achieve greater security of supply by having multiple and redundant production facilities.[5] In addition, operating in several nations may give a firm greater bargaining leverage in dealing with local governments or labor unions. Being multinational may also lower the *firm's risk profile* by reducing its dependence on the state of just one nation's economy. In fact, both Cohen and Rugman have found that earnings variability decreases as foreign activities increase[6] while research by Agmon and Lessard indicates that investors value the international diversification supplied by the multinational firm.[7]

It is true that ROI comparisons across subsidiaries might identify potential problems with current operations. However, as we will see in the next section, more direct methods of receiving early warnings of trouble are possible.

Perhaps the most important comparison that can be made is between *actual results and ex ante budgeted figures*. A postinvestment audit can help a firm learn from its mistakes as well as its successes. In the multinational corporation, where so many additional complexities enter into the capital budgeting decision, it is easier to make errors due to a lack of experience. Reviewing the record of past investments can enable a firm to determine whether there is any consistency in its estimation errors such as generally under- or overestimating the impact of inflation on costs or of devaluations on dollar revenues from foreign sales. Correction factors can then be included in future investment analyses. Even if estimation errors are random, a firm may be able to place limits on the relative magnitudes of these errors and thereby supply useful inputs to an investment siimulation model.

In analyzing actual results, it is necessary to recall the previously mentioned nonfinancial strategic rationale that may have prompted the original investment. Otherwise, an investment undertaken for one reason may be judged on the basis of different criteria resulting in a misleading comparison.

Evaluation of Current Subsidiary Performance

Frequent monitoring of operations in an uncertain environment is useful to determine whether any tactical or strategic changes are warranted. The appropriate measure(s) to use in controlling foreign operations, though, will vary by company and subsidiary. For marketing-oriented companies, market share, sales growth, or cost/sales dollar may be the most relevant measures. A manufacturing subsidiary may be most concerned about unit production costs, quality control, or the labor turnover rate. Others may find return on assets or a working capital to sales ratio most helpful. The important thing is to use those measures which experience has determined are the key leading indicators as to when an operation is out of control. In evaluating foreign operations, though, it may be necessary to employ different standards than those used in controlling the domestic business.

Inventory turnover may be lower overseas due to the larger inventory stocks required to cope with longer lead times to delivery and more frequent delays in intracompany shipments of goods. Where foreign production occurs, it may be necessary to stockpile additional supplies of imported raw material and components given the possibility of a dock strike, import controls, or some other supply disruption.[8]

Receivables may also be greater abroad, particularly in countries experiencing rapid rates of inflation. During times of inflation, consumers normally prefer to purchase on longer credit terms, expecting to repay their debt with less valuable future money. Furthermore, local credit standards are often more relaxed than in the home market, especially in countries lacking in alternative credit arrangements. To remain competitive, MCCs may feel compelled to loosen their own credit standards. This is not always the best policy, however. The multinational corporation should weigh the profit on incremental credit sales against the additional carrying costs, including devaluation losses and bad debts, associated with an easier credit policy.[9]

Different cost standards are usually necessary for foreign operations due to local value-added requirements (which mandate the use of more expensive local goods and services), import tariffs, government limitation on the choice of production processes, and a frequent inability to lay off or fire workers. In the latter case, labor becomes a fixed rather than a variable cost.

Most firms find it helpful to design budgets based on explicit assumptions on the internal and external environment. In a foreign environment, with greater uncertainty, *flexible budgeting* will probably be even more useful than it is domestically. Flexible budgeting involves computing alternative budgets based on different projections of the future rate of inflation, exchange rate changes, wage settlements, and so forth.

It is obviously impossible to develop a different budget for each potential future scenario. Instead, a limited number of the most likely scenarios should be selected for further study. If the firm selects these scenarios carefully, it should have an advantage in coping with foreseeable changes in its operating environment. Furthermore, these alternative budgets will provide a firm with a more reasonable and reliable basis for evaluating the performance of its overseas managers. This is the subject of the next section.

Evaluating Managerial Performance

The standards used to evaluate managers will also serve to motivate them. A key goal, therefore, in designing a management evaluation system is to ensure that the resulting managerial motivation will be congruent with overall corporate objectives. A good strategy which managers are not motivated to follow will be of little value. Thus, it is necessary to anticipate the likely response of a rational manager to a particular set of evaluation criteria.

For example, manangers evaluated on the basis of current earnings will likely emphasize short-run profits to the detriment of longer-term profitability. This is particularly true if executives are frequently transferred, enabling them to escape the long-run consequences of their actions. These actions might include reducing advertising and maintenance, cutting back on research and development (R&D) expenditures, and investing less money on employee training. Managers judged according to return on investment will also concentrate on short-run profits. Furthermore, they will likely be slower to replace used equipment, particularly during a period of rapid inflation, even when economically justifiable. This is both because new investments will increase the investment base and also because ROI measured on an historical cost basis will be greater than ROI on a replacement cost basis. If return on equity is used as the measure of performance, managers will have an incentive to substitute local debt for retained earnings and parent-company equity. The effect of this will be to increase the MNC's worldwide debt ratio causing a deterioration in the parent company's credit rating and an increase in its cost of capital.

Consistent with the goal of properly motivating employees is the principle that *a manager's performance should be judged on the basis of results in those areas over which he has control.* Assigning responsibility without authority will lead to frustrated and disgruntled employees. Furthermore, it is unreasonable, as well as dysfunctional, to reward or penalize a manager for the impact of economic events beyond his control. Thus, headquarters must carefully distinguish between managerial performance and subsidiary performance.

As noted earlier, *a subsidiary can be doing quite well despite the poor performance of its management* and vice versa. For example, during a time of rapid inflation, a subsidiary selling to local customers will show a proportional increase in its dollar profitability. Poor management will just hold down the increase in profits. After the inevitable devaluation, though, dollar profitability will invariably decline even with good management in control. Furthermore, a consistently poor profit performance by a manager may simply be evidence of a past mistake in approving the original investment.

Rather than evaluate managerial performance on the basis of a subsidiary's profitability or ROI which are subject to uncontrollable events, it would be more useful to compare *actual results* with the *budgeted figures*. Revenue and cost variances can then be examined to determine whether these were likely to have been caused by external economic factors (such as inflation or devaluation), by corporate policy shifts (such as transfer price adjustments), or by managerial decisions (a new product strategy).

The keys to this analysis are the explicit assumptions which are incorporated in the budget and the knowledge of how changes in these assumptions are likely to affect the budgeted numbers. Exhibit 2 illustrates the likely impact of exchange rate changes. As the exhibit points out, the main factors which determine this impact

Exhibit 2
CHARACTERISTIC ECONOMIC EFFECTS OF EXCHANGE RATE CHANGES ON MNCs

Cash Flow Categories	Relevant Economic Factors	Devaluation Impact	Revaluation Impact
Revenue		Parent-currency revenue impact	Parent-currency revenue impact
Export sales	Price-sensitive demand	Increase (+ +)	Decrease (− −)
	Price insensitive demand	Slight increase (+)	Slight decrease (−)
Local sales	Weak prior import competition	Sharp decline (− −)	Increase (+) Slight increase
	Strong prior import competition	Decrease (−) (less than devaluation %)	
		Parent-currency cost impact	Parent-currency cost impact
Costs			
Domestic inputs	Low import content	Decrease (− −)	Increase (+ +)
	High import content/inputs used in export or import competing sectors	Slight decrease (−)	Slight increase (−)
Imported inputs	Small local market	Remain the same (0)	Remain the same (0)
	Large local market	Slight decrease (−)	Slight increase (+)
Depreciation		Cash-flow impact	Cash-flow impact
Fixed assets	No asset valuation adjustment	Decrease by devaluation % (− −)	Increase by revaluation % (+ +)
	Asset valuation adjustment	Decrease (−)	Increase (+)

Note: To interpret the above chart, and taking the impact of a devaluation on local demand as an example, it is assumed that if import competition is weak, local prices will climb slightly, if at all; in such a case there would be a sharp contraction in parent-company revenue. If imports generate strong competition, local-currency prices are expected to increase, although not to the full extent of the devaluation; in this instance only a moderate decline in parent-company revenue would be registered.

are the sector of the economy in which a firm is operating (export, domestic import-competing, domestic nonimport-competing) and the source of its inputs (imports, domestic traded goods and services, domestic nontraded goods and services).

By including allowances for training programs, research and development, and other vital functions in the budget, the natural tendency to neglect these areas can be reduced. However, it is necessary to consider other, less tangible, factors as well when evaluating performance.

A profit-oriented manager may allow relations with the host country to deteriorate. A study by Negandhi and Baliga indicates that, in contrast to the typical American MNC'S concentration on profits, European and Japanese multinationals emphasize cultivating and maintaining harmonious relations with host government officials and others in the local environment.[10] Given the difficulties facing multinationals abroad, qualitative determinants of long-run profitability and viability are likely to be more important in the future and should be included in any performance evaluation. The inability to objectively measure the state of host country relations is not a reason to ignore it. Ultimately, any performance measure is subjective, even if it is quantitative, since the choice of which measure(s) to stress is a matter of judgment.

The next section deals with three areas of current concern in performance evaluation: transfer pricing, adjusting intracorporate fund flows, and the choice of appropriate exchange rates for internal use.

Transfer pricing. In a decentralized profit center, transfer prices on goods and services (fees and royalties) can be a significant determinant of a manager's performance. Therefore, unless the manager is not held accountable for the influence of transfer prices on his reported profits, he is likely to react in ways which are counterproductive to the organization as a whole. Cases have arisen, for example, where managers selling to subsidiaries which are forced to buy from them behaved as monopolists and attempted to gouge their captive customers. On the other hand, purchasers of goods and services from other units of the MNC may try to act as monopsonists and underpay their suppliers.

Even if a manager wanted to act in the best interests of the corporation, his perspective would be too limited. Thus, individual managers are likely to ignore or be ignorant of the broader legal, tax, and liquidity calculations involved in setting a corporate-wide transfer pricing policy.[11] For these reasons, transfer pricing is too important to be left to subsidiaries. However, budgeted profit requirements for individual subsidiaries should recognize and adjust for the distorting influence of less-than-arm's length transfer prices. In other words, managerial evaluations should be decoupled from the particular transfer prices being used. This can be done by charging managers who are buying goods the marginal cost of production and shipping while managers who are selling goods would be credited with a reasonable profit on their sales. Managers of subsidiaries only producing for sale to other units of the corporation should be evaluated on the basis of their costs of production rather than profits since they have no control over their revenues.

One manufacturing firm which set transfer prices on the basis of cost plus an allocation for overhead and then used these prices for evaluation purposes found that its sales managers were pushing low, rather than high, margin products. Due to their high overhead costs, the high margin products were less profitable to the sales managers than to the company. Further investigation showed that demand for these high margin products was quite elastic and that significant potential profits were being lost due to the transfer pricing strategy in effect.

Decoupling may present problems at times, however. For example, the transfer prices of multinational drug companies are closely monitored worldwide, and this information is shared by a number of governments. Thus, it may be necessary to keep transfer prices at the same level worldwide. Given the low elasticity of demand for many branded pharmaceuticals, these prices are normally set quite high. However, due to competitive circumstances, some individual subsidiaries may be penalized by the necessity to market these drugs at high prices. To sell to these subsidiaries at lower prices, though, would jeopardize the firm's worldwide pricing strategy since other countries would wonder why they had to pay higher prices. These effects would have to be considered to evaluate management performance fairly, particularly when making comparisons across subsidiaries.

Exchange Rates for Evaluation Purposes. Firms must choose the exchange rate(s) to use when setting budgets and evaluating performance.[12] When setting the operating budget, for example, two exchange rates are possible—the actual spot rate at the time or the forecast rate. In addition, if the budget is revised when exchange rate changes occur, the updated rate can be used. In evaluating performance relative to the budget, there are three alternative rates that can be used: the actual rate at the time the budget is set, the projected end-of-period rate, or the actual end-of-period rate. There are, thus, six exchange rate combinations possible.

A study of 200 MNCs, however, revealed that only three budget evaluation combinations were actually used.[13] Half of the firms surveyed used a projected rate of budgeting but measured performance with the end of period rate, 30 percent used a projected rate both for budgeting and performance evaluation, while the remaining 20 percent used the spot rate for budgeting and the end-of-period rate for tracking performance.

In choosing the appropriate combination of budgeting and evaluation rates to use, it is necessary to consider the behavioral consequences involved. If at the one extreme, the budget and evaluation rates assume no exchange rate change (by using the actual beginning-of-period rate for both purposes), then managers will have no incentive to incorporate anticipated exchange rate changes in their decisions. For example, a marketing manager rewarded on the basis of the spot rate prevailing at the date of sale rather than the anticipated rate upon collection of the receivables generated will likely engage in an uneconomical expansion of credit sales. At the other extreme, if exchange rate changes are ignored in the budget, but the end-of-period rate is used for evaluation, the manager will probably behave in an overly risk averse manner since he or she will bear the full consequences of any exchange rate fluctuations. The harmful effects of such a system will likely include "padding" of the budgets as well as decentralized hedging by managers to reduce their perceived risks.

The use of forecast rates at both the budgeting and evaluation stages appear to be the most desirable combination since it excludes unplanned currency fluctuations but recognizes expected fluctuations at the budgeting stage. Clearly this combination will dominate all other combinations which hold managers responsible for unforeseen exchange fluctuations but do not force them to consider likely currency changes at the budgeting stage. This standard seems most fair since the local decision maker receives no blame or credit for anticipated currency fluctuations. It is also most realistic since it serves to make decentralized decision making congruent with corporate-wide goals and information. Lessard and Lorange call these projected rates internal forward rates.[14] One means of constructing these internal forward rates, which may differ considerably from the actual forward rate, is presented by Shapiro and Rutenberg.[15]

If the exchange rate changes dramatically, it may be necessary to adjust the projected rate during the operating cycle. The need for adjustment will depend on the magnitude of these changes as well as the degree of exposed assets and local currency earnings. Most importantly, it will depend on the extent to which operating decisions can be changed in response to a new exchange rate. Lessard and Lorange point out that if decisions are irreversible, then the evaluation rate should not be adjusted.[16] Such a change would violate the principle of insulating operating managers from random currency changes. If decisions are reversible, albeit at a cost, new plans should be drawn with updated rates. However, any change in budget and evaluation rates should apply only for the remainder of the period—the time during which new operating decisions can be made. In all cases, it would appear that updating the projected rates when appropriate is preferable to holding operating managers responsible for actual exchange rate changes whether anticipated or not. Furthermore, adjusting these rates would permit sharing the results of unforeseen developments rather than imposing them on operating units.

Adjusting Intracorporate Fund Flows. The ability to adjust intracorporate fund flows by speeding or slowing payments on intracorporate accounts is a valuable and widely used technique in liquidity and exchange risk management. However, use of this tool, known as leading and lagging, is likely to distort the various working capital ratios of subsidiaries. For example, a subsidiary ordered to extend longer credit terms to another unit will show an increase in its receivables to sales ratio. Furthermore, its interest expenses will increase while its customer's working capital costs will decline. Since leading and lagging is a corporate policy, its effects should not be included in any evaluation of subsidiary management. It would be advisable, of course, to consider these effects when evaluating the financial staff at headquarters.

Motivating Managers. Implicit in the comments in this section is *the idea that these evaluations will serve as inputs for promotion and salary decisions. The connection should be made obvious to managers.* Otherwise, these evaluations become irrelevant data, useful neither for motivational purposes nor for selecting and promoting a highly qualified cadre of international executives.

Managers who feel they are not rewarded (or penalized) for their job performances may put less effort into the work. However, the real damage is the loss of the entreprenurial spirit that appears to be necessary to cope with a rapidly changing environment. The incentive to take risks is encouraged by the existence of significant rewards for success. Without these rewards, a manager's initiative may be severely diminished, perhaps resulting in work as hard as before but only in more traditional areas rather than embarking on new ventures which offer great potential but are risky.

To implement these evaluations, an effective reporting and control system is necessary. This is the subject of the next section.

Reporting and Control Systems

Many multinationals have found it useful and sometimes necessary to require more frequent reporting by their affiliates due to the increased likelihood of problems arising overseas. Different methods of reporting and communications may also be useful, such as a worldwide telex system and more personal visits with headquarters staff both in the field and at the home office.

Choosing an Appropriate Exchange Rate

Almost by definition, multinational firms have transactions in more than one currency. Thus, MNCs face the problem of which exchange rate(s) to use when reporting the results of foreign operations. A number of alternative exchange rates possibilities exist but interviews with a number of MNCs disclose certain distinct preferences.

Multinational corporations appear to use either the end-of-period rate to book all transactions during the period or else a predetermined rate. This predetermined rate is revised only when the actual exchange rate differs from it by more than a given percentage, usually between $2\frac{1}{2}$ and 5 percent. Another possibility, the average rate during the period, is rarely used because of the additional complexity involved. It should be noted, however, that each of these methods could present measurement problems if care is not taken in the application.

The end-of-period rate, for example, could seriously distort actual profitability if a major exchange rate change occurs during the period unless most sales take place at the new exchange rate. Otherwise, if sales are uniformly distributed throughout the period, an average rate could most accurately represent the period's income. On the other hand, use of an average rate is inapporpriate if sales are bunched and a major currency change occurs.

When using a predetermined rate, the limits within which fluctuations are permitted must be set so that changes within these margins will not seriously distort the period's income. Clearly, a firm with a 5 percent profit margin on its sales should not use a predetermined rate with 5 percent fluctuation limits.

Capital goods manufacturers or other firms which usually have only a few large sales during a period should probably use the actual exchange rates at which each transaction took place. The basic criterion then in deciding on which reporting rate to use should be that the approach chosen will not seriously distort the period's actual income.

Centralization versus Decentralization

A key concept in the design of a reporting system is responsiblity reporting. This involves flowing information from each decision area to the manager accountable for the results of these decisions. A general rule of thumb in organizational design appears to be to decentralize responsibility as much as possible. The fewer the linkages between activity areas, the better decentralization will function. However, in the multinational corporation, the interactions among various units is often so great because of tax factors or economies of scale in risk management (to be discussed later), for example, that complete decentralization will be suboptimal.

Some firms have partially decentralized operations by establishing regional headquarters for the different geographical areas of the world. This shortens the lines of communication and enhances the dispersal of geographically-centered information. The more similar business conditions are within, as compared with between, geographical regions, the more valuable regional headquarters are likely to be.

In companies with a dearth of experienced international financial managers, there is an added incentive to centralize decisions. It is often felt that the talents of this limited number of experienced managers can best be utilized at headquarters where fullest advantage can be taken of their knowledge. Working against centralization is the complexity and size of the multinational corporation which makes it difficult, if not impossible, for any headquarters group to completely coordinate financial activities worldwide.

A Conference Board study on the level of corporate involvement in certain key multinational financial decision areas indicated that the wider the perspective required, the more likely it was that a particular decision would be controlled by headquarters.[17] The following are some of the results of the Conference Board study.

Repatriation of Funds. Of the companies surveyed, 85 percent indicated that decisions involving repatriation of funds were made at the corporate level. However, respondents appeared to have little control of the repatriation decision in joint ventures where they were minority partners.

Intersubsidiary Financing. In most companies, either the chief financial executive of the parent company or the treasurer, with the advice of tax counsel, decided on which intracorporate fund flows should take place.

Acquisition of Funds. Of the firms studied, 85 percent indicated that all medium and long-term financing was approved at corporate headquarters. Many firms, though, allowed their subsidiaries much more leeway with regard to short-term financing.

Protection of Assets. Many of the firms questioned did not have any formal plans for asset protection although a number indicated that they were beginning to change toward greater centralization. The advent of FASB 8 has accelerated the centralization of exposure management.[18]

Planning and Control. The responses here were quite varied. The more financially oriented (as opposed to marketing oriented, for example) that firms were, the more likely they were to have a centralized planning and control function.

A more recent study by Stobaugh indicated significant differences in attitudes towards centralization among small (average annual foreign sales of $50 million), medium (average foreign sales of $200 million annually), and large (average of $1 billion in annual foreign sales) multinationals.[19] Small MNCs generally allowed subsidiaries considerable leeway in financial management, perhaps because of the lack of sophistication in international financial management at headquarters. The tendency among medium-sized firms was to try to optimize worldwide results, treating each subsidiary as just one unit in a global system. These firms required very sophisticated control and reporting systems. Large MNCs appeared to reverse the centralization trend somewhat, providing subsidiaries with formal guidelines but allowing them considerable intiative within those guidelines. This was apparently due to a recognized inability to optimize in such a complex system. The author will now examine two particular areas—currency and cash management—where controversy has developed over the optimal degree of headquarters control.

International Cash and Foreign Exchange Risk Management

In the areas of cash and foreign exchange risk management, there are good arguments for both centralization and decentralization. Arguing for centralization is the reasonable assumption that local treasurers want to optimize their own financial and exposure positions, regardless of the overall corporate situation. To a local treasurer, a subsidiary's cash reserves may appear too low while to the corporate treasurer, the subsidiary is holding excess liquidity relative to the corporation's ability to supply liquidity from its worldwide reserves. Similarly, a study by Rodriguez has concluded that *foreign exchange risk aversion increased with decentralization of the financial function.*[20] Local treasurers ignored the possibilities available to the corporation to *trade off positive and negative currency exposure* positions by consolidating exposure worldwide. A further benefit of centralized exposure management is the ability to take advantage of the economies of scale in risk management effect,[21] that is, the fact that the *total variability or risk of a currency exposure portfolio is less than the sum of the individual variabilities of each currency exposure considered in isolation.* This is due to the less-than-perfect positive correlation that exists between the various currencies. Thus, centralization of exchange risk management should reduce the amount of hedging required to achieve a given level of safety. This can be valuable given the high costs of hedging. The company can then select the cheapest option(s) worldwide to hedge its remaining exposure. Tax effects can be crucial at this stage,[22] but only headquarters wil have the required global perspective.

These are all powerful arguments for centralization of cash and currency risk management. Against these benefits, though, must be weighed the loss of local knowledge and the lack of incentive for local managers to take advantage of particular situations with which only they may be familiar. However, this conflict between centralization and decentralization is more apparent than real.

As the section on evaluation noted, the use of internal forward rates can enhance the advantages and suppress the disadvantages of both centralization and decentralization. Similar advantages can be achieved by using internal interest rates. This can be done by providing local managers with interest rates and forward rates which reflect the opportunity costs of money and exposure to the parent corporation. Thus, headquarters can make full use of local knowledge while ensuring that local managers act in the company's best interests. With regard to exchange risk, headquarters, in effect, is offering to *sell insurance* to local managers to cover their exposure. If a manager decides it is cheaper to hedge locally, fine. At least he has taken into consideration the cost of hedging to the corporation.

In setting internal interest rates, the corporate treasurer, in effect, is *acting as a bank,* offering to borrow or lend currencies at given rates. By examining these internal rates, local treasurers will have a greater awareness of the opportunity cost of their idle cash balances as well as an added incentive to act on this information. In many instances, they will prefer to transfer at least part of their cash balances (where permitted) to a central pool in order to earn a greater return. To make pooling of funds work, though, it is essential that managers have access to the central pool whenever they require funds.

Mechanisms of Control

When designing a control system for use overseas, there may be a tendency to use the most sophisticated system available due to the complexity of the problems encountered abroad. Furthermore, since headquarters is not bearing the most of furnishing subsidiary reports, it is likely to demand a good deal of information which is rarely, if ever, used merely on the off chance that it might be needed. However, *a sophisticated and complex system may yield worse results than a simpler, less ambitious system* if local managers are not top caliber or local operations are of small size. A system which is more sophisticated than the managers it is supposed to control can lead to suspicions, frustration, and, ultimately, to sabotage attempts. Where operations are small, a complex reporting system can become burdensome and take managers away from their primary function which is to manage.

According to Zenoff and Zwick, a new and relatively sophisticated management group took control of Singer Corp. in the early 1960s. Despite their desire to bring more sophistication to Singer's international business, though, the new management felt that the quality of many of their field managers precluded the adoption of a complex system of performance standards and evaluation criteria. Instead, they opted for a system of simple standards and reports that were comprehensible and provided some degree of control.[23] Over time, a simple system can evolve into a successful sophisticated system. However, local managers must understand the system. Otherwise, they will defeat it, either deliberately or inadvertently.

Even with sophisticated managers, however, a relatively small operation may not warrant the reporting requirements and elaborate control mechanism of a larger affiliate. *The value of gathering additional information must be balanced against its cost in terms of taking up scarce management time.* A small company may not have the resources to hire additional personnel to fill out reports, and thus the job is left to the existing managers, adding to their workload.

A possible solution is to require fewer reports from smaller subsidiaries while at the same time monitoring several key performance indicators. As long as these indicators remain within bounds, a subsidiary is allowed considerable freedom. If problems appear, then, additional controls can be imposed. In effect, this is reporting and control by exception. The danger here is that these additional controls may be perceived as punishment and reacted to accordingly. Tact and a truly helpful attitude will be necessary to convince a manager that these new reports and controls are designed to help him do a better job.

A zero-base information system would aid in this process of reducing information requirements. This would involve an audit of all the information which is currently being provided and the uses of that information. Unless information is being used in decision making, it should be discarded.

Traveling teams of auditors are another device used to facilitate communications and control with the multinational corporation. Quite often, though, it is difficult to find qualified people willing to be constantly on the go, living out of suitcases. Furthermore, these teams may be perceived as spies and met with hostility, unless they demonstrate their helpfulness to the local managers. The attitudes of the team members will be dependent on whether headquarters actually is using them as spies or instead intends for them the more constructive role of assistants and consultants to managers in the field.

Feedback is an important element in any evaluation and control system. Local managers, sophisticated or not, from large or small operations, are likely to complain about overreporting and overcontrol if they feel that headquarters demands information without providing a commensurate amount of feedback. Since the reporting system is normally tailored to the needs of headquarters alone, preparing reports is seen as a waste of time for subsidiary management. Redesigning the reporting system so that it provides more useful information to subsidiary management along with more feedback from headquarters will increase the incentive of local management to cooperate with headquarters.

Sometimes only negative feedback is received. According to some managers, "I only hear from headquarters when I am doing poorly, never when I am doing well." This lack of symmetry is difficult to understand since praise can be an equally effective motivating force. After all, almost everyone likes to feel that his or her work is recognized and appreciated.

Many of the problems referred to in this paper are caused by a lack of communications between headquarters and its subsidiaries. One suggested approach to facilitate headquarters-subsidiary communications is to require all top headquarters staff personnel to spend at least two years in the field becoming acquainted with the problems faced by subsidiaries. At the same time, subsidiary managers would be required to spend time at headquarters to gain a broader perspective of the corporation's activities.

Conclusions

As stated at the beginning of this paper, there is no set of scientific principles that can guarantee the development of a successful evaluation and control system. However, a truly geocentric system, to use Perlmutter's terminology,[24] should encourage a free flow of ideas and information worldwide. Headquarters must avoid the temptation of trying to overcontrol field operations or else run the risk of stifling local initiative. In addition, local managers should have the opportunity to explain their operating results and seek help for their problems. The lack of such a safety mechanism will cause the kinds of problems associated with a too rigid adherence to strictly numerical criteria. In the final analysis, it appears that in the multinational corporation, as in any social institution, a system characterized by mutual understanding works best.

Notes _____

1. Irene W. Meister, *Managing the International Financial Function* (New York: The Conference Board, 1970).
2. Ibid., and Business International Corporation, "Evaluating Foreign Operations: The Appropriate Rates for Comparing Results with Budgets," *Business International Money Report,* May 20, 1977, p. 154.
3. David P. Rutenberg, "Maneuvering Liquid Assets in a Multinational Corporation," *Management Science,* June 1970, p. 671.
4. Sidney M. Robbins and Robert B. Stobaugh, *Money in the Multinational Enterprise* (New York: Basic Books, 1973).
5. David P. Rutenberg and Ram Rao, "Robust Plant Location for the Stochastic World of a Multi-National Manufacturer," GSIA Working Paper, Carnegie-Mellon University, 1973.
6. Benjamin I. Cohen, *Multinational Firms and Asian Exports* (New Haven, Conn.: Yale University Press, 1975). and Alan M. Rugman, "Risk Reduction by International Diversification," *Journal of the International Business Studies,* Fall—Winter 1976, p. 75.
7. Tamir Agmon and Donald R. Lessard, "Invester Recognition of Corporate International Diversification," *Journal of Finance,* September 1977.
8. Alan C. Shapiro, Howard C. Kunreuther, and Pascal E. Lang, "Planning Horizons for Inventory Stockpiling," University of Pennsylvania Working Paper, 1977.
9. Alan C. Shapiro, "Optimal Inventory and Credit-Granting Strategies under Inflation and Devaluation," *Journal of Financial and Quantitative Analysis,* January 1973, p. 37.
10. Anant R. Negandhi and B. R. Baliga, "Quest for Survival and Growth: A Study of American, European, and Japanese Multinational Corporations," International Institute of Mangement Working Paper, 1976.
11. Edgar M. Barrett, "Case of the Tangled Transfer Price," *Harvard Business Review,* May—June 1977, p. 20, and Rutenberg, "Liquid Assets," p. 671.
12. Donald R. Lessard and Peter Lorange, "Currency Changes and Management Control: Resolving the Centralization/Decentralization Dilemma," *Accounting Review,* July 1977, p. 628.
13. Business International Corporation, "Evaluating Foreign Operations," p. 154.
14. Lessard and Lorange, "Currency Changes," p. 628.
15. Alan C. Shapiro and David P. Rutenberg, "When to Hedge Against Devaluation," *Management Science,* August 1974, p. 1514.
16. Lessard and Lorange, "Currency Changes," p. 628.
17. Meister, *Financial Function.*

18. Financial Accounting Standards Board, "Accounting for the Translation of Foreign Currency Transactions and Foreign Currency Financial Statements," Statement of Financial Accounting Standards No. 8 (Stamford, Conn.: FASB, 1975).
19. Robert B. Stobaugh, "Financing Foreign Subsidiaries of U.S.-Controlled Multinational Enterprises," *Journal of International Business Studies,* Summer 1970, p. 43.
20. Rita M. Rodriguez, "Management of Foreign Exchange Risk in the U.S. Multinationals," *Journal of Financial and Quantitative Analysis,* November 1974, p. 849.
21. Harry Markowitz, "Portfolio Selection," *Journal of Finance,* March 1952, p. 89.
22. Alan C. Shapiro and David P. Rutenberg, "Managing Exchange Risks in a Floating World," *Financial Management,* Summer 1976, p. 48.
23. David B. Zenoff and Jack Zwick, *International Financial Management* (Englewood Cliffs, N.J.: Prentice Hall, 1969), p. 457.
24. Howard V. Perlmutter, "The Tortuous Evolution of the Multinational Corporation," *Columbia Journal of World Business,* January–February 1969.

ANNOTATED BIBLIOGRAPHY

NOTE: The annotated bibliography in this section is organized into five major sections to allow a more focused literature search.

I. Multinational Corporation and Its Environment _____

Adler, Michael, and Bernard Dumas. "Exposure to Currency Risk: Definition and Measurement." *Financial Management,* 13 (Summer 1984): 41–50.

This article defines and differentiates between exposure and currency risk as they pertain to the prices of financial and physical assets. The Appendix demonstrates how hedging the amount of exposure can minimize the variance of the hedged asset and cause the residual value to be independent of exchange rates. The practical implications of this method are discussed.

Boddewyn, Jean J. "Theories of Foreign Direct Investment and Divestment: A Classificatory Note." *Management International Review,* 25 (1985); 57–65.

This article provides a comprehensive review of theories of foreign direct investment and divestment. The author suggests that although none of these theories singlehandedly explains why foreign investment or divestment occurs, an integration of the three theories into one simple pedagogical model would eliminate some of the weaknesses of each.

Collins, J. Markham, and William S. Sekely. "The Relationship of Headquarters Country and Industry Classification to Financial Structures." *Financial Management,* 12 (Autumn 1983): 45–51.

The authors conducted a study using two-way analysis of variance to determine which factors affect capital structure of a firm. Evidence showed the location (country) was more important than the industry. Even when economic factors such as tax-rate, ROI, and size were included, the same relationships were maintained. Therefore, the authors conclude that country norms are institutionally or culturally based, rather than economically based.

Eaker, Mark R. "Denomination Decision for Multinational Transactions." *Financial Management,* 9 (Autumn 1980): 23–29.

This article examines the denomination decision within a multinational corporation and how that decision can affect cash flow and taxes. A decision rule is developed and a simulation performed to demonstrate the benefits it can have for a firm.

Edwards, Franklin R. "Financial Institutions and Regulation in the 21st Century: After the Crash?" *Columbia Journal of World Business,* 17 (Spring 1982): 82–87.

Economic, technological, and regulatory changes are bringing about a structural revolution in financial markets. The primary goals of regulation should be to maintain effective monetary control and sound financial structure. The author discusses current structural changes, their implications, and makes recommendations for future long-term policies.

Errunza, Vihang R., and Lemma W. Senbet. "The Effects of International Operations on the Market Value of the Firm: Theory and Evidence." *The Journal of Finance,* 36 (May 1981): 401–417.

This article examines the presence of monopoly rents connected with international operations resulting from the flaws in the product, factor, and financial markets, and the dissimilarities between international taxation factors. Empirical evidence, based on multiple partial correlation coefficient methods, shows that there is a positive correlation between the present amount of international involvement and excess market value.

Fielske, Norman S. "Dollar Appreciation and U.S. Import Prices." *New England Economic Review* (November-December 1985): 49–54.

The sharp increase in the dollar's value between 1980 and 1984 benefitted U.S. consumers, but increased foreign price competition of U.S. producers. The author highlights several specific aspects of this occurrence, including country-by-country (Canada, Germany, and Japan) and product-by-product (textiles, apparel, nonrubber footwear, steel, and passenger cars) analyses of import price behavior. It was found that these prices perceived as threatening imports behaved in the same way as prices paid for "non-threatening" products.

Hitzenberger, Robert H., and Jacques Rolfo. "An International Study of Tax Effects on Government Bonds." *The Journal of Finance,* 39 (March 1984): 1–22.

This article analyzes the effect taxes have on the relative pricing of fixed-income securities in Germany, Japan, the U.K., and the U.S. Evidence shows that coupon bonds by themselves are insufficient to span time-dated claims or ordinary income, capital gains, and non-taxable wealth. It was found that coupon-bond pricing is consistent with the tax status of major government debt holders in each country. These findings concurred with earlier studies performed by Skelton (1979) and Trzcinka (1982).

Hoffman, Dennis L., and Don E. Schlagenhauf. "Real Interest Rates, Anticipated Inflation, and Unanticipated Money: A Multi-country Study." *The Review of Economics and Statistics,* 67 (May 1985): 284–296.

This article analyzes the behavior of real interest rate in Canada, West Germany, the U.S., and the U.K., relating it to monetary growth shocks, and expected inflation and inflation variance. Results show that anticipated inflation increases drive interest rates downward, unanticipated money shocks relate to real interest, but inflation variance does little to explain real interest rates. These findings are compared to previous studies.

Jacque, Laurent L., and Peter Lorange. "Hyperinflation and Global Strategic Management." *Columbia Journal of World Business,* 19 (Summer 1984): 68–75.

> *Despite the fact that hyperinflation is short-lived and changeable, most MNCs automatically assign such countries a high risk factor, thereby providing a narrow-minded basis for decision-making. This need not occur if one realizes the extent to which hyperinflation distorts the foreign exchange and factor/goods market. The article develops a normative framework by which to analyze potential opportunities and existing operations.*

Kennedy, John Whitcomb. "Risk Assessment for U.S. Affiliates Based in Less Developed Countries." *Columbia Journal of World Business,* 19 (Summer 1984): 76–79.

> *Newly industrialized nations offer considerable opportunities for multinational corporations. Careful risk assessment and strategic planning greatly reduce the chances of failure. The author demonstrates how techniques for identifying exchange risk can allow MNCs to decrease their economic exposure and capitalize on new growth.*

Rugman, Alan M. "Internalization Theory and Corporate International Finance." *California Management Review* 23 (Winter 1980): 73–79.

> *This article analyzes certain aspects of corporate international finance; more specifically, international diversification, transfer pricing, and the financial structure of multinational firms in relation to the concept of internalization. Internalization, the process by which firms acquire the advantages to succeed in a less than perfect market, is only a theoretical supposition. Further empirical evidence is needed to confirm it.*

Scott, Bruce R. "OPEC, the American Scapegoat." *Harvard Business Review,* 59 (January-February 1981): 6–30.

> *Contrary to popular belief, OPEC is not the price-fixing, conspiratorial cartel U.S. government officials would have us to believe. Nor is it responsible for inflation, the recession, and other economic problems. The author argues that deficit spending for imports and the increased demand for oil have led to these financial difficulties. The U.S. needs to decrease consumption and acknowledge the need for energy interdependence.*

Wu, Friedrich W. "External Borrowing and Foreign Aid in Post-Mao China's International Economic Policy: Data and Observations." *Columbia Journal of World Business,* 19 (Fall 1984): 53–61.

> *Since 1978, when the "open-door" policy began, People's Republic of China has purposefully sought expansion of transnational economic relations with nations across the globe. The author has amassed historical and current data on China's external*

borrowing and economic assistance situations. The implications of these observations are discussed.

II. Foreign Exchange Risk Management —————————

Akhtar, M. A., and Bluford H. Putnam. "Money Demand and Foreign Exchange Risk: The German Case, 1972–1976." *The Journal of Finance,* 35 (June 1980): 787–794.

Here the authors use the example of the German economy to empirically test several theories in support of the argument that foreign exchange risk uncertainty influences the demand for money. Their evidence shows that while income and interest rate variables are more influential, foreign exchange risk does effect real money balances. Therefore it should be considered when formulating the money demand function.

Bergstrand, Jeffrey H. "Money, Interest Rates, and Foreign Exchange Rates as Indicators for Monetary Policy." *New England Economic Review* (November-December 1985): 3–13.

This article analyzes the significance of fluctuations in a monetary aggregate, an interest rate, and the trade-weighted average foreign exchange rate for predicting shifts in income and the general price level in several countries. Evidence demonstrates that neither of the three produce consistent results when used alone. However, these combined with other information variables should be utilized when setting domestic monetary policies.

Choudhri, Ehsan U., and Levis A. Kochin. "The Exchange Rate and the International Transmission of Business Cycle Disturbances." *Journal of Money, Credit and Banking,* 12 (November 1980): 565–574.

The authors use the Great Depression to demonstrate that, contrary to popular belief, a flexible exchange rate is helpful in protecting a country from foreign business cycle disturbances. In examining eight small European countries during that time, the authors found that those with flexible exchange rates were virtually unaffected by the Depression. Those with fixed rates were severely affected. Finally, the countries that allowed their exchange rates to float during this time were less adversely affected than the fixed-exchange-rate countries.

Cornell, Bradford. "Inflation, Relative Price Changes, and Exchange Risk." *Financial Management,* 9 (Autumn 1980); 30–34.

Many claim that firms operating in a world economy with floating exchange rates must cope with exchange risk. This author claims that there is no need to consider exchange risk once one has taken account of inflation and relative price risk. The implication is that both international and domestic firms face the same difficulties and require similar strategies in this regard.

Cushman, David O. "Real Exchange Rate Risk, Expectations, and The Level of Direct Investment." *The Review of Economics and Statistics,* 67 (May 1985): 297–308.

> *This article examines four direct investment models in terms of assorted inter-relations between foreign and domestic production. Evidence supports the original hypothesis that as a result of risk, MNCs reduce foreign exports but counter-balance that by expanding foreign capital input and production.*

Dince, Robert R., and Peter N. Umoh. "Foreign Exchange Risk and The Portfolio Approach: An Example From West Africa." *Columbia Journal of World Business,* 16 (Spring 1981): 24–29.

> *This paper examines the advantages and disadvantages of using the mean/variance (Sharpe) portfolio approach as a means of reducing risk exposure. Assumed is that the investing multi-national corporation operates under foreign exchange restrictions and has limited hedging capabilities. Also assumed is a regional economic community that has freely convertible local currencies. An example of an U.S. MNC conducting business in the Economic Community of West African States (ECOWAS) demonstrates this method.*

Dufey, Gunter, and Rolf Mirus. "Forecasting Foreign Exchange Rates: A Pedagogical Note." *Columbia Journal of World Business,* 16 (Summer 1981): 53–61.

> *This article examines several exchange rate forecasting methods and illustrates how each of them fails to furnish superior returns, properly measured.*

————, and S. L. Srinivasulu. "The Case for Corporate Management of Foreign Exchange Risk." *Financial Management,* 12 (Winter 1983): 54–62.

> *This paper answers six common arguments against corporate management of foreign exchange risk. The arguments basically state that if there is a problem of foreign exchange risk, corporations should not hedge these risks. The authors maintain that there is a case for corporate management of foreign exchange risk. Whether or not it can succeed is a matter for later discussion.*

Fielcke, Norman S. "The Rise of the Foreign Currency Futures Market." *New England Economic Review* (March-April 1985): 38–47.

> *This article discusses the foreign currency futures market, its characteristics, the reasons behind its growth, and how it contrasts with the forward market in terms of transaction type and cost.*

Giddy, Ian H. "Measuring the World Foreign Exchange Market." *Columbia Journal of World Business,* 14 (Winter 1979): 36–48.

> *Based on personal interviews, published and unpublished data, Giddy attempts to estimate worldwide trading volume of foreign exchange, its make-up, and the un-*

derlying determinants of volume. The author concludes that the phenomenal growth of the world foreign exchange markets in recent years will stabilize as the market reaches maturity.

Jacque, Laurent L. "Management of Foreign Exchange Risk: A Review Article." *Journal of International Business Studies,* 12 (Spring/Summer 1981): 81–101.

This article reviews recent literature on Foreign Exchange Risk Management. The author examines forecasting and measuring exposure of exchange risk from a normative perspective and reviews existing decision models for dealing with same. Further research areas are recommended.

Khoury, Sarkis J. "Stability of Predictors and the Forecasting of Foreign Exchange Rates." *Journal of Business Research,* 14 (February 1986): 37–46.

This study reviews the pitfalls and merits of existing foreign exchange rate fore-casting approaches, and introduces a new element to the model: the stability of predictors. The findings show that stability variables do improve the forecasting ability of an econo-metrically based model. The model developed here is shown to be transferable from one currency to another.

Longworth, David. "Testing the Efficiency of the Canadian-U.S. Exchange Market Under the Assumption of No Risk Premium." *The Journal of Finance,* 36 (March 1981): 43–49.

This article analyzes the efficiency of the Canadian-U.S. exchange market from July 1970 to December 1978, as well as subperiods within that time frame, using two semi-strong-form tests. These tests disclose the possible predictive ability of the lagged spot rate. The stronger statistical tests reject the dual null hypothesis of an efficient exchange market and no risk premium through October of 1976, but not for the period as a whole. In general, the current spot rate was better than the current forward rate in predicting the future spot rate.

Madura, Jeff, and E. Joe Nosari. "Utilizing Currency Portfolios to Mitigate Exchange Rate Risk." *Columbia Journal of World Business,* 19 (Spring 1984): 96–99.

This article evaluates exchange rate factors for eight major currencies from 1970 to 1983. While it is impossible to predict currency standard deviations and correlations exactly, it is realistically attainable to assess each currency characteristic relative to other currencies. The authors suggest means by which to construct a currency portfolio, thereby decreasing exchange rate risk.

Maldonado, Rita, and Anthony Sauders. "Foreign Exchange Futures and the Law of One Price." *Financial Management,* 12 (Spring 1983): 19–23.

This article examines U.S. multinational stocks being traded on both the New York and London exchanges, in order to determine if the Law of One Price is true for homogeneous financial assets which are traded at the same time in different countries. The authors found that in order for investment restrictions to be effective enough to violate LOP, both foreign and domestic investors must be regulated.

Maxwell, Charles, and Nicolas Gressis. "Parity-Based Valuation of Foreign Exchange Options." *Management International Review,* 26 (1986): 45–55.

This paper examines four of the six foreign currencies being traded on the Philadelphia Stock Exchange through issuance of foreign currency options contracts. This study finds little evidence of informational redundancy between this and companion markets. It does, however, find evidence of possibly mis-priced options contracts, thereby lending support to the existence of arbitrage profits.

Meese, Richard A., and Kenneth J. Singleton. "On Unit Roots and The Empirical Modeling of Exchange Rates." *The Journal of Finance,* 37 (September 1982): 1029–1035.

The authors conducted tests to determine if unit roots are present in the auto regressive representations of spot and forward exchange rates logarithms. They discuss the tests for unit roots and provide their results for forward and spot dollar exchange rates with three additional currencies. These results offer an explanation for some of the conflicting conclusions seen in recent papers on the foreign exchange market. Additional implications are also discussed.

Raker, Mark R., and Joan Lenowitz. "Multinational Borrowing Decisions and the Empirical Exchange Rate Evidence." *Management International Review,* 26 (1986): 24–32.

Empirical evidence provides a strategy for determining the currency of denomination for the borrowing decisions of multinational corporations. Effects are shown of a five-year implementation period. Evidence suggests that this strategy will reduce borrowing costs but increase risk.

Soenen, Luc A., "The Optimal Currency Cocktail: A Tool for Strategic Foreign Exchange Management, "*Management International Review,* 25 (1985): 12–22.

The move to a multi-currency reserve system has greatly increased the volatility of exchange rate markets. This paper shows how the optimal currency cocktail for an international company can be derived and how to use it as a tool for defining a strategy for foreign exchange risk management. An example of a U.S. MNC headquartered in Europe illustrates the approach.

Srinivasulu, S. L., "Strategic Response to Foreign Exchange Risks," *Columbia Journal of World Business,* 16 (Spring 1981): 13–23.

The author emphasizes the importance of foreign exchange risk analysis, using Volkswagen as an example. Translation, transaction, and economic exposures are discussed, as well as strategies to withstand these risks. Marketing, financial, and production strategies of Volkswagen for 1970 and 1980 are also examined. A guideline for MNC strategy concludes the article.

Wihlborg, Clas., "The Effectiveness of Exchange Controls on Financial Capital Flows: A Framework For Analysis," *Columbia Journal of World Business,* 17 (Winter 1982): 3–10.

This article examines the costs and effectiveness of exchange controls, and analyzes their effects on firms in terms of fixed, temporary, and marginal costs of acquiring a satisfactory portfolio. Also, the effects on the loanable funds market are investigated. Finally, several possible control effectiveness tests are considered.

III. Foreign Investment Decision _____

Anderson, Erin, and Hubert Gatignon, "Modes of Foreign Entry: A Transaction Cost Analysis and Propositions, " *Journal of International Business Studies,* 17 (Fall 1986): 1–26.

The objective of this paper is to provide a transaction cost framework for investigating the entry mode decision. The paper illustrates the feasibility of clustering 17 modes according to degree of control. The paper then proposes that the most efficient mode is a tradeoff between control and the cost of resource commitment. It also advances a number of testable propositions delineating the circumstances under which each mode maximizes long-term efficiency.

Brewer, Thomas L. "Political Risk Assessment for Foreign Direct Investment Decisions: Better Methods for Better Results." *Columbia Journal of World Business,* 16 (Spring 1981): 5–11.

The author gives three methods of improving political risk assessment. First, types and sources of risks should be explicitly defined, for which several political models are offered as aids. Second, due to the complexity of political analysis, a wide variety of theoretical frameworks should be used. Finally, capital budgeting calculations should be developed such that they consider the results of political risk assessment.

Burton, F. N., and H. Inoue. "An Appraisal of the Early-Warning Indicators of Sovereign Loan Default in Country Risk Evaluation Systems." *Management International Review,* 25 (1985): 45–56.

This article analyzes the value of country risk evaluators held in common by American, European, and Japanese international banks as set forth in a survey. The results display inadequate theoretical and empirical bases for most economic aspects and virtually no quantification of political risk.

Calvet, A. Louis. "A Synthesis of Foreign Direct Investment Theories of the Multinational Firm." *Journal of International Business Studies,* 12 (Spring/Summer 1981): 43–59.

This article classifies several foreign direct investment theories since Kindleberger's market imperfections paradigm. Second, the appropriability, internalization, and diversification theories are examined. Finally, the MNE is viewed within a markets and hierarchies framework. Areas for further research are suggested.

Elsaid, Hussein H., and M. S. El-Hennawi. "Foreign Investment in LDCs: Egypt." *California Management Review,* 24 (Summer 1982): 85–91.

This article examines foreign investment climate in Egypt from the 1960s to present and how it has improved since the early 1970s. When surveyed, over a hundred Fortune 500 firms ranked political variables as being important in influencing investment decisions. Implications of these findings and further suggestions for reform in Egypt are discussed.

Eun, Cheol S., and S. Janakiramanan. "A Model of International Asset Pricing With a Constraint on the Foreign Equity Ownership." *The Journal of Finance,* 41 (September 1986): 897–914.

This paper derives a closed-form valuation model in a two-country world in which the domestic investors are constrained to own a fraction of the number of shares outstanding of the foreign firms. The authors derive optimal portfolio choices and equilibrium asset pricing relationships within the constraints of the model.

Finnerty, Joseph E., James E. Owers, and Ronald C. Rogers. "The Valuation Impact of Joint Ventures." *Management International Review,* 26 (1986): 14–26.

This article discusses the potential value and the problems associated with joint ventures. A study of domestic and international joint ventures provides little evidence that international joint ventures provide any valuable diversification benefits from the shareholder's short-term perspective.

Juhl, Paulgeorg. "Economically Rational Design of Developing Countries' Expropriation Policies Toward Foreign Investment." *Management International Review, 25 (1985): 44–52.*

Foreign direct investment expropriations in LDCs supposedly have a detrimental effect on future foreign investment inflows. However, contrary to this assumption, most LDCs pursue rational economic policies with regard to volume of investment. The main detrimental consequence seems to be loss of potential jobs.

Little, Jane Sneddon. "Foreign Direct Investment in New England." *New England Economic Review* (March-April 1985): 48–57.

Foreign investment in the U.S. has become especially important in New England. This article looks at how foreign business has affected New England. It has apparently eased the transition from a manufacturing to a high-technology area by keeping unemployment down and increasing New England's strength in high-tech industries.

Mantell, Edmund H. "Accounting for Sources of Risk in International Portfolio Diversification." *Journal of Business Research,* 14 (June 1986): 225–236.

The objective of this paper is to develop an analytic method of disentangling the distinct components of the risk to a U.S. investor of his holdings of foreign assets. The paper suggests practical application of the analytical results in the context of portfolio optimization.

Stern, Richard. "Insurance for Third World Currency Inconvertibility Protection." *Harvard Business Review,* 60 (May-June 1982); 62–64.

A great number of MNCs need to protect their investments in developing countries from delays in converting currencies, adjustments in foreign exchange laws and controls, and other risks involved. The author demonstrates the benefits of inconvertibility insurance, which is offered by the Overseas Private Investment Corporation (OPIC), and certain private insurers. The history of OPIC and how it works is also discussed.

Stoever, William A. "Endowments, Priorities, and Policies: An Analytical Scheme For The Formulation of Developing Country Policy Toward Foreign Investment." *Columbia Journal of World Business,* 17 (Fall 1982): 3–15.

In dealing with multinational corporations and their foreign investment policies, many less-developed host countries have paid too high a price for the limited benefits they have received. The author provides an analysis method by which LDC governments can rationally develop a policy which will enable them to evaluate foreign investment proposals in terms of endowments, priorities, and policies.

————. "LDC Governments: Takeovers and Renegotiations of Foreign Investments." *California Management Review,* 22 (Winter 1979): 5–14.

An examination of eight case studies of full and partial takeovers demonstrate how host countries have erred in past negotiations. These errors, a result of poor management, include ideological singlemindedness, wrong or incomplete information, overcentralized decision-making, and the pursuit of political goals at the expense of economic goals. The author makes several suggestions for improvements.

Wells, Louis T., Jr. "Foreign Investment from the Third World: The Experience of Chinese Firms from Hong Kong." *Columbia Journal of World Business* (Spring 1978): 39–49.

The author attempts to explain and elaborate the Chinese-owned Hong Kong firms' leading position in foreign investment in developing countries, which was once the domain of industrialized nations. The investment strategies, the competitive edge of Hong Kong, as well as the complementary skills that contribute to the facts, are studied. These are carried over in lessons that will be useful in looking at the foreign activities of firms from other developing countries besides Hong Kong.

IV. Financing Decision _____

Abrams, Richard K. "The Role of Regional Banks in International Banking." *Columbia Journal of World Business,* 16 (Summer 1981): 62–71.

The author discusses activities, organizational approaches, and special problems of regional banks operating in international banking. Recent trends and possible reasons for success or failure of these banks are also mentioned.

Allan, Iain. "Return and Risk in International Capital Markets." *Columbia Journal of World Business,* 17 (Summer 1982): 3–23.

This article contains 23 tables and 11 charts showing statistical data of several international capital markets between the years of 1972 and 1981. First, local currency rates and variability of total returns are considered. Next, the effects of conversion to U.S. dollars and how fluctuations of currency increase variability of market returns is explained. The author concludes with an examination of the correlation between bond and equity markets.

Biger, Nahum, and John Hull. "The Valuation of Currency Options." *Financial Management,* 12 (Spring 1983): 24–28.

The authors provide two different methods for valuation of foreign currency put and call options. In these valuation formulas, the foreign exchange rate is very important. An example shows how to use options for hedging foreign exchange risk.

Brecher, Charles, and Vladimir Pucik. "Foreign Banks in the U.S. Economy: The Japanese Example." *Columbia Journal of World Business,* 15 (Spring 1980): 5–13.

This article examines the reasons for entry, type of business, and direct and indirect economic ramifications of the Japanese banking industry in the United States. Research shows that Japanese banks come to the U.S. to serve Japanese clients operating in the U.S., to take part in the International Capital Market, and to compete in the American market. Approximately 9,200 U.S. residents are employed by Japanese banks. It is estimated that their operations provide nearly 11,000 additional jobs in the U.S.

Chew, Ralph H. "Export Trading Companies: Current Legislation, Regulation And Commercial Bank Involvement." *Columbia Journal of World Business,* 16 (Winter 1981): 42–47.

The recently passed Export Trading Company Act (S.734) does allow banks to own ETC's, but the industry is still so heavily over-regulated that it severely hampers American export entrepreneurs. A new export trading law, written with ETC industry members' involvement, would greatly benefit U.S. exports. The author examines these issues and challenges export traders and government officials to cooperate with one another.

Crane, Dwight B., and Samuel L. Hayes, III. "The New Competition in World Banking." *Harvard Business Review,* 60 (July-August 1982): 88–94.

This article examines the historical roots, current foreign competition, and possible strategies of the U.S. commercial-investment banking industry. Competition within the fast-growing international capital markets has several implications for banks, corporations, and banking regulatory agencies. The authors conclude with a brief discussion of much-needed regulatory reform and the importance of global strategy for U.S. banks.

Dale, Richard S. "A Proposal for the LDC Debt Problem." *Columbia Journal of World Business,* 17 (Winter 1982): 36–42.

The weaknesses of the current international banking regulatory system pose several threats to the economic community. The author discusses the regulatory provisions of other countries besides the U.S. Finally, analyses of the natures of risk and security lead to regulatory implications and recommendations for regulatory reform.

Dotan, Amihud, and Arie Ovadia. "A Capital-Budgeting Decision—The Case of a Multinational Corporation Operating in High-Inflation Countries." *Journal of Business Research,* 14 (October 1986): 403–410.

This article examines a lease vs. borrow problem in the case of a U.S.-based parent company making capital budgeting decisions for a subsidiary operating in a high-inflation country. It shows that, because of existing tax codes, inflation affects both the cash flow of a project and the discount rate. Consequently, all factors affected by inflation should be analyzed in order to reach the right decision.

Edwards, Franklin R. "Financial Institutions and Regulation in the 21st Century: After the Crash?" *Columbia Journal of World Business,* 17 (Spring 1982): 82–87.

With the recent onslaught of deregulation of financial institutions, it becomes necessary to review the original purpose of financial regulation. The author examines the fundamental problems caused by the economic changes of financial institutions and markets. Regulatory implications are discussed, as well as some general recommendations for reform.

————. "The New 'International Banking Facility': A Study in Regulatory Frustration." *Columbia Journal of World Buisness, 16 (Winter 1981): 6–18.*

This article traces the key events which led to the creation of IBF's and their general relationship to the economic and regulatory history of the Eurodollar market. The author defines several key terms relating to this topic and offers an explanation for these new regulatory arrangements.

Feder, Gershon, and Knud Ross. "Risk Assessments and Risk Premiums in the Eurodollar Market." *The Journal of Finance,* 37 (June 1982): 679–691.

The authors try to identify a correlation between lenders' risk assessments of individual countries and interest rates in the Euromarket. A model desdribed in the paper helps establish this relationship. Evidence shows that credit pricing in the market is apparently influenced by the subjective risk perceptions of lenders. Further credit pricing judgments should examine the quality of these assessments.

Friedman, Benjamin M. "The Financing Must Come—But Where From?" *Harvard Business Review,* 58 (September-October 1980): 52–56.

The needs of financing increasing domestic capital formulation and decreasing international imbalances during unstable inflationary times presents a great challenge to the Western world financial markets. Since the customary sources (such as banks and securities markets) are offering less, innovative methods are necessary in order to raise funds.

Korth, Christopher M. "Risk Minimization for International Lending in Regional Banks." *Columbia Journal of World Business,* 16 (Winter 1981): 21–28.

International lending by a commercial bank opens the door to a vast array of new risks not ordinarily encountered in domestic banking. Not only do the familiar domestic lending risks appear with unfamiliar aspects, but new risks found only with international lending are also present.

Marsh, Paul. "Valuation of Underwriting Agreements for UK Rights Issues." *The Journal of Finance,* 35 (June 1980): 693–716.

This paper describes the use of the Black and Scholes model for valuing underwriting agreements for United Kingdom rights issues from 1962 to 1975. The author attempted to determine if the fees charged for underwriting were competitive. Evidence showed that underwriting, taken by itself, was highly overpriced. Marsh suggests that issuing companies should use caution in choosing to underwrite and should actively participate in pricing of same.

Mirus, Rolf, and Bernard Yeung. "Economic Incentives for Countertrade." *Journal of International Business Studies,* 17 (Fall 1986): 27–39.

This paper examines countertrade, using standard economic theory. The authors show that in many circumstances contertrade is a rational response to transaction costs, information asymmetry, moral hazard-agency problems, and other market imperfections. This paper integrates counter-trade into existing international business theories and some preliminary hypotheses.

Park, Y. S. "The Economics of Offshore Financial Centers." *Columbia Journal of World Business,* 17 (Winter 1982): 31–35.

International or "offshore" financial centers have played a large part in integrating national capital markets on regional and global bases. This article examines the reasons for their growth, provides a classification system based on types of service offered, and assesses their economic effects on local and regional economics.

Philippatos, G. C., A. Christofi, and P. Christofi. "The Inter-Temporal Stability of International Stock Market Relationships: Another View." *Financial Management,* 12 (Winter 1983): 63–69.

The inner-temporal stability of the interrelation among the fourteen nation stock exchanges are examined for the period from January 1959 to December 1978. Evidence supports the existence of structure and stability of those relationships for investment horizons greater than two years. Also, the results reveal the presence of international economic elements which increase stability of the relationship.

Rabino, Samuel. "The Growth Strategies of New York Based Foreign Banks." *Columbia Journal of World Business,* 16 (Winter 1981): 29–35.

The increasing prevalence of foreign banks in the U.S. has caused both respectful regard and alarm in the American banking industry. A study was conducted to evaluate New York-based foreign banks' marketing strategies in terms of organizational form and regional affiliation, as well as their planning strategies.

Ryder, Frank R. "Challenges to the Use of the Documentary Credit in International Trade Transactions." *Columbia Journal of World Business,* 16 (Winter 1981): 36–41.

For the past 50 years, the documentary letter of credit has operated successfully as a facilitator of international commercial trade. Nevertheless, their susceptibility to fraud and forgery, coupled with potential jurisdictional problems arising out of international transactions, are examples of the weaknesses in this fundamental tool to international trade.

Schuster, Falko. "Barter Arrangements With Money—The Modern Form of Compensation Trading." *Columbia Journal of World Business,* 15 (Fall 1980): 61–66.

This article examines the most common forms of modern barter arrangements. It also shows how even businessmen who typically do strictly for money sales may participate in reciprocal dealings. Finally, the author presents the advantages of using sophisticated barter constructs.

Theobald, Thomas C. "Offshore Branches and Global Banking—One Bank's View." *Columbia Journal of World Business,* 16 (Winter, 1981): 19–20.

Separate domestic vs. offshore banking is being replaced by global banking. The Eurodollar, a result of government regulation of money flow, demonstrates not only the global market, but sophisticated communications as well. The author states that many governmental concerns are unfounded and irrelevant.

Wellons, Philip. "International Bankers: Size Up Your Competitors." *Harvard Business Review,* 60 (November-December 1982): 95–105.

In order for U.S. banks to become more competitive in the world banking industry, they must adopt aggressive economic strategies instead of maintaining reactive policies. They should examine the economic and likely banking strategy of each home country. The author uses Japan, France, and Germany as illustrations. Questions to ask oneself in conducting an analysis are offered as a general guideline.

White, Betsy Buttrill, and John R. Woodbury, III. "Exchange Rate Systems and International Capital Market Integration." *Journal of Money, Credit and Banking,* 12 (May 1980): 175–183.

The authors applied factor analysis to the covered yields in call money, bond, and equity markets in order to determine effects of floating rates on capital market integration. Although they used the same basis technique as Logue, Salant, and Sweeney, looking at asset-yield covariation, the authors' results were significantly different. The authors found that no generalization could be made concerning the exchange rate systems and their impact on capital market integration.

Wynant, Larry. "Essential Elements of Project Financing." *Harvard Business Review,* 58 (May-June 1980): 165–173.

The author discusses several advantages of using project financing for very large ventures. These include spreading risk and increasing borrowing capacity. Future customers, suppliers, and governments may help share the risk, even though they have little or no financial recourse.

V. International Financial Planning _____

Dietemann, Gerard J. "Evaluating Multinational Performance Under FAS No. 8." *Management Accounting,* 58 (May 1980): 49–55.

This article compares several methods of presenting foreign earnings in terms meaningful to U.S. management with the Financial Accounting Standards Board Statement No. 8 (FAS No. 8), which has been blamed by the business community for fluctuations and distortions of foreign subsidiaries earnings. The author argues that official U.S. dollar results per FAS No. 8 of foreign operations cannot be completely ignored as a basis for evaluation of foreign operations.

Hekman, Christine R. "On Revising FASB 8–Use A Band-Aid or Major Surgery?" *Harvard Business Review,* 58 (May-June 1980): 38, 42, 44.

In January 1976 the FASB issued Statement 8, a declaration concerning foreign exchange translation. Despite the criticism of FASB 8, Hekman maintains that it is the most reasonable solution to date. However, in order to stabilize corporate and investor interests, more data is required from multinationals.

Horwitz, Bertrand, and Richard Kolodny. "Has the FASB Hurt Small High-Technology Companies?" *Harvard Business Review,* 58 (May-June 1980): 44, 48, 52.

FASB 2 became effective as of January 1, 1985. The authors examined 131 companies in terms of R&D expenditures and whether those costs were deferred or expensed. Study results show that FASB 2 has damaged those companies which deferred R&D costs prior to 1975. Furthermore, the statement has also detrimentally affected earnings, ability to raise capital, and innovativeness.

Mathur, Ike. "Managing Foreign Exchange Risk Profitably." *Columbia Journal of World Business,* 17 (Winter 1982): 23–30.

The heightening dynamism and changeability of the foreign exchange market has uncovered an ever growing need to effectively manage foreign exchange risk. A survey was conducted of U.S. companies to determine their foreign exchange policies and practices.